THE ULTIMATE BOOK OF
FRESHWATER
FISHING

THE ULTIMATE BOOK OF
FRESHWATER
FISHING

KEN SCHULTZ

MASTERS PRESS

Acknowledgments
All photographs by Ken Schultz, except:
34 Bruce Holt; 67 Berkley, Inc.

All illustrations by Oxford Illustrators, with
the help of. 3M/Scientific Anglers (page 38)
and Great American Tool Co (page 154)

Published by Masters Press
A Division of Howard W. Sams & Company
2647 Waterfront Pkwy E. Dr, Suite 100,
Indianapolis, IN 46214

First trade paper back edition published in 1997 by
Masters Press.

ISBN 1-57028-154-8
Library of Congress CIP 97-17865

96 97 98 99 00 01   10 9 8 7 6 5 4 3 2 1

Printed in Hong Kong

CONTENTS

INTRODUCTION

The world of freshwater fishing is a broad, sometimes complex, but always intriguing one. The freshwater scene does not offer such leviathans of the deep as are found in the saltwater realm, yet freshwater anglers are blessed with opportunities to catch a lot of hard-fighting, strong-pulling, active species. In most cases these angling opportunities can be enjoyed all year long, and with a variety of techniques and tackle in many different environments.

Unfortunately, not all techniques, tackle, bait, and lures, are suitable for all of the fish species to be caught. For example, fishing for Atlantic salmon is as different from fishing for crappies as eating oysters on the half shell is from eating a bologna sandwich.

One thing for certain is that the cast of characters in freshwater fishing includes some of the gamest fish that swim. Largemouth bass, for example, probably win the popularity honors. They are the most widely distributed of the top freshwater species; they grow to sizes large enough that the bigger specimens provide real excitement and trophy status; and they are dynamic in their topwater feeding abilities.

However, it is generally recognized that the smallmouth bass will outfight a largemouth of equal size. Though cousin to the largemouth, smallmouth bass are less widely spread because of their preference for cooler, cleaner environments. Smallmouths also don't grow as large, but they fight to the finish, pulling and tugging with every ounce of strength, making them an exceptional gamefish on appropriate tackle. Smallmouths jump repeatedly, too, even if they have to swim 20 feet to the surface to do so. They've been called "ounce for ounce and pound for pound the gamest fish that swims", which they may just be.

In terms of meanness and just a contrary attitude, consider the muskellunge. There is an aura, a mystique, that veils this not-so-widely-available fish, fueled no doubt by its appearance and behavior. Perhaps the hardest freshwater fish to catch with frequency, it is truly unpredictable. Most muskies, particularly large ones, provide an impressive short-term fight, and those that leap clear of the water (not all do) are fish an angler never forgets.

For size, strength, and general hard-to-bring-to-the-net qualities, there are two freshwater fish that rate tops, yet whose paths never cross. One of these is the striped bass, a transplant to many southern waters and a veritable eating machine that grows to 50- and 60-pound sizes in landlocked environments. It is as hard-fighting and strong-pulling a fish as you'll find in freshwater, and, characteristically, anglers need stout tackle and ample heavy line to contend with the larger members of this species.

Much the same can be said about chinook salmon, which are found in Western coastal waters and which have been very successfully transplanted into the Great Lakes. Chow hounds like stripers, they grow to 30 to 40 pounds in three to five years. Their fight is particularly dogged, and, unlike stripers, they occasionally jump.

Then, of course, there is the venerable Atlantic salmon, considered the king of gamefish by many anglers though geographically limited and unavailable to many anglers; steelhead, which grow large, jump, are found fairly abundantly in the Northwest as well as the Great Lakes; and walleyes, which lack something in fighting ability, but make up for it in edibility and challenging fishing.

All of these fish, in fact, can be a challenge to catch, as much as they can be fun to fish for and hard to land. A great deal has to do with the tackle used and the conditions under which they are caught.

A lot also has to do with the skills and knowledge of the fisherman, some of which is learned quickly, some of which comes through on-the-water experience. That's where *The Ultimate Book of Freshwater Fishing* comes into play. As concisely as possible, it distills the pertinent aspects of freshwater fishing – species knowledge, equipment, techniques, and savvy – in words and illustrations to help the reader focus on what is important to angling success.

Additionally, it reflects the many different faces of freshwater fishing pictorially. The one regret that I have is that this book could not contain more photographs. The selection process for this book was as long and arduous as for any of my previous books, because I wanted the photographs to reflect the very broad here's-what-you-can-expect scenario of angling in rivers, creeks, ponds, lakes, and reservoirs in all areas of North America. The pictures here, in fact, were taken from Florida to Labrador, Washington and British Columbia to Texas, and scores of points in between. They are truly representative of all types of North American freshwater fishing.

The information disseminated in *The Ultimate Book of Freshwater Fishing* is applicable to all of the fish profiled here and to all of the environments in which they are found, and is as up-to-date as it can possibly be in a sport that has seen many changes in the past several decades.

Ken Schultz

SPECIES

BASS

LARGEMOUTH BASS

Largemouth bass are the most popularl pursued and perhaps most abundant North American freshwater fish. They are found in all states but Alaska, and as a warmwater species they do especially well in relatively fertile bodies of water, primarily being found in reservoirs, lakes, ponds, and large slow rivers with quiet back-waters.

They orient toward cover and most of their food is found in or near some form of cover, whether it is visible in relatively shallow water or existing beneath the surface out of visible sight. Favored haunts include logs, stumps, lily pads, brush, weed and grass beds, bushes, docks, fence rows, standing timber, bridge pilings, rocky shores, boulders, points, weed line edges, stone walls, creek beds, road beds, ledge-like dropoffs, humps, shoals, and islands.

Largemouth bass and their cousins spotted bass (also known as Kentucky bass and found in some of the same waters in the mid-South) are most active in waters ranging from 60 to 78 degrees; 65 to 72 degrees is likely their optimum range, but they do well in temperatures much higher and lower, being caught in waters that touch the 90-degree mark as well as in frozen lakes where mid-30s water exists.

These fish have an extremely catholic diet, foraging on shiners, bluegills, shad, alewives, minnows, and crayfish. They will also consume more exotic items, but primarily eat what is most abundant, most accessible, and easily preyed upon, with most fish being of fingerling size. One of the charms of angling for largemouth bass is that the lures used needn't necessarily closely imitate specific forage. As a result, there is probably no other freshwater gamefish for which there is such a wide range of lure types, sizes, colors, and actions.

Spring is the most popular time to fish for these species in most areas (a few states have seasons on bass and there is little or no spring fishing), as bass spawn during this time and are relatively shallow and close to shore. Water temperature is a big factor in fish activity in the spring, and this varies on any given day between geographic locales. Small lakes and ponds are best for early season bass fishing, since they warm up quickly. On large lakes, shallow flats, coves, feeder creeks, and tributary areas are gen-erally warmer than the rest of the lake in the early season and are better places to fish.

Many lures catch spring bass, but few are more consistently effective than spinnerbaits and crankbaits. Of the latter, the type to use varies. If the water is very cold, you will likely have to use a lure that gets down 5 to 10 feet and is worked on points, steeply sloping banks, and shores with a breakline (a distinct dropoff to deeper water) at the 5- to 10-foot level.

In shallow lakes that have a lot of stumps, flat with cover (which is just starting to emerge), and the like, a shallow-or intermediate-running crankbait is best. As the water warms and cover – which may be grass, milfoil, hydrilla, or cab-bage weeds – begins to grow up, the same crankbaits can be used to skim the edges and tops, and only speed of retrieval may vary. Crankbaits are especially productive in places with a lot of deep water and where submerged creek or river channels meet the shore.

Spinnerbaits are generally fished close to the

The largemouth bass, shown here in an early spring setting, is the most popularly pursued freshwater gamefish in North America, and one that succumbs to a variety of fishing tactics.

surface and within sight in the spring. Being rel-atively snag- and weed-free they are particularly well worked around moss, lilies, milfoil, and other forms of vegetation, and around stumps, standing timber, fallen trees, and docks.

Bass are generally harder to catch in the summer than in the spring, in part because anglers as a whole are not as persistent, and in part because bass become less accessible, going deeper or become more ensconced in thick cover that is difficult to fish.

On big bodies of water with little vegetation, the midsummer trick is to locate deep-water places (15 feet or more) that hold largemouths, fish the edges of those spots, and present lures

Smallmouth bass differ in appearance from largemouths, and generally do not grow as large. This one was caught on a minnow-imitation plug.

in a precise way. Look for submerged humps, long points, and old roads well away from shore. In other places, focus on the heaviest cover that a bass could hide in. That will probably not be very deep, but the cover will provide security, comfort, and many opportunities to ambush unsuspecting prey.

Generally, such surface lures as plugs or buzz baits work best early and late in the day in the shallows, with plastic worms the preferred offering otherwise, and jigging spoons or weed-less spoons also of value. With heavy cover, you often have to get into the midst of it to be suc-cessful, plodding along, working spots deliberately, and probing carefully.

The most obvious, most frequently employed, and most easily managed method of catching summer bass is working the edges of vegetation. In large, fairly thick concentrations of vegeta-tion, the easiest fish to catch are those that are close to the edges, especially where that is readily observed. Pinpointing the edges of sub-merged weed lines, however, is not as easily done, but often important, as much vegetation, especially in clear northern waters, does not grow above the surface. A plastic worm, rigged with a slip sinker, is the main vegetation lure, but sometimes it is good to use a lure that moves more enticingly, such as a weedless spoon with plastic skirt or pork chunk, or a weedless surface product.

Bass are often found in flooded timber in the summer, and here, plastic worms, jig-and-pork combinations, and occasionally deep-diving crankbaits are the ticket. The junction of two old channels, the outside bend of a channel, clumps of timber, and timber adjacent to boat lanes with a depth change are good locales. If bass suspend in the midsection limbs, a jigging spoon, worked vertically, is the lure of choice.

In fall, bass are coming off their summer behavior and gradually moving shallower as the water cools. Temperature and habitat conditions vary greatly by geographic area and far southern bass waters experience favorable conditions for a longer period of time than northern ones. Ponds and small lakes are especially worth fishing, although they cool off quickly after a succession of cold fall nights. Shallow and near-shore environs become worthy of greater up on, and fly tackle is also of merit at times, especially when fishing with deer hair bugs and poppers for shallow fish.

SMALLMOUTH BASS

The smallmouth bass is one of the most impressive of all freshwater fish and is coveted for its fighting ability. It is the smallmouth to which the famous Dr. James Henshall quote "inch for inch and pound for pound the gamest fish that swims" quote is ascribed. A relative of the largemouth bass, it is less tolerant of very warm environs and is not as widely distributed, with most of its abundance occurring in the northern states and southern Canadian provinces; therefore, many freshwater ang-lers have not made this fish's acquaintance.

In lakes, ponds, and reservoirs, smallmouths prefer a rocky bottom, cool water, and crayfish. Crayfish make up an important part of their diet wherever these creatures are found, but other forage includes small bass, panfish, perch, and assorted fingerling-size minnows. In lakes, smallmouths are mainly located around rocky points; craggy, cliff-like shores; rocky islands and reefs; and riprap banks, preferring small rocks but also being found around boulders.

Smallmouths also exist in creeks and rivers, where they are frequently abundant though small. River smallmouth are even spunkier than their lake-dwelling brethren, and tend to be more streamlined and without a drooping belly. In flowing water, smallmouth bass concentrate around boulders, smaller rocks, gravel, stone, shale, and various obstructions (fallen trees, bridge pilings, etc.) that offer holding and feeding benefits. Minnows, crayfish, hellgrammites, nymph larvae, and leeches comprise the diet of river smallmouths, and these delectables often converge around structures.

In rivers, anglers primarily tend to fish below structures or objects, which is fine in spring and during high water flowage. Later in the season, you should also try above those places. Always work with the current to represent the natural movement of fish in a river. That doesn't always mean retrieving downstream, however, except when fly fishing on the surface. Most casts should be made upriver at a 45-degree angle and offerings should be retrieved across and down. In smaller flowages where there is not as much midriver structure, work the undercut banks, sunken logs, stumps, and rock walls.

Fishing for smallmouths with live crayfish, especially the softshell variety, is very popular among bait anglers. Another good natural bait is a nightcrawler. Live crayfish and worms can be worked behind various bottom bouncing rigs in flowing water, and on bobbers in still water.

Crayfish-imitating crankbaits are a popular river and lake lure for smallmouths. These look and act a bit like a crayfish, and can be produc-

Largemouths are found around various objects and forms of cover, and put up a scrappy fight.

attention in the fall, but fishermen should not be averse to working deeper water if shallow prospecting fails to bring dividends. Spinnerbaits, crankbaits, jigs, and surface lures have merit at this time.

Since most bass fishing is a matter of casting, and since boats equipped with an electric motor are very widely employed by bass anglers, it is important to achieve proper positioning with your boat and to make accurate casts and proper presentations. The important point to always consider is how to present a lure most effectively and how to position for thorough fishing.

Pinpoint presentations are more important in largemouth bass angling than in many other forms of freshwater fishing. When casting to potential largemouth-holding spots, accuracy is a must. The first cast to a likely bass hole is often the most important one, so it pays to be able to make each cast count. Make casts to all sides of likely cover, and learn to feather your casts so that lures don't crash into the water like a bomb.Since serious bass fishing involves a range of angling conditions, lure styles and sizes, and fishing methods, there is no one type of tackle that will suit all needs.

Most fishermen are partial to bait-casting rods for most bass fishing, particularly when using crankbaits and worms, fishing in heavy cover, and fishing for very large bass. Bait casting tackle offers good casting control and is conducive to the use of big lures. Ten or 12-pound-test line is standard, though lighter and heavier is used where appropriate.

Spinning gear is also employed, though generally with lighter line and not in places where there is a lot of cover for lures and fish to hang

Frequently found in rocky environments, as in this river, smallmouth bass are a great fish to catch on light tackle, and are one of the spunkiest of all freshwater species.

tive all season long if smallmouths aren't too deep; they are especially worthwhile in the spring. Bottom scratching is critical with these. Another good smallmouth lure is a floating/diving plug, worked by twitching on the surface or by a stop-and-go underwater retrieve.

Surface lures have most merit in the springtime and early and late in the day in the summer. Poppers, wobblers, and the aforementioned plugs are of most merit, and fly fishing with bugs and poppers is also effective when the fish are fairly shallow. Streamer flies and dry flies may also work in flowing water.

Perhaps the best all-around smallmouth lure, however, is a jig. Hair-bodied, soft plastic, and rubber-legged jigs are tantalizing and very effective in the hands of a good angler. Rocky banks and sharply sloping shorelines are very suitable for jig fishing, although it is critical to get the jig down and working along the bottom. I'm partial to dark jig colors, such as black and brown, for smallmouth bass, but many other anglers have success with yellow and white jigs with soft-plastic curl-tail bodies.

In many lakes and reservoirs, smallmouth bass are fairly deep in summer when the water warms up. Fishing vertically with jigs or jigging spoons is necessary and in some environs trolling with deep diving plugs or with assorted lures run behind downriggers or off planer boards is even employed.

Spinners are a good flowing-water lure for smallmouths at times, incidentally, especially in the spring. They may also be effective when fished on a slow-and-deep retrieve in the spring on lakes along rocky shores where bass are staging prior to spawning. Spinnerbaits can

sometimes produce good smallmouth action as well, though they are not universally appealing. When bass are shallow and aggressive, especially early in the season, spinnerbaits are very effective (and better than a multi-hooked plug for releasing fish), but later, as these fish move deeper and become warier, spinnerbaits don't produce unless you want to spend time fluttering single-blade models off deep ledges.

Light-and medium-duty spinning gear will handle the majority of smallmouth bass fishing situations. Light (6- and 8-pound) and ultralight (2- and 4-pound) lines are practical, even desirable, because smallmouths are residents of open water for the most part, and when hooked do not have to be muscled away from obstacles other than the bottom, unlike with largemouths.

In many places, smallmouths inhabit relatively clear, deep lakes and are an especially wary fish, so delicate presentations involving light, thin-diameter line, small lures, and corresponding rod and reel combinations make light and ultralight tackle a fundamental part of smallmouth fishing success. Using heavier gear, including bait casting tackle, is usually overkill, although some plugs and large jigs are worked a little better on that.

The freshwater striper is a transplant from saltwater environs and, like its cousins, eats voraciously and travels widely.

STRIPED BASS

Although striped bass have their origins in saltwater, landlocked stripers are one of the largest-growing and strongest-fighting freshwater fish. They are very similar to their ocean-roaming brethren, although they are found in large freshwater impoundments, some rivers, the tailrace flowage below dams, and in estuarine waters. Pure strain stripers, as well as hybrids (crosses between striped and white bass) have been transplanted into over thirty states, and have become a premier gamefish.

Stripers are predominantly open-water nomads in big reservoirs and lakes, which is where they are most abundant, and locating these fish is sometimes a more formidable task than catching them. Striped bass are very vigorous predators, however, and their environments are usually blessed with abundant forage populations, especially threadfin shad, gizzard shad, and alewives, as well as panfish in waters without shad. Since they do a lot of eating, they are a good target for various angling techniques.

Stripers migrate in the spring up tributaries (if they exist) to spawn, usually when the water is around 55 degrees. Fishing on channel bends is popular during the spring. After spawning, stripers scatter, migrating back to the lake and often following the path of channels and streambeds into deep water. They may locate over old creek beds and channels, near sunken islands, along ridges with quick dropoffs, at the deep end of points, near bridges and adjacent causeways, and near any natural funneling point for baitfish to travel. In the fall, they move into shallow flat areas and chase schools of bait. In winter, they stay deep and in many of the same places as summer, though they travel less.

In striper fishing it is generally important to have some type of sonar, either to find the types of places that attract stripers, to locate catchable fish, or to determine the depth at which stripers are located so you can place your lures or bait at the right level.

Because stripers wander a good deal and exist in open water environs on lakes, a lot of trolling is done, primarily by flatlining a diving plug or using assorted lures behind downrigger weights. When stripers are within 25 feet of the surface, most trollers flatline by tradition; plugs, spoons, flies, and jigs can be used for shallow fishing, but only plugs have merit from 10 to 25 feet unless sinkers or weighted lines are used.

Downriggers have taken on a greater presence in striper trolling in recent years, and the use of these devices is affording deep striper trollers

Right: A lot of open-water angling takes place for stripers, chasing schooling fish in the fall, and trolling and jigging at other times.

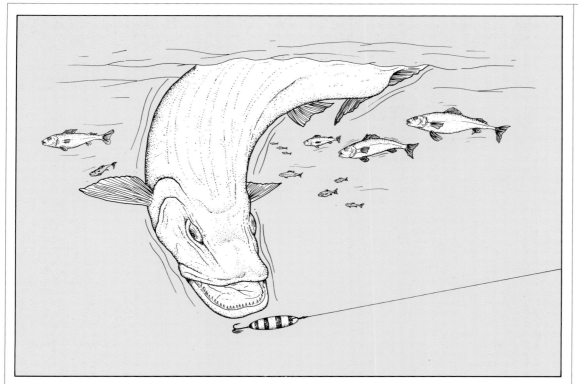

When stripers school and chase bait near the surface, they are extremely aggressive.

a greater range of lure presentation and more precise lure placement and control. There are some places, however, where striper trollers are reluctant to use downriggers, mainly where there is a lot of standing timber. Such timber often holds baitfish and stripers and does pose a trolling problem, but this can usually be solved by astute anglers working as a team.

Fishing with live bait is also very popular, especially in the spring. The primary baitfish used are gizzard and threadfin shad, herring, bluegill (where it is legal to do so), alewives, shiners, and assorted minnows. Which one to use depends on the species present naturally and its availability. Live bait is still fished while the boat is at anchor or slowly adrift. Depending on the depth to be fished, the size of the bait, and whether there is current or wind, you'll need from 1 1/2 to 4 ounces of lead in the form of a bead-chain weight to keep the bait at the proper depth and right below the spot where you have positioned it. The weight should be about 2 feet ahead of the bait. Use a 2/0 or 3/0 hook for small baitfish like threadfin shad and 4/0 to 6/0 hooks for larger baits. Hook them through the top of the back so they can swim freely if they are large or through the top of the nose if they are smaller (while using smaller hooks). Sometimes it is best to keep the weight just off the bottom, but when you already know where the stripers are, keep it slightly above the depth at which you've pinpointed them. Keeping bait fresh and lively is extremely important, and difficult with alewives, herring, and threadfin shad. Circular livewells are used for those. Cut bait is also effective in some places.

Although casting lures for open-water stripers is seldom done other than when the fish are schooling (more about that in a moment), there is a fair amount of jigging that takes places, usually when you have located stripers holding in deep water in a defined area, or when fishing submerged humps or mounds that stripers visit to feed. Metal and slab-sided jigging spoons are almost exclusively used for this, and both standard and speed jigging techniques are employed to good effect.

In many locales in the fall, striped bass, hybrid stripers, and white bass chase and consume pods of baitfish (usually threadfin or gizzard shad) and roam over a wide area as they keep up with the bait and maraud them. Often this phenomenon is best observed in early and late daylight hours. With white bass, it happens on points and along rocky shores as well as in open water, but with stripers it may happen anywhere. The key to finding it is observation.

Striper anglers usually motor to places where schooling fish are frequently observed or were seen the morning or evening before. They shut the outboard motor off, and watch and wait. When a sudden splashing occurs in the distance, and/or a flock of seagulls is seen hovering expectantly and diving to the water, that's a giveaway and also the signal to shift into breakneck gear.

The tactic is to race to the site of the commotion, glide to the outer edge of it, cut the motor, and cast into the melee. Sometimes nearly any lure will do; sometimes it must be close in size and shape to the baitfish being pummeled. Two or three anglers may get into fish this way, and if the school moves on you try to move with it, being careful not to put the fish down (which often happens anyway, due to the fish you catch or the intrusion of your boat or that of others) and trying not to lose their direction.

A jig is a good lure to use in these situations, as is a noisy surface lure, which can imitate the type of noise and action — gamefish slashing at prey trapped near the surface — that such fish make. A diving plug or sinking vibrating lure (plug or lead) is another good choice because it can cover different depths, has an attention-getting type of action, and can be fished erratically.

Most striper anglers use 20- to 30-pound-test line; 20 is adequate and 12 to 17 will do well in most open water circumstances provided you can fight a fish properly and use the appropriate reel drag setting.

WHITE BASS

White bass are a popular, important gamefish in many regions of North America, particularly south of the Mason-Dixon line and in large river systems. Also called sand bass, sandies, stripes, and silver bass, they are truly a member of the temperate bass family, which also includes yellow bass, white perch, and striped bass. Unlike their striped bass relatives, white bass aren't heavyweight fish. However, their savage strike and vicious darting fight surely place

White bass are usually found in schools, and it is possible to catch a number of fish on such lures as those shown here.

them in the middleweight division.

These are a schooling fish, and it is common to catch quite a few white bass in one location. The average size white bass is about 3/4 to 1 1/2 pounds in most places, and a 2-pounder is considered large; generous limits and fine tasting flesh make it desirable to keep a good number. Light tackle is highly suitable for these fish, which are aggressive fighters. Spinning or spincasting rods loaded with 4- to 8-pound line are ideal, although a fly rod may be used as well.

White bass feed primarily on small shad, smelt, alewives, or minnows. Lures that correspond to the size and likeness of these baitfish are best. This includes small crankbaits, bucktail or marabou jigs, silver jigging spoons, spinners, sinking lures, and tailspinners, but also small stick baits and buzz baits. Some fish are caught trolling, and in northern environs where anglers are using plugs off planer boards for walleyes, they are accidentally catching a slew of white bass. However, jigging, casting, and live bait account for most success.

In the spring, white bass run up tributaries to spawn and provide a lot of action. Spring white bass runs are renowned on many large lakes and river systems, and this movement seems to generally take place once the water temperature in the tributaries exceeds 55 degrees. Late in the summer and into fall there is some exciting angling for schools of white bass that feed near the surface on shad. There are many fish in such schools and they are literally frenzied while tearing into the baitfish. Many boats follow these schools and enjoy fast fishing, similar to that experienced for striped bass (which see). Shallow, wind-blown, gravelly points are also a prime fall white bass locale. In rivers, look to those areas where streams enter, where bridge pilings disrupt current flow, above wingdams, along riprap, downstream from lock-and-dam structures, and on rocky points.

Since white bass are on the move so much, an angler who relies on one spot may be disappointed. In lakes and reservoirs, it is wise to pick out a dozen or so areas where white bass have been caught before and return to each one when you are pursuing these fish specifically (many anglers catch whites while fishing for other species, such as largemouth bass or stripers). At other times, look for riprap on shorelines, rocky points, reefs off islands, old river channels, sand bars, dropoffs, and stony flats where depth holds constant at a level between 10 and 16 feet.

White, yellow, or chartreuse marabou jigs are favored where casting is involved, usually swimming them just off the bottom. For surface action a small propellered floating plug twitched like a wounded baitfish is favored. Virtually overlooked is the effectiveness of a 1/8-ounce white or chartreuse buzz bait with a plastic blade; this is a killer off rocky points in the fall. Wind-blown points and adjacent shore-

lines are the best spots then, as they often have schools of baitfish, which in turn attract whites.

PEACOCK BASS

Peacock bass are one of the world's hardest fighting freshwater fish, and one destined to become more of a phenomenon in appropriate North America waters (they must be warm all year long) through stocking efforts. These fish are not native to North America, and are found primarily in South American jungle rivers and reservoirs, but they have been transplanted, both legally and otherwise, into some southern U. S. waters, most notably in canal systems in Florida and warm water reservoirs in Texas.

These fish not only fight well, but they are attractive looking, with golden yellow sides, an

The colorful peacock bass is becoming more of an attraction to freshwater anglers, and is known for its hard-fighting characteristics.

alternating orange or bronze tinge, dark vertical bars, and a large black spot at the base of the tail which resembles the eye of a peacock tail plume, explaining the name of the fish. Bodily they resemble largemouth bass, although they are more sleek, appearing muscular and without the sagging belly that big largemouths develop; also, males have a hump at the top of the head. Also known as pavon and tucunare, they take a variety of flashy diving and surface plugs, as well as jigs, flies, and live bait. Several fish can be caught out of a given school, and they jump and fight much like a strong largemouth bass, to which they are not related.

CARP

Although many North American freshwater anglers have a distinct affinity for certain species of fish, they often have a clear dislike for others, and carp usually top the list of the latter. Carp, which are imported fish of European and Asian origin, don't get much respect because they seldom take artificial lures or standard natural baits, and have a tendency to roil the water when feeding and spawning. However, they are a fish that can grow quite large and that will provide a strong fight.

Although attempts have been made to eradicate carp in North America, they have not been successful because these are hardy, durable fish. They can live in lake and river waters that will not sustain other fish species, including places with little oxygen, and can withstand extreme changes in water temperature, although they are not active in cold water.

Carp spawn in shallow bays, stream tributaries, or flooded fields and marshes from mid to late spring or early summer, and are quite noticeable then as they thrash about and disturb the water. Often their backs are exposed, providing an obvious target for spear fishermen or bowfishermen. At other times of the year they are frequently seen leaping out of the water or rolling or finning in shallow water.

Look for carp primarily in shallow water, realizing that they can find bait better on a sand or gravel flat than in thick weeds. In back waters, work narrow, open areas between deep-water locales. Carp funnel through these while feeding. Look for them in rivers at the head of pools, eddies, slow-moving slicks, and beneath undercut banks. They also hold along bottom structures where there is some current relief. In big rivers they can be found en masse below dam structures where eddying currents rotate against lock-and-dam walls or roll off gate ends. Carp scour the bottom when feeding, often uprooting water plants in the process. They consume much vegetation, as well as insect larvae, crustaceans, and small mollusks, and are often found quite shallow.

In large lakes and reservoirs, and in slow-moving backwaters, carp anglers fish with worms, corn, grubs, marshmallows, potatoes, and dough balls. In rivers, anglers use these same baits but also live crayfish and hellgram-

The hardy carp, like the one held here by a delighted angler, is abundant in most river and lake systems, but is seldom caught on lures by casting or trolling anglers.

mites. Sometimes carp are caught accidently on artificial lures, usually on a small dark jig that is tipped with a piece of worm, or on a small diving plug. Dough balls are the most popular item used specifically for carp; these homemade concoctions are made from a variety of ingredients such as corn meal, flour, syrup, anise oil, vanilla extract, etc., and rolled into a ball.

Tackle for carp varies. Ten-pound line is adequate, as is the standard tackle used in casting for such species as bass or walleye. Lengthy rods with long handles are used by shore fishermen, who prop these into rod holders while waiting for their bait to be picked up.

CATFISH

Catfish are widely spread and often undervalued and overlooked fish that are important to many bank, pier, and shore fishermen, especially those without boats and with a minimum of tackle. Some species are caught in prodigious sizes (over 20 pounds and even over 40 in a few places), however, and are pursued in a more sophisticated manner. The ugly face and bulldog-like fight of catfish do not lend them to great prose and they are considered repulsive by many people, although the flesh of these creatures, especially the smaller ones, is as fine as that of any freshwater fish, which is one reason why they are farmed extensively and why catfish is a prime southern menu item.

BULLHEAD

The smallest of the catfish clan is the bullhead, also known in New England as a horned pout, and found in both black and brown colorations. They are a popular species, widely found in many small lakes and ponds. They do not grow particularly large as a rule, and anglers catch them while stillfishing with an assortment of baits. They are mainly nocturnal and are caught mostly on nightcrawlers, but occasionally will strike a slow-moving crankbait.

CHANNEL CATFISH

Perhaps the most popular of the whiskered clan is the channel catfish, which is found from western Montana to southern Texas and eastward, and as far north as southern Ontario and Manitoba. They spawn in late spring or early summer, when the water temperature is between 75 and 85 degrees, and may migrate into rivers or current areas during that time, especially being found around bank holes, log jams, pockets beneath stumps, and other darken spots. They may be found in schools in rivers, particularly around gravel and rock bottoms, deep-cut banks, channels, and current cuts.

Their natural food consists mainly of aquatic insects when very young, graduating to crabs, mayflies, clams, minnows, varying mollusks, caddisflies, crayfish, and other delectables. In northern regions, sucker minnows are the principal minnow-type food, while in the south, shad are predominant. In making angling presentations, various forms of bait work; channel catfish prefer fresh bait more so than their flathead or blue cousins, although rank-smelling stink baits work better in still environments,

Channel catfish grow to much larger sizes than this specimen, and are fairly widespread in North America. Note the frozen smelt, which was used for bait.

such as farm ponds and man-made lakes.

For channel catfish bait, fresh frozen chicken liver and gizzard shad are tops. Sucker or smelt can be used if shad are not available. Nightcrawlers, hellgrammites, shrimp, clams, and crayfish are popular, too. Although rotten or unfrozen chicken livers are used by some people, they are hard to keep on a hook; frozen ones stay on longer, can be cast better, and exude scent for a longer period.

Like all catfish, channels have a keen sense of smell. They take bait with less reticence in the spring, and mouth it more in the summer, and they have an excellent ability to steal bait, meaning that a lot of strikes are missed by anglers. Therefore, it is important to pay close attention to strike detection, which is usually done by observing a feintly slack line, which indicates that the fish has picked up the bait but not moved off with it.

For channel cat fishing, many anglers use egg sinkers above a barrel swivel or other stopper, which allows a channel cat to move off with a bait. This is good in slow water, where catfish pick up the offering and move sideways with it, mouth it for a while, then swallow. In current, however, these fish move backward after taking a bait; here, a bottom-bouncing sinker rig with a 2-foot leader to the bait is used, fished directly down-current, with constant pressure on the rod tip, which droops significantly when

a catfish takes the offering (whereupon you lower the tip, reel up the slack, and set the hook).

Most channel cat anglers use stiff rods loaded with very heavy line when going for these fish, especially where large ones (20 pounds and up) might be encountered. That's okay for big fish and for working where there is a lot of brush and logs. Generally, however, a medium-action baitcasting outfit, with 10-to 15-pound line, is adequate, and a lot of fun can be had with a medium-action spinning reel and 8-pound line. Channel cats can fight pretty well on tackle that gives them a chance, but you do have to be able to steer them free of obstructions.

FLATHEAD CATFISH

If there was ever a truly ugly fish it is the flathead catfish, with its huge mouth, puny eye, blotchy brown-and-gray color, and prehistoric tail structure. Flatheads are less common than channel cats, but they can grow to huge sizes.

Flatheads are a river species first, reservoir species second, and lake species last. Sluggish rivers provide a multitude of wing dams (man-made structures placed in large rivers to divert

Large catfish, such as this flathead, are quite a handful, in the boat or on a strong line.

current flow toward the center channel) and navigational structures, and flatheads prefer to hold below these. Wing dams, in particular, are a favorite place for young flatheads. Most large adult fish, however, prefer deep, big-water rivers and lakes. Fish over 35 pounds are more apt to be found below a dam, holding below open, churning gate waters where dead, stunned, and mutilated prey is easily snatched.

This species' diet consists mostly of fish and crustaceans. Anglers often take these catfish on deep-diving crankbaits, jigs tipped with sucker minnows, or large live bait that is left to lie on the bottom. Though flathead will take almost anything at some time, they prefer live fish, such as suckers, bluegill (where legal), or stone cats, and they produce a tenacious battle.

BLUE CATFISH

Not as abundant as the other species, but growing as large and equally favored, is the blue cat. They lack spots but have a pale blue coloration on top with a whitish-blue to gray belly, a distinctive forked tail, and an upper jaw that carries well over their chin. They are most abundant in large rivers and impoundments, but also exist in lower river estuaries and backwaters, and in some small waters. They are frequently caught below dams, and are found in schools.

Though blue catfish are noted for striking the worst of stink baits, their diet is extremely broad. Minnows, crabs, clams, snails, rotten flesh, and much more are on their menu, and assorted stink bait concoctions are favored by many anglers. The same methods hold true for blues as for flatheads and channel cats, and tackle needs are similar as well.

Catfish are especially fond of locating in rivers below dams, especially just below humps that are formed by the digging current. Channel cats hold along the upstream sides and flatheads and blues are more likely to be found downstream. The riprap shoreline below dams is worth working for catfish, perhaps floating a crayfish, leech, or other bait along under a slip bobber. The area around and just ahead of wing dams is good for cats, especially at dusk.

Deep holes or pools also present a good river fishing opportunity. Channel cats work up into shallow water to feed and move back to deeper water. Though some cats are caught during daylight hours directly from deep holes, they are best caught as they move into the shallower areas upstream from the hole. Flatheads, however, may not feed during the day but begin only at dark, venturing a shorter distance from the hole to feed and not as shallow.

Catfish will strike artificial lures, incidentally, although these are seldom used deliberately for catfish and are much less productive. Flatheads are more likely to be the targets, however, with crankbaits of first choice. Tipping a jig hooked with a minnow, a common practice for walleyes, does result in some catfish, and a large and scented jig-and-pork combination does the trick, too.

Trolling with large plugs or fishing with jigging spoons or bucktail jigs may catch catfish in impoundments, though this is usually an accident while fishing for striped bass. Live or cut bait (shad or herring mostly), fished off the bottom, is the main ticket, and it is best to use a 4/0 or larger hook and 2-foot leader tied to a swivel, above which is a heavy sinker. In noncurrent areas of impoundments, look for catfish primarily along river and creek beds, concentrating on curves, bends, deep holes, and the junction of two creeks, as well as at breaklines where the bottom drops off deeply.

Remember that catfish are a bottom feeder and must be sought on the bottom almost exclusively. Stillfishing and drifting with some form of bait is really the best overall approach. Don't overlook fishing at night, either. Anglers spend as many hours working these fish after dark as they do during daylight hours. Lastly, be careful in handling catfish. They have pain-inflicting mad-tom spines near the front of each dorsal and pelvic fin. These spines can inflict ripping wounds. To avoid getting stuck, approach a catfish from the underside of the fish, placing your thumb against the back side of one pectoral fin and your index finger against the other. Grasp firmly with palm across the catfish's stomach. It will be securely held and can be unhooked.

ARCTIC CHAR

The Arctic char bears the scientific appellation *Salvelinus alpinus*, which means little to the ordinary fisherman but which helps the technicians differentiate among the char genus. That is important because this is a rather puzzling and confusing fish, befitting its remote high-Arctic environs. It is a distant relative of trout and Pacific salmon, a closer relative of brook trout, lake trout, Dolly Varden, and bull trout. It is not just a char, but an Arctic char. A true char. The fact is that its brook trout and lake trout cousins should have other names, such as brook char in place of brook trout, and lake char instead of lake trout.

In any event, Arctic char are found all across the North American Arctic, although they are pursued by relatively few anglers annually, and then only for a few weeks. The largest appear to come regularly from Victoria Island rivers and from the Tree River, both of which are in Canada's uppermost Northwest Territories. Geographically these locales are not far from one another, yet their char are distinctly different. Tree River char in their spawning colors have a dark back and are not fully swathed in red or orange. They have a humped back, too, and often a more pronounced kype. Char are also found eastward in Alaska and westward in northern Quebec and Labrador, as well as at Baffin Island and along the tributaries to Hudson Bay.

Arctic char are reknowned for their beauty and for their sporty virtues. Their pinkish, orange, and bright red coloration is only found when the fish are migrating inland to spawn, as they are silvery otherwise. They are as royal a fighting fish as is found in freshwater, known for blistering runs and salmon-like leaps, especially in river environs, and their vivid pink flesh is coveted when fresh.

Char are found in both sea-run and land-locked forms. They are anadromous, and the larger fish are those that migrate from Arctic oceans into freshwater rivers and lakes. No Arctic char remain in the ocean during the winter. In late August and early September they run up the rivers and into holding lakes, where they stay through winter. When ice leaves the rivers, most of the char descend rivers and return to the ocean for the brief summer. Fish that don't make the seaward journey are those that will be spawning; they change color and inhabit the rivers and lakes, eventually to spawn beneath the winter ice.

Arctic char angling can be a feast or famine affair. Char sometimes are clustered so thickly that a river seems full of these fish, or they can be scarce. Fishing is sometimes fast, with continuous action, but these are spooky fish; when a school is spooked, it will move off, and it will be necessary to rest the locale for an hour or two.

River fishing is more dependable, with the fish often holding at the head of a pool. Where current drops over a gravel bar and dumps into a deep pool is a particularly good location. In lakes, concentrate on inlets, where the river dumps into a lake.

Early in the season, char in lakes can be seen and caught as they wander along the edges of ice floes that are breaking up, and a spoon, jig, or streamer fly will take them. Light to medium spinning tackle, using spinners and spoons that are all or partly colored red, is used, with 6- to 10-pound line standard.

Fly fishermen need a reel with ample backing, and use streamers on sinking or sink-tip 7- or 8-weight fly lines.

The Arctic char in its spawning colors is a colorful fish in a fairly bleak and gray northern setting. This rather large char is being revived for release.

CRAPPIE

Crappie are like that Chinese dog called a Shih Tzu. Most people don't say the name of that dog in a way that comes out very flattering. Ditto for the poor crappie, which, if it was pronounced by more folks as if it had the letter "o" instead of "a", as in "crop", we would all be better off. Actually, these are a fish of many names. They are known regionally as calico, speckled perch, strawberry bass, barfish, and sac-a-lait.

Technically, there are two species of crappie, the white and the black, but they look very similar and their range overlaps. The black crappie prefers cool, clear lakes and slow-moving rivers. It is a little more particular about its environment than the white crappie, which flourishes in warm and more silted water. Among the most popular freshwater fish in the U. S., and resembling sunfish in shape, crappie are widely distributed and intensely pursued, being perhaps the most favored of all the so-called panfish species. Crappies are delicious fish, which is a prime reason for their popularity. In many places crappies are quite plentiful, and creel limits are liberal, so it does no harm to keep a batch of these fish for the table.

Crappies feed primarily on insects and small fish. In southern reservoirs, gizzard or threadfin shad are major forage and in northern states, insects are more dominant. Crappies also consume the fry of many species of game fish.

In the spring, when water temperatures reach about 60 degrees, crappies move shallow to build nests and spawn, and this is a particularly favorite time for angling, much of which is done around some form of wood or brush. Spawning-time crappies are reasonably predictable and easy for anglers to catch. After spawning, crappies move to deeper water and gather in schools. They congregate tightly in sunken weed beds, dropoffs, offshore brushpiles, river channel drops, shoreline riprap, flooded timber, and sunken cribbing. Many crappies are caught in 10 to 15 feet of water among tree limbs in standing timber. During the hottest part of the day, they are situated on the cool, shaded side of such structures. Other shaded areas that may attract these fish, though not necessarily in large numbers, include bridges, piers, docks, and the bases of old tree stumps. Massive schools of crappies may form at different levels of the lake, and usually are situated horizontally.

In the fall, crappies may move into deeper water to gather around underwater structures such as old channels, rocky ledges, or weed beds. Though they will move around a bit, they

A father and son with differing baseball allegiances seem to agree that this crappie is a pretty good catch.

generally remain in deep water until spring. Crappies also offer a prime opportunity for winter fishing, and many northern ice anglers make these fish their number one pursuit.

In many bodies of water without timber, especially large reservoirs, where it is legal, anglers plant brushpiles in order to attract and hold crappies (other fish, too). In places where it is allowed, anglers may plant many brushpiles, often in places known only to them and sometimes in front of their own docks or boathouses, and will visit them often.

Although some trolling is done for crappies, the vast majority of anglers drift or anchor, and either jig or stillfish with minnows. Unquestionably the favored crappie catcher is a small, fine-wire jig. Marabou or soft-plastic bodies (grub especially) are favored. White and yellow are the standard colors, but silver, green, chartreuse, and multi-colored tinsel versions are useful. These should be small, with 1/8-ounce perhaps most useful, going a little lighter or heavier as depth and wind warrant. A small, single-bladed spinnerbait, with a plastic grub or curl-tail body, is another good crappie taker, as is a small jig tipped with a tiny minnow (hook it from the top of the head through the mouth). Crappie have tender mouths and strikes are

often delicate, and the most regularly successful anglers are those who develop a fine jigging motion and subtle feel.

Crappies don't usually strike a large minnow or lure, although it happens occasionally, especially in places where there is an abundance of these fish; 1 1/2- to 2 1/2-inch-long offerings are best for jigs, spinnerbaits, and plugs. Few small crankbaits will dive very deep unaided, though they can be fished deep with the assistance of bottom-walking sinkers. These crankbaits can be cast or trolled.

These fish also are not prone to striking fast-moving baits. You have to get down to their level (usually bottom) and work your offering slowly. Many anglers work lures too quickly for crappies, even though they think they're retrieving pretty slowly. When jigging, there is also a tendency to go too fast, so you have to put some effort into maneuvering your boat properly over crappie structures and fishing carefully. Rather than fight wind, many anglers (or tie off to brush or stumps) or drift. A moderate wind will move a boat along at a speed conducive to drifting, especially if you use an electric motor to control location and rate of drift. With the right wind speed and direction, you can drift slowly over deep-water channels, weedbeds, or dropoffs, or through timber, using a slow lift-and-drop method with jigs, spinnerbaits, or plug-and-sinker combinations.

Crappie fishermen primarily use ultralight spinning or spincasting reels equipped with 4- or 6-pound-test line and 5- to 5 1/2-foot-long rods. Fly rods, telescoping fiberglass rods, and cane poles are used as well. Cane poles or telescoping glass rods play a large, traditional role in crappie fishing. Eight- to 12-foot poles work well for boat anglers, but bank fishermen prefer 16- to 20-footers. The line is seldom longer than the length of the pole. Live bait is used, and dabbled in place after place.

Favored crappie lures include a jig with plastic body (top), marabou hair jig (middle), and jig tipped with minnow. The jig and minnow combo also catches bass and walleyes.

GRAYLING

Grayling are an admirable gamefish known to comparatively few anglers. Technically known as Arctic grayling, they are found primarily in the northern part of North America. These distinctive-looking fish with the sail-like dorsal fin are seldom the primary quarry of distant-traveling anglers, although they serve as a desirable secondary attraction to anglers primarily seeking lake trout, walleye, northern pike, or char. They have, however, saved a trip for more than one traveling angler who found that his main quarry was unavailable or uncooperative, and was geared with a light spinning rod or fly rod to take advantage of the 1- to 2-pound feisty grayling that were available, more likely than not feeding in the evening on the surface.

Although these fish are also known as American grayling, there are few grayling to be found in the continental U. S., and those are primarily in Rocky Mountain waters. Grayling are most abundant in clean, cool, swift-flowing streams and rivers from southern to Arctic regions of Canada and Alaska, and in many cold Arctic lakes.

Grayling are a member of the salmon family, but they don't attain typical salmon sizes. A 3-pounder is a large grayling, and most are in the 1-pound class, although some waters are noted for large average-size fish. They are routinely found in groups, and feed heavily on aquatic insects in all stages of development. Grayling are most commonly observed in flowages while dimpling the water and feeding on surface insects, which are usually mosquitoes; they often do this very daintily, but occasionally feed dramatically by clearing the surface and coming down on the insect.

Primarily caught by fly fishing, grayling provide a challenge and thrill. Dry fly fishing with 5- to 7-weight lines is most practiced and certainly preferred. When not rising freely to insects, grayling may better be pursued with a wet fly or nymph. A floating fly line is used most of the time, but a sink-tip line may be necessary. Grayling can be leader-shy, and they pursue flies and often strike at the end of a drift, so attention to detail is sometimes important. Fly size ranges from No. 12 through 18, and the general rule is skimpy and dark. Exact representations aren't usually critical, but a black or brown color is.

Grayling are an excellent fish to catch on light

Grayling are a fine light-tackle fish of the north, though one that few anglers are familiar with.

or ultralight spinning tackle too, using 2- through 6-pound-test line. Small spinners and spoons are often used, but the best artificial is a small dark jig. Black or brown marabou or soft-plastic-bodied jigs in 1/16- to 1/8-ounce sizes produce very well, in flowing and still water.

While most grayling are caught in the slick water of rivers and streams, and sometimes where it flows quite fast, they can also be found in lakes near river inlets, usually along small-rock-studded shores. There, in calm water, they may be seen cruising and inhaling surface insects, and caught with flies, jigs, or spinners.

Grayling have small mouths and many fish that strike are lost. They are scrappy, feisty fish that jump and fight to the end, but they must be handled gently, as they die quickly when held out of the water or if manhandled. Grayling are one of those fish that bleed easily and profusely, and unfortunately squirm and wiggle all the time, making it difficult to unhook them in the water and worse to grasp them.

MUSKELLUNGE

The short story on muskies is like this: they are hard to catch. They are similar in shape and looks to northern pike, but are distinguished from that species by barred or spotted markings and six to nine pores along each side of the lower jaw. They are caught by trolling diving plugs and by casting with bucktail spinners and diving or surface plugs. And they are found in rivers and lakes, usually around weeds, but also on points and in open water.

But there is much more to the story of muskies. Muskellunge are generally harder to catch than any other freshwater species, and are quite unpredictable. They are fervently pursued by a coterie of devoted admirers, most of whom voluntarily release nearly all of the muskies that they catch.

Musky fishing is the one form of freshwater angling (Altantic salmon runs a close second) in which it is highly regarded merely to glimpse the quarry; a 'follow'–when a a musky trails a lure to the boat–is as meaningful as tossing a horseshoe close to the peg.

Technically speaking, muskellunge are cool-water fish that are close relatives of pickerel and northern pike. They are most abundant in upper Midwestern states, southern Ontario, and Great Lakes drainages, but have been stocked outside those areas. Hybrid muskellunge, which are a sterile offspring from pure musky and pike parentage, and which are called tiger muskies, have been introduced widely.

Muskies generally lurk in or near places where they can lie relatively concealed to ambush forage fish, so anglers must seek places that provide feeding opportunities. Muskies are large fish that have big mouths and that strike big lures, perhaps because they are prone to eating big fish. A 15-inch walleye isn't that big to a 40-inch musky, which positions itself in certain places that attract prey large enough to make an ambush attack worthwhile. The nature of that cover, the depth of water there and nearby, and the presence of current will determine which places are better than others. Here are some prime locations to concentrate on:

SUBMERGED VEGETATION. Muskies are attracted to the edges of vegetation; at the breakline where weeds end and deep water begins; and at the corners, pockets, or other irregular contour features. In the fall they will move away from dead and decaying vegetation; at that time you should look for green and healthy weeds.

POINTS OF LAND. Whether they extend from the shore or from islands, points are natural impediments to fish movement and attractants to prey and predator alike. Concentrate on points with a long underwater slope adjacent to deep water, especially if they break sharply from 10 feet off to 20 or 25 feet, or those that have some form of heavy vegetation around their perimeter, or those that have rock piles on the underwater breaklines.

SHOALS, BARS, SUBMERGED ISLANDS. With or without a hard bottom or vegetation, these structures attract baitfish and gamefish, making them reliable feeding areas.

CONFLUENCES. Near and just below a warm-water discharge, feeder creek, or other tributary is a prime place to seek muskies. In the fall, for example, the immediate area near a warm-water discharge is affected, and may be attractive to forage fish and muskies. Where a tributary meets a major flow is a promising locale as well, especially in summer when the tributary may be dumping cooler and more oxygenated water into the main flow.

CURRENT. A point or shoal that is washed by a strong current is a promising place to find muskies. A locale where strong current can bring bait washing by, or which retards the movement of weak, crippled, or wounded fish, is also a top spot. Back eddies, slicks, and current edges are worth a look, too.

Although muskies may inhabit deep water, they are seldom caught very deep. Most fish are taken in less than 30 feet of water—generally from 15 to 30 feet deep. In many places, they are located in much shallower water. Most

casting musky anglers catch fish from 5 to 15 feet deep; trollers usually catch them from 8 to 30 feet deep.

Casting and trolling both have its advocates and devotees, partially by law (trolling for muskies is not legal in a few places), but mostly by traditional preference. Trolled lures are fished on fairly short lines. There is seldom much reason to put out more than 75 feet of line. Muskies are not spooked by boat noise, and some trollers catch them right in the prop wash, within 10 to 25 feet of the boat and just a few feet below the surface.

The primary advantage of trolling for these fish is the ability to cover a lot of territory on large bodies of water, though heavy vegetation on some waters hinders trolling efforts. Also, trollers don't see fish that might follow their lures, but casters often do. Muskies will pursue a cast-and-retrieved bait right to the boat, occasionally striking at boatside, but more often vanishing. This activity shows an angler where a fish is located; good musky casters remember all of the places where they have caught and seen fish on their favorite waters, and they continue to visit those places regularly. The choice of whether to cast or troll is yours, and should be based on your own interests and abilities as well as the habitat and angling situation.

Musky fishing lures don't have the diversity found in lures for other types of fish. And though there is no sure-fire lure, there are some contenders. Large jigs, jerk baits, a few surface surface plugs, bucktail spinners, and assorted diving plugs are the common lures, with bucktails the runaway favorite for casting, followed by jerk baits. Some muskies are caught on large jigs and on surface plugs, but it is best to focus on bucktails and diving plugs and only experiment with peripheral lures after you've become a proficient angler.

Bucktail spinners are weighted in-line spinners heavily dressed with bucktail hair over one or two treble hooks. They are mainly used in shallow- to mid-depth casting, over the top of submerged cover, and along the edges of shallow submerged cover. They are seldom used for trolling. They are found in a host of color combinations, but black is the hands-down top musky producer. If you're new to the musky casting scene, start with a black bucktail around cabbage beds.

Among diving plugs, shallow-running

Left: *Muskellunge are an unpredictable fish, though one that has a devoted following. This 44-pounder, caught by trolling, was at one time a line-class world record.*

Right: *Casters fish points, weed beds, and shoals for muskies, with bucktail spinners (barely visible in the mouth of this fish) being one of the principal lures.*

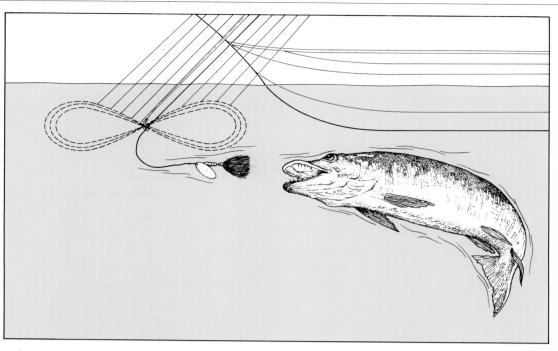

When a musky follows a lure to the boat, it will sometimes strike when the angler makes a series of quick figure-eight movements, with the lure just a short distance from the rod tip.

---

minnow-style baits account for a lot of muskies. They can be used around the edges of weedy habitat, and sometimes are retrieved over the top of deeply submerged vegetation.

Deeper diving plugs can be both cast and trolled. A good tactic with deep-diving plugs is to reel them down until they hit vegetation, then stop the retrieve (which allows the lure to float upward), then reel it in a few feet until you hit vegetation, then stop, and so forth. This is like using a jerk bait except that the lure is far more enticing when retrieved. Deep-diving plugs are better than other lure types for casting around reefs and points and quick-current edges that don't allow vegetation on them. Shallow, medium, and deep divers all have trolling application. Five- to 8-inch long plugs are customary for this, preferably in single- or double-jointed versions, but also in unjointed models. Popular musky plug colors include black, black-and-white, chartreuse, silver-and-black, and yellow, plus perch, walleye, bass, and musky patterns, but there is no clear favorite.

No matter what lure you tie on, the way you use your boat and equipment to cope with the conditions can be a factor in your success. Drift along the side of, rather than through, prime habitat. This permits many casts around an area without alarming any fish that might be there. A musky caster can use an electric motor as much as a bass angler, primarily for boat control and positioning benefits. Sonar can be a substantial aid here, too. In most cases, proper boat positioning over areas likely to hold muskies but not visible to fishermen can only be accomplished through the use of some type of sonar.

Most musky anglers use heavy tackle. Twenty-five to 40-pound line and a stiff rod is standard, but some anglers are very successful with 12- to 20-pound line and a 6-foot fast-action bait casting rod. Muskies fight well but not laboriously, although they can provide some spectacular jumping action. They are noted for being hard to drive a hook into, and for escaping from anglers who thought they had a well-hooked fish. The use of a steel leader is advised because of a musky's formidable dentures.

PANFISH

There are many so-called panfish that provide great sport and table fare for legions of anglers. Much of the attention paid to panfish is through very casual fishing, yet there are many panfishes that are pursued fervently by some anglers, using very sporting tackle and prizing their catch for food value. Crappies are probably foremost of these, and they are treated separately in this section. Under this heading we will deal with the three most prominent fish that anglers refer to as panfish.

ROCK BASS

The range of these fish, which are also called goggle-eyes in some places or redeyes in others, is primarily northerly, in many of the same environments in which smallmouth bass are found. They inhabit lakes and rivers, spending much time around rock areas and wood structures and generally feed deep below the surface. Rock bass are a gregarious fish, and it is often possible to catch several or more from the same locale.

Sunken logs or tree stumps are prime places to locate these fish, as are deep-water rocky ledges, quiet still pools along river banks where large rocks are present, deep-water gravel beds where a large weed structure begins, and beneath overhanging willows along a river or lake shoreline. They spawn in late spring or early summer, making a nest in shallow water when the temperature is about 65 degrees.

The primary forage for rock bass is crayfish, insects, and small minnows of various species. Many are caught by live bait anglers using garden worms, nightcrawlers, small crayfish, and small minnows. The most common tactic is placing a small worm on a short-shanked No. 4 hook with a few small split shot above it and stillfishing with a bobber, allowing the bait to sit about 6 inches above the bottom. Among artificials, small crankbaits, spinners, and spoons may work, as well as fly rod poppers or bugs. These should be retrieved very slowly.

SUNFISH

Known as "bream" in many locales, bluegills are the most widely distributed panfish, and are found with, or in similar places as, such companion and related species as the redbreasted sunfish, green sunfish, pumpkinseed, shell-cracker, and longeared sunfish, all of which are similar in configuration but different in appearance. These species, collectively known as sunfish, are highly respected fighters even though they are diminutive fish. They are most commonly pursued in the spring and early summer while they are spawning in shallow water and where their round clustered nests are readily visible along the shoreline of ponds and lakes. Vegetation is a prime place to seek sunfish, followed by stumps, logs, and fallen trees.

A lot of fishing for sunfish is done with live worms and bobbers in relatively shallow water, although the bigger fish are usually found deep. A long-shanked # 8 or 10 hook is employed, since sunfish don't have very large mouths, and is used unweighted or with just a small split shot. Other baits include crickets, tiny minnows, and meal worms. Small jigs are a fine lure, and small spinners and spinnerbaits can be productive, as well as dry flies, nymphs, and popping bugs used with a fly rod. A slow retrieve is best. Sunfish are popular in winter, too, where small jigs, flies, and meal worms are used.

YELLOW PERCH

Yellow perch, which are predominantly a northern coolwater fish, are among the most favored panfish for edibility, tasting much like their walleye relations. Not a member of the sunfish family, yellow perch are in fact a true perch. They are schooling fish, and while they are caught in open water they are most avidly sought through the ice in winter and while in the midst of their spring spawning runs in which they ascend tributaries and seek warm shoreline areas in bays and back eddies. Yellow perch primarily like cool water and will school deep in places where surface temperatures get warm, although they will move shallower to feed.

Perch are caught on a variety of baits and lures, with live worms, small minnow-imitating plugs, jigs, spoons, and spinners being among the best attractors. Bobbers are frequently employed with live bait; nightcrawler rigs, sporting a No. 2 hook and No. 2 spinner, are also effective.

The tackle used for panfish needn't be stout. Light spinning or spincasting outfits are more than adequate, and in many areas, long cane poles without reels are used to dabble bait into selected pockets for various sunfish species. Four- to 8-pound-test line is ample. Fly fishing is also an excellent way to pursue panfish, particularly bluegills and other sunfish species, and even perch when they are in shallow water in the spring. Floating and sinking flies, small streamers, and poppers are the terminal items.

A good-sized yellow perch, such as the one that this angler caught on a jig, will provide excellent table fare.

PICKEREL

Pickerel are lean, sporty, evil-eyed bandits, yet they are not widely acclaimed. They are virtually neglected by most non-winter fishermen, rarely specifically pursued by open-water anglers, and often downgraded by people who catch them unintentionally while seeking more popular fish. Yet, pickerel have fine sporting attributes. They are an aggressive, available fish, offering a good chance of angling success, and they are good battlers on appropriate tackle.

Not too many other gamesters will follow a lure right to the boat with impunity. It is common for pickerel to strike viciously just as a lure is about to be lifted from the water. They often make a vee wake in shallow water when dashing out from cover to intercept a lure, and they may hit a lure three, four, or five times in a row while chasing it. Long, slimy, toothy, camouflaged in chain-like markings and green-brown colors, and sporting cold-blooded eyes, the pickerel is a smaller but equally fearsome-looking version of his northern pike and muskellunge cousins.

Pickerel are referred to as chain-sides, jacks, jackfish, pike, and other names. They are not a jack but a member of the Esox, or pike, family. They are sometimes confused with walleyes, particularly in southern Canada where walleyes are called yellow pickerel, but the walleye is a member of the perch family and is unlike the true pickerel in nearly all respects. Pickerel are abundant where pike and muskies are not found or are not very abundant. They range from Nova Scotia to Florida and from Texas through most of the easterly states, though their primary abundance is in Florida and Georgia and from the mid-Atlantic states north.

The habitat of pickerel is somewhat similar to that of largemouth bass, particularly in regard to vegetation and abundant cover. Found in ponds, bogs, tidal and nontidal rivers, streams, lakes, and reservoirs, their primary habitat is lily pads and various types of weeds, and sometimes lay near such objects as stumps, docks, and fallen trees. Invariably the waters with the best pickerel populations are those with abundant vegetation, much of which is found near shore.

Mostly pickerel consume other fish, such as small minnows and fry, but they are fond of mid-size fish like yellow perch and other pickerel in the 4- to 6-inch lengths. They will often go

The chain pickerel, shown here, is fond of flashy, brightly colored plugs and other lures, and is both voracious and aggressive.

for larger fish, too, and it is not uncommon to catch a large pickerel that is still trying to digest another pickerel half its own length.

Pickerel are primarily attracted to movement and flash. Nearly any lure with a spinning blade or sparkle-like appearance will catch at least one pickerel in its lifetime. Standard spinners and small spoons are traditionally effective lures, but they are prone to hanging up in thick cover. Spinnerbaits, weedless in-line spinners, and weedless spoons are a better option. Worms and jigs are also taken by pickerel, but the result is often a line severed by the fish's teeth. Fly fishing is also worthwhile for pickerel, with streamers being especially ravished. Tandem-bladed spinnerbaits with a white or chartreuse skirt are probably the single most popular pickerel lure, fished with a trailer hook and equipped with silver, copper, chartreuse, white, or yellow blades. A variety of colors works in other lures, but silver and shad are among the favorites.

Live bait may be the top pickerel catchers for most anglers, certainly in the winter. Minnows or shiners up to 6 inches long are used. Pickerel often strike their prey to stun or cripple them so they can re-attack and consume the prey head first. Therefore they usually take bait sideways in their mouth and run off with it a bit, maneuver it around, then swallow it head first. Because of this, an angler should give the fish time to swallow the bait before setting the hook.

In typical pickerel water, the best fishing is had in the spring. Pickerel spawn in shallow bays and marshy areas after ice-out in the North and in the mid-to late-winter in the South. Water temperature and the development of cover are usually two indicators of progressing pickerel activity. Pickerel feed all year and can be caught in modest numbers in the cold water of early spring. When the water temperature passes 50, they become more active, and 55- to 70-degree water temperatures offer excellent conditions. At this time, weed growth is developing, providing more cover in which to lie motionless for the inevitable bait fish ambush. When vegetation becomes thick, which will be in the late spring or early summer, there is usually more forage available; these two conditions generally combine to lessen fishing productivity. From this time through mid-fall, it is important to be able to fish heavy cover effectively. In the cold water conditions of early spring and fall, fish slowly for pickerel, as would also be done for bass. Shallow-running crankbaits and minnow-imitation plugs are best.

Pickerel are unfortunately caught by many anglers using tackle that is too heavy to allow the fish to make a good showing. The best gear for pickerel fishing is a spinning outfit with 4- or 6-pound line. Considering that the average pickerel weighs no more than a pound and a half, such thread seems to be appropriate. On light tackle or fly rods, pickerel will run, jump, and cavort in a pleasing manner. Only the large pickerel put up a really good fight on medium to heavy tackle. Where cover is really thick, and where largemouth bass are also being pursued, you'll have to temper this go-light advice with practicality.

NORTHERN PIKE

The evil-eyed, spear-shaped northern pike is a fish that might well have been named "water wolf". It is often likened to the notoriously vicious barracuda of saltwater. Although disparaged by a few fishermen who catch pike while seeking other species of fish, the pike is a worthy angling quarry, one that grows fairly large, fights well, and accommodates sportsmen often enough to be of substantial interest to a lot of anglers in the areas where they are found.

This toothy, slinky, coolwater fish is most prominent in the northern U. S. and across Canada, with the majority of larger, trophy-size specimens coming from mid-to northern Canadian rivers and lakes. Born in weedy waters, pike spend much of their life in similar habitat, holding motionless in the vegetation, camouflaged for suddenly striking passersby. Menacingly, the northern pike waits in ambush for a moment of attack.

Key habitat structures in lakes include weedy bays, river inlets where weeds are plentiful, shoreline points with beds of cabbage weeds on their open-water sides, reefs with coontail weeds, marshy shorelines, lily pads, and reedy pockets along sandy and rocky shorelines. There are many others, but some form of vegetative structure obviously holds a major portion of the pike population. Some pike, especially large ones, are found in open waters where they will forage on schools of bait, so it is not necessarily the case that every pike in a given environment will be in the weeds.

Pike are found fairly shallow in the early part of the year, and some pike (mostly smaller ones) will be in shallow water throughout the season. Bigger pike, however, usually gravitate to deeper, heavy-cover haunts as the water warms. During early summer they move to cabbage weeds, for example (also called pike weeds), in water that exceeds 6 or 7 feet and drops off to 15 or so. Look to the outer edge of this for trophy fish, and especially pockets or indentations.

In rivers, pike are a lazy fish and usually try to establish an easy ambush position. Look for them where small rivers and streams merge with the main flow; in the small eddy below a beaver hut; downstream from islands; in shallow backwaters; under docks; on shorelines just below riprap or wing dams; on the inside of large eddies; and where brush and slow water meet.

Pike are a voracious predator and consume various small fish, including other pike, and they sometimes attack other fish that are quite

Left: *This large northern pike is a prized catch for nearly any freshwater fisherman. Note how its markings are different from those of the pickerel in the preceding photograph.*

Right: *Shallow running plugs, as shown here, plus spoons, spinnerbaits, and spinners, top the list of effective pike catchers.*

large, bigger than any lure in your tackle box. Even relatively small pike may attack a big lure, so the big lure/big fish theory doesn't necessarily hold with these game creatures. Often, smaller pike are more eager and more vulnerable to angling, and they out-hustle a larger fish to a lure of any size. This is especially true in places where pike are very abundant. However, using fairly large lures is nonetheless advantageous in pike fishing, as they will discourage some smaller fish from attacking and will represent more of a meal to a larger pike than a diminutive lure, thus being more worthy of pursuit.

Pike lures include the traditional red-and-white spoon, plus a fluorescent orange-bladed spinnerbait or bucktail spinner; an orange-and-yellow-backed minnow imitation plug; a yellow, Five-O-Diamonds pattern spoon; a black bucktail with a single fluorescent spinner; and various shallow-and deep-diving plugs in gaudy and metallic colors. Good pike lures often tend to be brightly colored and to work with a broad, wide-wobbling type of action.

Pike are attracted not only to size and shape in lures, however, but to swimming action, flash and visibility, and noise. They are one of the most curious of freshwater fish, and getting their attention is one of the keys to catching them. That would seem true of most fish, but there are many other freshwater species that are keenly aware of the presence of certain lures in their domain, yet otherwise disinterested.

Lure types and the techniques used to present them vary greatly for northern pike, although many would-be pike catchers stick to the simplicity of casting spoons in and around weeds. Casting weedless spoons directly into a mass of shoreline vegetation and retrieving outward can have merit, and is a standard tactic, though one that suffers in heavily fished waters.

All types of plugs can be useful in catching pike – surface plugs, shallow-running plugs, and medium to deep divers – but shallow runners are most popularly used, as are long and slender plugs that imitate small fish. Most fishermen think only of shallow-running minnow-style plugs for pike. These are useful, of course, and are perennial pike catchers. Anglers should broaden their horizons, however, where plugs are concerned. Many of the larger minnow-shaped plugs used for striper and musky trolling, for example, are effective pike catchers, both in casting and trolling applications.

An overlooked hot pike plug is a super-shallow-running (1 foot and less) bulbous crankbait that rattles very noisily, which not only calls pike up out of deep weeds in the summer, but can be worked in back-bay shallows in the spring. In lieu of this particular lure, you could try a surface plug such as a walking-type stick bait or a propellored plug (perhaps even a popper), to get a pike's attention and bring it up for a strike. Another option would be to use a medium- or deep-diving crankbait that possesses rattles, working it in a stop-go fashion over and through the weeds. Still another option is to use a non-rattling deep-diving plug; this should first be worked around the edges of the vegetation to entice a pike out, and then through it in a slow twitching style.

Another good plug is the diving minnow variety, used for parallel casting to banks and weedlines, and also for shallow pull-pause retrieves; it's helpful to use the same lure – which has good flash and looks like a small fish – for deep edges as well as for relatively shallow work. Barbless hooks, incidentally, are the only way to go where multi-hooked lures, especially plugs, are used for pike, and some plugs can be switched to single barbless hooks, which diminishes the chances of being hurt (you and the fish) and facilitates unhooking.

Spinnerbaits have become a popular northern pike lure in recent years, fished through weed beds, a round timber, up against stuimps, in and about brush, and across rocky points. Their weedless nature is especially beneficial, and they work especially well in the spring when pike stage in extremely shallow water during spawning and post-spawning periods.

Jigs work well for these fish, although when used without a wire leader, many jigs are lost to a pike's toothy maw. Newer pike jigs include plastic eel-like versions, or those formed of natural hair, and with bright colors. Sometimes these are slow-trolled long the deep edge of weed beds, slowly lifting and lowering the rod tip. Casting along the edges is also productive.

Bait casting, spin casting, and spinning gear are all suitable, though bait casting is most preferable where large lures or bait are used. Some fly-rodding, using large streamers, is also done. Line capacity is not a big factor with reels in pike fishing. Rods should be 5 1/2 to 7 feet, with a stiff butt and midsection and rather fast tip. Most pike fishermen prefer heavy line, with 12- to 17-pound-test favored, but many opt for 6- to 10-pound line where the cover is not thick.

Steel leaders are used by many pike anglers, but avoided by others. A large pike may take a lure deep or get some of the line in his mouth, and certainly many lure-hooked pike get free when they cut an unleadered line. Yet many fish are caught without the use of leaders, although this is sometimes pure luck. You have to make your own judgment here; I opt for small (6-inch) 20-pound-test leaders so as not to hamper casting but to afford some protection.

Pike aren't hard to subdue. They do a lot of thrashing and short-distance darting, and some don't really fight until they eyeball the boat or fisherman. The one difficulty with light lines is the heavy weeds in which these fish are found.

Big pike tend to make long, steady runs through thick vegetation. A leader can be very helpful there. too.

SALMON

ATLANTIC AND LAND-LOCKED SALMON

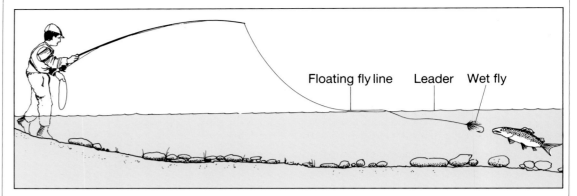

Despite its relative scarcity today, the Atlantic salmon is still considered the premier salmon. Dubbed "the leaper" by Romans, this salmon is revered for its sporting quality, succulent flesh, general tenacity, and mysterious lifestyle. Today there are fishable runs in only a portion of their original range, mostly in eastcoastal Canadian provinces.

These fish migrate great distances from their wintering grounds in the North Atlantic to their natal tributaries. It is during their limited spawning run period that seagoing Atlantics are pursued by sport fishermen in rivers; there is virtually no ocean sport fishing done for this species. The average fish weighs less than 15 pounds, and one over that is considered quite large, though even the smaller fish fight extraordinarily well. Some Atlantic slmon live to spawn more than once; some die in the process through natural means, but they differ from Pacific salmon, which all die upon completion of their spawning ritual.

The seagoing Atlantic salmon is the only Atlantic salmon species but it is also found in a "landlocked" form. Landlocks are fish that are confined to natural lakes and impoundments, and which usually utilize the major tributaries for spawning. Landlocked salmon, also known as ouananiche in eastern Canada, are generally small, and found in sizes from 1 to 3 or 4 pounds, although larger fish are caught in some environs. A big landlock is usually one over 5 pounds, but they have been caught to 20 and may grow larger in the Great Lakes. Landlocked salmon are found primarily in the Northeastern part of the continent and the Great Lakes, and then not in great abundance. In the U. S., most of the landlocked salmon population is supported by stocking efforts. They are, however, a highly desirable fish, known for long runs and superior fighting ability, and they are widely sought by anglers in lakes and rivers.

Seagoing Atlantic salmon begin their life in the fall in the upper reaches of streams and rivers, where, as eggs, they are buried under gravel. The fry hatch in late winter or spring. Young fish, called parr, remain in the river until they are roughly 6 to 8 inches long, at which

The author holds a grilse, a young sea-run Atlantic salmon. A typical northern river salmon pool is seen in the background.

time they are called smolts. Smolts eventually migrate to sea. Some return after one year and are called grilse. Most return after several years, and all cease feeding as they enter spawning tributaries. The life history of landlocked salmon is quite similar to that of the seagoing Atlantic, the principal difference being that the latter will enter tributaries from summer through early fall prior to spawning, while the former don't enter tributaries until September.

Atlantic and landlocked salmon hug the bottom in rivers, resting in pools and deep-water sections. They are not usually caught in the fast-water reaches, although they will be located at the head and tail of pools, and in slick-water runs. It is common when fishing for them to start fishing above the head of a pool or run, and methodically work your way down through the entire stretch, casting down and across and letting your fly swing at the end of each cast. Most fish are caught when the fly makes its swing or hangs momentarily in the current at the end of the swing.

Fly fishing is the angling method by law or tradition in most of North America for seagoing Atlantic salmon, which are usually found shallower than other salmon and are often caught by sight fishing, i. e., casting to a specific fish that has been seen, rather than casting blindly for unobserved fish as is usually done in coho and chinook angling. On some waters there are also restrictions on the hooks to be used, with weighted hooks or flies illegal (in New

Atlantic salmon anglers use a floating fly line and leader, and cast wet or dry flies.

Brunswick, for example) to minimize accidental or deliberate foul hooking of fish.

Wet flies in various colorful patterns and sizes are popular for Atlantic salmon fishing, with the larger flies generally reserved for fast, high rivers. Dry flies work at times, too, which is an anomaly considering the nonfeeding disposition of these fish; the dries used, however, such as Bombers, are large flies and usually tied out of tightly packed deer hair.

Atlantics may take on the first, fiftieth, or one-hundredth cast, acting out of reflex or annoyance, and they may be put down easily or be relatively undisturbed by the angler's presence and activities. Unlike other salmon in rivers, Atlantics and landlocks are prone to jump high and often, in addition to making long, demanding runs. Long rods and reels with plenty of backing are required. Standard fly tackle consists of an 8 or 9 weight rod equipped with a floating fly line and a reel with 200 yards of 20 or 30 pound-test backing. Leader length should match rod length, or be slightly shorter. A sinking fly line or sink-tip fly line is not used. A 9-foot rod with 9 weight line is pretty standard, and useful considering the bulk of some of the flies that are cast.

Long casts in the 70- to 100-foot-plus range are the norm on many Atlantic salmon rivers, though that isn't always a necessity. Getting a

good drift on the fly, mending it where necessary, and at times even riffling it across the surface gently, are important aspects of presentation. The evening and early morning hours are particularly good times, and overcast days bode well for day-long fishing, although there is no guarantee on such matters.

Landlocked salmon in lakes are principally caught by trolling, with most activity taking place in the spring, after ice-out and until these fish move deep. While some salmon may be caught when the ice is breaking up and the water is in the 39- to 42-degree range, better action doesn't begin until the water hits the mid 40s. Landlocks are caught from the surface to 20 feet deep at this time and can be found near shore over relatively shallow bottom or in open areas over deep water.

As the surface temperature increases, landlocks are more likely to be found near tributaries if they attract large spawning runs of smelt, or inshore where schools of smelt or spawning alewives may be located. Water temperature then is in the low to mid 50s. This activity takes place in May and through June, but by mid to late June in a normal year, the surface water will be warming up, and landlocks will move to deeper water and locate in the thermocline, roughly staying in 52- to 57-degree water and roaming as widely as the size of the lake and water temperature zones will allow. They are usually hardest to locate and catch at that time.

The traditional and still widely practiced method of landlock salmon trolling is to use a fly rod and a streamer fly. The rod is between 8 and 9 feet long and equipped with a large-capacity fly reel loaded with 100 yards of backing, a level sinking line, and a long leader. The leader is between 20 and 30 feet in length, usually 6 to 10 pounds in strength. A streamer fly is tied to the end, and sometimes a split shot or two is added to the leader. The rod is often held in the angler's hand and kept parallel to the water and it is jerked backward frequently to give the fly a darting appearance.

Another traditional method is to use a fly rod or conventional rod with levelwind reel and lead core line, fishing a spoon or fly at the business end. Long rods are used and anglers hold them and pulsate them as with fly rods. Downrigger and sideplaner fishing have increased in the landlocked salmon scene, especially where spoons and plugs are employed, and are fished in conventional manners.

Lure selection should follow the baitfish patterns in a given lake. Smelt are the foremost, and preferred, landlocked salmon food. Alewives are a major forage in some locales. Elsewhere, ciscos, shiners, and yellow perch make up part of their lake diet. Smelt are usually the bread-and-butter prey, and most landlocked salmon lures are meant to imitate smelt. These lures

A nice landlocked salmon is revived for release. Landlocks are found in northeastern North America in rivers and lakes where they have no egress to the sea.

include minnow-imitating plugs in straight and jointed versions (from 4 to 6 inches), long thin spoons, and single or tandem streamer flies.

The best fishing, especially in spring, is often in the first few hours of the day, with a late afternoon or evening flurry common. Midday, particularly under bluebird conditions, is dubious. A relatively fast trolling speed is employed for landlocks, and while lines are usually set from 75 to 200 feet behind the boat on flatlines and 40 to 80 feet back on deep downriggers, some spring fish are literally caught in the wash of the propeller.

CHINOOK AND COHO SALMON

There are six species of salmon in North America. These fall under the categories of Atlantic (which see) or Pacific. Chinook, coho, sockeye (kokanee), pink, and chum (dog) salmon make up the Pacific grouping; chinook and coho are very prominent in North American sportfisheries in the Pacific Northwest from northern California to Alaska and in the Great Lakes, while chum, sockeye, and pinks are lesser catches, sought by river fishermen when they are abundant but not as highly valued for food.

These salmon are anadromous, spending their lives in open water and returning to their tributaries of birth to spawn. Open water has

traditionally meant the ocean; for chinook and coho, however, saltwater environs have also been replaced by large inland lakes in which these fish have been stocked. In either instance, salmon have a relatively short life of usually two to four years, which is characterized by wandering, and rapid growth through extensive feeding.

Chinooks are the largest members of either salmon genus. Also known as king salmon and as spring salmon, they are extremely strong-fighting fish, and pose a great angling challenge, especially in swift and narrow river environs. Along with cohos, which are also known as silver salmon, they were introduced to the Great

the rivers from mid- to late summer, spawning in the fall. In inland lakes, there is only a fall run. These fish do not feed once they enter spawning tributaries (and in the Great Lakes cease feeding when they gather near tributaries prior to running) and they all die after spawning.

Cohos are a popular sport fish in the West as well as in the Great Lakes, though not generally as abundant. While they are smaller on average than chinook, they are able fighters and active jumpers. Their coastal range parallels that of the chinook. Like chinooks, coho populations in the Great Lakes are supported almost entirely by hatchery production. They have brightly colored silver sides when they are in open water. Both

derings and are gathering in the vicinity of coastal rivers, waiting for rains to send new water out the rivers and signal the beginning of the "run".

Coho and chinook in the Great Lakes are widely pursued throughout the season in open water, as they have nowhere else to go. They are inshore early in the season and ultimately seek out a water temperature of 52 to 55 degrees, which occurs at the thermocline. The thermocline is usually deeper as summer progresses; however, due to shifting winds, its depth changes. Coho tend to be found closer to shore than chinooks, though the depth and location of each is a highly variable factor. These fish gather

Lakes, where they use these large bodies of water as if they were the ocean, and they have been a key factor in the revitalization of sport fisheries in those waters.

There are spring and fall runs of true seagoing chinooks; the former stays in the river for a year or more before migrating to the ocean, while the latter generally leaves after a three- to four-month period. The spring-run fish may enter the rivers from mid- to late winter, spawning late in the spring; the fall-run fish typically enter

Left: *Pacific Coast chinook salmon live most of their lives in the ocean, and are caught by sport fishermen when they return for the purpose of ascending natal waters*

Above: *Shown is a fairly large coho salmon; cohos are smaller on average than chinooks, but more acrobatic and energetic when caught.*

coho and chinook salmon are intensively sought by boat fishermen in coastal estuaries and bays and in the Great Lakes proper, and by boat, bank, and wading fishermen in the rivers.

Since coho and chinook salmon are found in various environments, there are many fishing methods utilized for them. Identifying habitat, structure, and so forth, as one might do for other freshwater fish, is less of a problem than either enticing nonfeeding river fish to strike through careful presentation, or locating the right depth and temperature of open water in which salmon schools will be located. Essentially, then, there are open-water and river-fishing techniques.

There is a significant ocean, tide-water, and estuary sportfishery for salmon in Pacific waters, which involves trolling with spinners and cut herring, as well as mooching (which see). This takes place from summer through early fall, when the fish have returned from their sea wan-

in schools and traverse great distances as they seek out desirable water conditions and alewife or smelt forage.

Since salmon do a great deal of migrating and are found at varied water levels in open water, particularly beyond 30 feet and as much as 70 to 100 feet deep in the summer, it is necessary at most times to search and fish deeply for them. A variety of trolling techniques are primarily used, with downrigger fishing being most popular. Some drift fishing and a limited amount of jigging is also done.

While open-water salmon fishing is essentially a boating proposition, the land-bound angler can score on open-water salmon in the spring and fall, and occasionally in the winter. Spring is the best all-around time for salmon in the Great Lakes. When the fish are in close to shore seeking out the most comfortable water temperature (influenced by wind direction and the introduction of warm tributary waters) they are just as accessible and vulnerable to shore-based fishermen as they are to boaters. The only edge that boaters have at this time is mobility – being able to cover a large expanse of water. Shorefishing close to the tributaries is generally best, as this is where the warmer water is. Breakwaters, piers, beaches, and other access points become jammed with long-rodded casters at this time. As the fish move out, shore fishing becomes markedly less productive. It increases in productivity again in late summer/early fall when many salmon return to migrate upriver.

Live bait fishing is a seldom-practiced technique among chinook and coho salmon anglers, principally due to the wandering nature of the quarry and the fact that a prodigious amount of natural forage (alewives, smelt, herring, anchovies, etc.) makes it difficult to get a hooked offering recognized. In the Pacific waters, cut bait fishing with herring is extremely effective for coho and chinook. Salmon eggs are very effective bait, and are used for drift fishing in coastal rivers and Great Lakes tributaries; they are usually fished in gobs or egg sacks, and are sometimes combined with crayfish meat or tails, frequently with just a pencil or ball lead rig or otherwise with a bobber.

Tributary fishing is the predominant Great Lakes method of catching chinook and coho salmon each fall. Fish that have just entered rivers or have only been in them a short while may still exhibit a feeding urge in the sense that they may strike a lure or fly as a conditioned, reflexive act. But the longer they are in the river the less this is so. Often it can be difficult to get these fish to strike any offering and it is usually vital to present the offering right in front of the fish. A precise presentation, therefore, particularly in regard to getting the bait or lure down to the bottom, is of foremost importance.

Long rods, medium-heavy lines, and small offerings are the elements in coho and chinook river fishing. In addition to eggs, spinners, spoons, and wobbling plugs have devotees as well. Fly fishing is more popular in the West than in the Great Lakes, primarily because the rivers in the former are bigger and longer than those in the latter, affording a greater expanse of fishing opportunities and somewhat less crowding. Shallower sections, however, provide the best opportunity. Bright flies and fast-sinking fly lines (usually the high density full-sink versions) get the nod.

Salmon hug the bottom, resting in pools and deep-water sections. They are also found in the tail of a run before swifter water, and in holes

This Great Lakes salmon is the same type of fish as the one caught on the Pacific Coast, but has been caught in the fall just prior to spawning, when it has darkened greatly and undergone a drastic physiological change.

and runs along deep-water banks. They are not usually caught in the fast-water reaches. Lures must be cast slightly upstream and quartered, drifting with the current to the end of the swing. Whatever the offering, it must bounce or swim along the bottom, and the right size sinker is critically important. Too little and the offering never reaches the bottom and is totally ineffective; too much and it drags in the current, acting unnaturally or hanging up repeatedly.

Much river salmon fishing is done by bank or wading anglers, but in large rivers, angling from boats for coho and chinook is not only practical but effective. Non-fly fishermen usually use wobbling plugs in the river more than they do other hardware, or they use salmon eggs or spawn sacks. Forward trolling here is not a popularly utilized tactic, and is not often prac-

ticed due to boat and angler traffic. Anchoring or controlled drifting (see backtrolling and back bouncing) are the primary boat-fishing methods. Those who anchor do so in or above selected pools, setting their lines out 50 to 75 feet behind the boat, allowing the plugs to work constantly in current, perhaps bouncing them back slowly and then retrieving to repeat the procedure.

In rivers, tackle ranges from 14- to 30-pound-test line, the latter used in narrow rivers and where heavy weights and big fish are encountered. Levelwind reels are preferred, and long (8- to 9-foot) rods are employed. Fly rods suitable for 9 and 10 weight lines with plenty of reel backing are necessary. In open-water trolling, 8- to 9-foot downrigger rods get most play, with levelwind reels most popular and line strength ranging from 12 to 20 pounds.

SHAD

American shad (Alosa sapidissima) and hickory shad are not to be confused with the smaller shad (threadfin and gizzard) found in southern and western reservoirs, which are baitfish that provide good forage for such species as striped bass, largemouth bass, and trout. American and hickory shad live most of their lives in the ocean and then ascend major Atlantic and Pacific Coast rivers to spawn, returning to the sites where they were born. American shad, which are the more widespread of the two species and the larger, generally weigh in excess of 2 pounds, with 3 to 5 pounds common, and the occasional fish weighing from 5 to 8 pounds. The males (called bucks) are usually smaller than the females (called roe fish or hens).

One of the primary appeals of these fish, which has been called the "poor man's salmon", is their active fighting ability. Shad provide drag-screeching runs, broadside-to-the-current fight, and frequent aerial maneuvers. They are as spunky a river fish as there is to be found. But they are also of limited availability seasonally. The shad spawning run only lasts for about a six- to eight-week period in the spring, and these fish often move through a river in stages or waves. They are affected by water conditions, and are often not present in the same locales on a day-to-day basis.

Shad are not much for mid-day activity. Often you can experience the best shad fishing in the evening, and early in the morning is considered prime time. The first two or three hours of the day may be the best because shad migrate upriver at night, and there is a new wave of migrants in the morning, and perhaps also because of the low level of light. Shad will move, however, during the day, particularly when it is cloudy or rainy, and may migrate from pool to pool or even move around in a large, slow-flowing section of water during the day, being visible on or just below the surface as they cruise en masse. This is often seen when the fish are on the spawning grounds, and they appear to be daisy-chaining, much like tarpon.

Shad basically stick to the river channels, preferring deep water to the swift, riffling, shallow sections. The primary place to fish for them is in the pools. This is slower, calmer, and deeper water than the rest of the river sections, and shad primarily rest in such spots before continuing upriver. You may find a large school of fish occupying a particular pool on a given day, or you may find few or none. Sometimes, when success tapers off in a given spot, you merely

need to move slightly up, down, or across the river to be back in action.

Light spinning tackle is standard for shad. A 6- to 7-foot light-action rod is good, using a spinning reel equipped with from 4- to 8-pound line. The reel should have a smooth drag, as large shad will take varied amounts of line during the fight. Terminal gear largely consists of shad darts; a dart is a lead-bodied buck-tailed form of jig with a tapered form and slanted nose. Darts are the perennially favored shad catcher, though some anglers have success with flies, small spinners, and tiny spoons.

Usually a fisherman must get these offerings down to the bottom, a task that is influenced by the depth of water, strength of current, weight of lure, and size of line. Shad do not feed during their spawning runs, and apparently strike out of reflexive action and thus don't seem to go out of their way to chase a lure. Your offering has to get in front of a fish's nose to be effective. For

this reason, it is common to get hung up and to lose a lot of lures in the pursuit of shad.

Shore fishermen, waders, and those casting from anchored boats should cast across and upstream, allow their lure to sink to the bottom, then with line tight, let the lure swing downstream with the current until it reaches the end of its sweep. Boat fishermen either troll into the current or anchor and still-fish their lures by letting them hang in the current. In either case, let out approximately 75 feet of line behind the boat, using a heavy enough lure (or weighting it with split shot about 18 to 24 inches ahead of the lure) to get just off the bottom.

Darts range in size from tiny to 1/2-ounce. Heavy versions are used in early spring when the river is high, swift, and roily, and it takes a lot of weight to stay down. But heavy darts are also large in size and may not attract fish even when they do stay down, so anglers often go to smaller sized darts with split shot; the extra weight keeps the dart down, but the smaller size dart is more favorable to the shad. One-eighth-to 1/4-ounce darts are most widely used.

A red-headed, white-bodied dart (with white

or yellow bucktail) is the time-honored, favorite color and it is a good fish catcher. But darts come in a host of colors and combinations, and it pays to have a selection of sizes and colors available. Black head/green body, green head/chartreuse body, red head/chartreuse body, and red head/yellow body are among the most successful combinations. It is a good idea to switch colors frequently, however, especially when you know there are fish in the area you are working, and they don't respond to your initial offering.

Very effective for trolling are tiny spoons with No. 6 hooks. A good shine is important, and the lure must have perfect balance to run properly, since action is critical. The spoon should twirl at a fast rate, and it is fished in a similar manner to darts, though it is not necessary to put out as much line; 50 feet or thereabouts will do if the river section is from 8 to 12 feet deep. Use a swiveling bead chain sinker (1/4-ounce is standard) with spoons, about 18 inches up the line.

A shad comes to two anglers as the sun sets; early in the morning and late in the day are preferred fishing times.

Fly fishing for shad is growing in popularity on both coasts. Rods should be suited for an 8 weight line (though you can do with less) and be in the 8- to 9-foot range. Sinking, fast sinking, and sink-tip fly lines are employed depending on river depth and current flow conditions. A short leader is fine. Flies are mostly short-shank streamers, sometimes brightly colored, and often weighted with bead eyes. The use of bead eyes and lead strips on the body, however, should be checked, as this is illegal in some places (especially New Brunswick) where weighted flies are prohibited (mainly for salmon fishing to avoid deliberate snagging of fish). It is usually necessary to get the fly down to the bottom, so an across, swing, and hang presentation is used, with most fish taking as the fly makes its down-current turn or when stripped back in retrieval. Some fly-caught shad can be taken close to the surface, usually when milling in slow pools, and a short stripping retrieve is used.

STURGEON

The sturgeon is somewhat of an anomaly. It isn't worthy of being classified as a gamefish, yet its eggs are nearly priceless. It reaches hundreds of pounds, spawning millions of eggs, grows to lengths exceeding 10 feet, and is a strong stubborn fighter; yet there is a general lack of interest in this fish, probably because so little is known about sturgeon and the dozen or so subspecies that comprise its family.

Sturgeon are river fish. Their range covers most of North America when all the members of their family tree are taken into consideration. Practically, however, they are only caught deliberately in the largest rivers, principally places like the Columbia River in the Northwest, where a small number of anglers deliberately seek these creatures, and in brackish or estuarine waters, such as San Francisco Bay in California and New York's Hudson River. Also common and fairly widespread is the so-called lake sturgeon, which is not the largest, but can grow up to 6 feet long and perhaps a few hundred pounds. They are occasionally hooked accidentally by Midwestern walleye anglers and succumb to a gob of nightcrawlers left lying on the bottom, although they usually escape, being too much of match for the moderately equipped angler. Sturgeon feed on such bottom matter as fish eggs, mollusks, insect larvae, leeches, crayfish, and hellgrammites; nightcrawlers are an effective angler's bait.

Proper equipage for these creatures is a large-capacity levelwind reel and fairly stiff rod. Line weight varies, with 25-pound-test the beginning point, and line of 80- to 100-pound strength used by those who are the specialists. Hooks do not have to be really large, with 1/0 to 4/0 short-shanked models doing the job. Sinkers are heavy, however, since most sturgeon fishing is done below high falls and dams, with slip, three-way, or walking sinkers utilized in 3- to 10-ounce sizes.

When seeking sturgeon, fish large, deep holes directly below dams and falls, along the outside edge of a bend, and in the main channel.walking sinkers being utilized in 3- to lO-ounces.

Sturgeon also hold directly downstream from a place where the river bottom shallows up and there is a hard rock area.

In smaller rivers, if the shallows are 2 to 4 feet deep, fast and running over rock and gravel, look for sturgeon to hold about 50 yards down from the structure where the surface water visibly smooths out. Here, the water should be about 8 to 10 feet deep.

When fishing a slow-moving, mud-bottom river that has a number of slowly twisting turns, look for sturgeon to hold along the outside edge of a bend. Look for places that are at least 2 feet deeper than other areas in the river channel. Stick to the center of the river channel if the river does little or no bending.

Where the river bottom consists of mud and loam, keep your bait slightly above bottom by using a floating jig tipped with a leech or nightcrawler or a tiny crappie float tied between sinker and bait. In fast river waters, fish channels areas with deep drops.

The bottom-scrounging sturgeon is one of the largest fish to be found in freshwater, and also one of the rarest for the average angler to encounter.

SUCKERS

There isn't any area of the United States, and few in Canada, that doesn't have one species of sucker or another. Although not a game fish per se, and usually of more importance in the diet of other fish, they are pursued by a small group of anglers every year, especially in the spring when ascending tributaries and rivers to spawn.

These fish are found in most watersheds in creeks, streams, rivers, lakes, reservoirs, backwaters, ponds, and sloughs. They will eat just about any fresh, natural baits found in their locale, but aren't crazy about artificial lures.

They are a bottom feeder, and offerings should be presented on bottom or within a couple inches of bottom. A host of sinker styles do the job. Sizes seldom exceed 1 ounce unless fast, heavy current is worked; common sizes are 1/4- to 5/8-ounce.

Garden worms and bits of nightcrawlers work on suckers better than anything else. Don't put an entire nightcrawler on your hook when fishing for suckers; this is simply a way to feed these hard-to-hook creatures. Use about a third of a worm at a time and bunch it on the hook. A single, No. 2, turned-up-eye hook with a short shank is a good hook for sucker fishing. There should be at least 24 inches between the hook and the sinker. In slow water, or no current, this may be shortened.

One of the biggest mistakes made by those attempting to hook suckers occurs at the first sign of a strike. Most anglers set the hook when they feel the initial tap, but they miss the fish. Let the fish tap your bait about three times. After the third time, point your rod tip directly at the fish, pick up slack line, and then set the hook hard; in this way you will hook about 85 percent of your strikes.

When fishing river systems, work the flats where current flows over rocks and gravel. It is the same structure where you might find catfish or walleye. Try eddies, small pools below islands, currents behind stumps, pockets downstream from large rocks, holes below bridge abutments, and small-stream channel areas where there is a gradual slope into deeper water. Cast bait downstream and allow it to rest directly below you.

A cup of worms, a fishing rod, and a small creek in spring will produce some sucker fishing action.

TROUT

From the viewpoint of distribution, abundance, and angling importance, the foremost fish of this classification are brown trout, rainbow trout, steelhead, and brook trout. The habitats and angling approaches for these fish overlap, and thus they are being treated as a group in this section rather than separately, like lake trout, whose habits and habitat differ greatly. Other trout species of some interest in North America, and found mainly in the western regions, include cutthroat trout; golden trout; and bull trout and Dolly Varden, both of which are actually char and found in the Pacific Northwest.

Trout are the foremost coldwater fish in North America. They exist naturally or through stocked introduction in mountain creeks, highland reservoirs, glacial lakes, beaver ponds, meadow streams, swift-flowing rivers, and other locales, and are found in a range of sizes, colors, and dispositions.

BROWN TROUT

Brown trout, which were imported to North America from Europe over one hundred years ago (they are still called German browns by some anglers), and which closely resemble their Atlantic salmon relation, are widely distributed fish, with a fair tolerance for intermediate-temperature water. They are most abundant in the Rocky Mountains from Calgary to the border plus all of Montana and Wyoming; in northern California; in Lakes Michigan and Ontario; from Pennsylvania through New Hampshire; and in the White River in Arkansas.

Brown trout are plentiful in streams, rivers, and lakes. They are similar to Atlantic salmon in appearance, although more heavily spotted, and with a more squared tail. They have a well-developed double row of vomerine teeth, which

makes differentiation absolute. Browns are caught in all waters by casting spinners, spoons, and many types of flies, and by trolling in lakes with plugs and spoons. They are cunning fish, often more difficult to catch than other trout.

Above: *The rainbow trout is aptly named; this native is nicely marked and colored, although some rainbows are more silvery.*

Browns grow large in some environments and they spawn in rivers in late fall or early winter.

BROOK TROUT

Brook trout, on the other hand, are a more diminutive native fish, less widely distributed and preferring cooler waters than brown trout. A colorful fish that spawns in late fall or winter in flowing water, the brookie is actually in the char family and more likely to be found in less

Left: *In a sizable flowage, look for trout to hold at the head and tail of pools, the deepest water in the main channel, behind boulders and large rocks, and on the edges of eddies.*

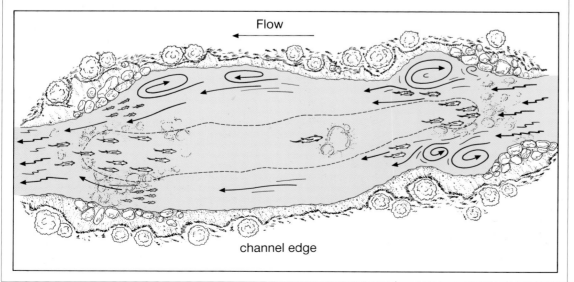

Flow

channel edge

fertile, elevated environs, in rivers, stream, lakes, and ponds. A brook trout has white-tipped lower fins; yellow, green, and red spots on its sides; squared tail; wavy lines on the top of its head; and bright orange-red lower flanks at spawning time. A hybrid brook trout that occurs naturally (though rarely) and which has been stocked in some places, is a splake; this is a cross between a brookie and a lake trout, and which looks more like a laker and is usually found in lake trout environs.

Also called speckled trout, coaster, and squaretail, the brookie is most abundant in the Northeastern U. S. and in the upper Midwest, as well as in southern Ontario, Quebec, and the Maritime provinces, with the largest specimens generally found in Labrador and portions of Quebec. It is supported by hatchery stocking in many well-populated areas, but occurs naturally in the more northerly and remote locales, and is sought almost exclusively by casting, using fly or spinning tackle.

Rainbow trout are a native North American fish that are as, if not more, widely distributed than brown trout and which have a higher tolerance for warm and/or lesser quality water than the other trout. They can grow large, are known for their spunky, acrobatic fighting, and spawn in the spring. Rainbows have many black spots and a broad red horizontal band on their side. These fish are also found in a more streamlined, silvery, anadromous version known as a steelhead. Steelhead trout can grow very large and fight well enough to be rated very highly for sporting values.

Rainbow trout and steelhead are principally residents of rivers and streams, but also inhabit

Above: *An angler unhooks a large river brook trout; native brookies are a highly prized catch, and colorful in the fall.*

large lakes. They are most abundant in Pacific coastal rivers, including British Columbia and Alaska; in Lakes Michigan and Ontario and their tributaries; the White River in Arkansas; and other large river/lake systems. Such bait as salmon eggs and worms are especially popular, but flies, wobbling plugs, and spoons – cast, trolled, or drifted – are productive.

Fishing activities for these species vary according to their environments, with fishing in flowing water being much different than that of fishing in lakes, reservoirs, and ponds.

RIVER FISHING

To some anglers, the thought of fishing for river trout brings to mind a gentle flowage and small fish dimpling the surface during a profuse insect hatch, and using a light fly rod and fine-tippet leader to daintily drop a tiny imitation fly among the rising fish. To others it means tossing a flashy spinner in a cold flow and prospecting for an intermediate size fish that will mistake the lure for a darting minnow. And to still others it means flipping a gob of fish eggs into a deep pool with a long rod and setting the hook into a 30-inch-long ball of silver fury that rockets out of the water and heads for the next county.

Each of these is a classic view of some type of river trout fishing, and this points out the extremes that exist in this facet of angling. Fishing for trout in rivers – and by river we refer to all forms of flowing water – is a diverse activity, one that requires proper presentation, a knowledge of the habits of the species, and an ability to analyze the water and determine what places will likely hold fish, to be consistently successful. There are a number of different size flowages in which brook, brown, and rainbow trout, plus steelhead, exist and portions of these can be extremely fast or dramatically slow. There are some excellent trout-holding areas which can be found in nearly any flowage; these fish may all be found in some of the same waters.

Below: *Early light bathes this river steelhead angler, who has started his day off with a fine catch; steelhead are also caught in the open water of the Great Lakes.*

Looking almost like a fat salmon, this chunky lake-dwelling brown trout was caught by trolling, which is the foremost method of pursuing this species in lakes and reservoirs.

Brown trout tend to lie in slower and warmer waters than brookies, yet they will both inhabit pools and slicks in rapid-flowing waters. Both primarily feed on various stages of aquatic insects, but also on small minnows. Rainbows and steelhead tend to stay in deep, main-flow water, and feed on aquatic insects as well as fish eggs and small fish. Yet, all of these trout are often found in some similar locations, such as pockets behind rocks; fishing the so-called "pocket water" is a standard river fishing ploy, especially in low water and where smaller fish

exist. Other such places include the slick water downstream from an eddy or pool; dark, swift water just above a falls or rapids drop; the sanctuary beneath a falls; and spring holes.

A great many river trout are caught by fly fishing. Fly anglers usually use a light outfit (7- or 8-foot rod for 4- to 7-weight line) in order to fish small streams, using perhaps an outfit on the upper end of this range for larger or more open waters and/or places where big fish might be found.

Leader length should be about 7 feet long for small waters, slightly longer elsewhere (equal to the length of rod is often a normal measurement), tapering to a 2X or 3X tippet. Flies must be selected according to the type of minnow or aquatic insect that needs to be imitated. There is

an enormous assortment of dry and wet flies, nymphs, and streamers to use on trout, depending on the circumstances.

Spring and summer insect hatches particularly attract river trout. In the spring these hatches may occur during the day, but later in the season they may be most most evident around sundown and last long into the night. Trout, especially browns, will feed on meatier forage in the night as well. Small fish are often preyed upon in a long, shallow, gravel flat above a deep pool.

Fly fishing tactics vary, of course. Nymphs must be retrieved in short, jerking movements, and at an angle downstream. Streamer flies, which represent minnows, are retrieved at a steady pace across or upstream in rivers. Dry flies are cast upstream and float naturally downstream while the angler gathers line rapidly. To work a fly across stream or retrieve upstream causes your offering to drag or move in an unnatural fashion, and fish will seldom strike a fly presented this way. In a very slow pool or a midstream beaver pond, a dry fly should sit motionless and drift with a breeze if there is one. Give the dry fly enough slack by mending line so it drifts without line pull.

Spin fishermen have a lot of success with river trout also, using small spinners, small spoons, occasionally a light jig, and sometimes minnow-imitation plugs, as well as live worms and salmon eggs where bait fishing is legal, and large spoons and spinners in big, swift-flowing waters. Spinning equipment should be light or ultralight, with lines ranging from 4- to 8-pound strength. In some smaller streams you might use 2-pound line and a 5-foot ultralight rod. Line capacity and drag is seldom a factor with reels used in spinning for trout. Where big steelhead are to be encountered, line capacity and drag are more crucial.

Steelhead, rainbow, and brown trout are sometimes targets for big-river drifting, backtrolling, or backbouncing presentations, too, which were described elsewhere. Most of this is done with diving plugs or bait; winter-run steelhead, for example, are caught with pencil lead-weighted spawn sacks or single-hook salmon eggs. Many different attractions, including plugs, spoons, spinners, flies, and bait, are used.

LAKE FISHING

Angling for trout in lakes — we'll use this term generically to mean not only lakes, but reservoirs and ponds — is a completely different sport than angling for trout in flowages, not only because lakes usually harbor larger fish, but because such waters often provide suitable year-round water temperatures, have abundant forage fish, and their trout are not readily accessible.

Trout in lakes move a lot and aren't always

Lake trout dwell in the cold, deep waters of lakes, and are caught primarily by trolling, but also by jigging. This one took a popular five-of-diamonds pattern trolling spoon.

confined to readily identifiable terrain. Primarily they move in search of food, which is not made up principally of aquatic insects but such forage as alewives, smelt, ciscoes, chubs, sculpin, assorted species of shiners and darters, and even yellow perch and crayfish. It is usually a certainty that the prominent forage species in any environment constitutes the major part of the diet of a trout.

After ice-out or in late winter and early spring, trout lakes begin to warm on the surface. Trout may be found at any level at this time, and are often within the upper strata (20 feet or less) of a lake or in shallow water close to shore. Thermal discharges, tributaries, rocky shorelines, and the like contribute to warmer water locales. In large lakes, a vertical surface distinction between water temperature may exist until the weather warms. Known as a thermal bar, and found offshore in the spring, it is particularly attractive to steelhead.

Trout seek preferred temperature zones in lakes as they get warmer. Brown and rainbow trout prefer water in the upper 50s and low 60s, and once the water warms on the surface, they usually are found in this temperature water, whatever depth it may be, provided that there is ample oxygen at that level. Often, their forage is found at or close to the same level. With

brown and rainbow trout, the place where those temperatures meet with the bottom of the lake can be a very strong area for catching fish, especially if they are prominent aspects of underwater terrain, like a point or near-shore ledge.

An ideal situation in large lakes is to find a place where temperature, forage, and shore structure coincide. If you are looking for schools of baitfish, and monitoring preferred water temperature, try to find both of these where the thermocline intersects the bottom. This would be a prime place to begin looking for trout in the summer on large lakes. Trout may be more concentrated, incidentally, along a sharply sloped shoreline than a moderately sloped one.

Trout orient to objects and edges. By identifying physical terrain, from depth contours to irregularities in the shore or bottom, you can get an idea what places attract baitfish as well as trout and pinpoint possible ways to fish them. A good locale is where baitfish get funneled, or where they might routinely pass by. The deep-water/shallow water interface near islands can be similarly productive. The edges of long underwater bars or shoals are places where bait migrate naturally by, and logically present feeding opportunities for trout. In midsummer, deep trout may cruise over a large area, so in big lakes you may have a lot of scouring to do.

Fishing for trout in lakes is like blind prospecting. To have regular success means covering a lot of water. When trout are shallow and near the surface they can be caught by trolling,

casting from shore or in a float tube, or drifting with bait. Although casting is the most fun, trolling is often more popular, because it allows you to cover a lot of ground and look for active, aggressive fish, particularly trout that perhaps have not been spooked or otherwise bothered by other fishermen and boaters. Drift-fishing with a boat usually is a live-bait proposition, but it is slow and, where motors are permitted on lakes, less productive than lure trolling. If you cast from shore, you may simply be limited to one spot, such as a pier or breakwall, and must cast repeatedly in hope of attracting a moving, incoming fish to strike your lure. This can pay off in tributary areas where warm river water attracts a significant number of fish. In most lakes, however, it is better to be mobile, concentrating shore-casting efforts near prominent points, inlets, steep banks, rock- and boulder-studded shores, shorelines with sharp dropoffs to deep water, and warm bay and cove areas. Try casting spoons and plugs (crankbaits or sinking minnow-style baits) from shore.

Once the trout are deep, it becomes tough, if not impossible, to catch them from shore, and here the boater with the ability to get his lures down, to scout for fish with some type of sonar, and with the ability to ply a lot of water by trolling, has a distinct advantage.

In fishing for trout in lakes, once you have established some idea of where and how deep to fish, the consideration becomes what type of lure to fish, what color, and at what speed. Spoons, plugs, and spinners all catch trout, as do jigs at times. Many flat-line trollers use fairly heavy spoons to help them get down, but light spoons are preferred on downriggers. Fly fishing is predominantly done in small, shallow lakes and ponds, to rising fish with dry flies or to near-shore fish with streamers and sinking lines.

There is seldom any reason to use heavy tackle for trout in lakes, although large browns and steelhead can be powerful fish and line capacity may be a factor. Spinning and bait casting tackle is used for trolling, and spinning and fly equipment for casting. Rods are usually long, in the 7- to 9-foot range for all but brook trout fishing, and line strengths from 4- to 10-pound are usually adequate, although big-water anglers who troll simultaneously for trout and chinook or coho salmon may use heavier line.

LAKE TROUT

Lake trout are really in the char family and a relative of Arctic char and brook trout, although they grow much larger than either of those species, and behave quite differently from other char and trout. Known as mackinaw and togue in a few places, their range is limited in the U. S. outside of the Great Lakes, but they are widely distributed across northern Canada, especially the Northwest Territories, northern Manitoba, northern Ontario, and northern Saskatchewan.

Lakers have white-tipped fins and light-colored spots on a dark gray body with a forked tail, although their coloration differs in certain waters. They are generally one of the least accessible freshwater game fish, frequenting the cold, dark, and mysterious nether depths, and sometimes found in far northern rivers.

Although lakers do not have the reputation of being an exciting sportfish, this is partially due to the heavy tackle many anglers traditionally use, the depths from which they are often dredged, and the nature of the lakes in which they are found. There is a distinct difference, however, between north-country lakers, which reside in waters that seldom warm up enough to establish a thermocline, and those which live in lakes where the upper strata becomes quite warm. Fish in the former are strong-pulling, head-shaking runners who give an able account of themselves in all sizes.

Lake trout feed on sculpins, smelt, alewives, ciscoes, and similar bait. They are predominantly caught by trolling with flashy spoons and diving plugs, especially around reefs and rocky structures. Jigging for lake trout is possible, as is casting with spoons, spinners, and flies in northerly locales.

In most places in the southern part of the lake trout's range, trolling for these fish is mainly

Flowing water in the background indicates a major tributary, which attracts large lakers in far northern waters as the ice recedes.

done at relatively deep levels. This is because lake trout are attuned to very cold water (mid 40s to low 50s) that is situated below the thermocline, and because they are often near bottom and some form of hard structure (primarily shoals or reefs) from late spring to early fall.

Not all trolling for lakers is done at decompression depths. Rocky islands and reefs are prime foraging grounds for lake trout, which move into such spots to feed (even in the summer and even if the water temperature is higher than they generally prefer), then retreat to deep water. Also, early and late in the year are good times to find lake trout in the upper 20 feet of a lake or reservoir if the water temperature is favorable.

Lake trout are one of the most curious of freshwater fish, a fact that can make you more successful at catching them when you know how to appeal to this trait. Lakers may follow a lure a considerable distance, sometimes nudging the lure and sometimes just staying right behind it for a long while like a bird dog. When holding a rod, jerking or pumping the rod tip periodically, as well as dropping it back a few feet or speeding it up momentarily, are tactics that provoke these fish into striking. When rods are set in holders, changes in boat speed, turns, and manipulative boat operation momentarily affect the swimming pattern of a lure, and these are often factors that cause a lake trout to strike. It isn't the faster or slower speed of the lure that draws strikes so much as it is change in behavior. Lakers basically like a slow presentation, quite slow, in fact, compared to salmon and other trout.

It is because of the laker's preference for slow-moving lures that the most successful lake trout tactic on the Great Lakes is to run a small plastic

wobbling bait (called a Peanut by some) about 12 to 18 inches behind a dodger or cowbell attractor. Some spoons and small diving plugs are also worked in this fashion. In areas where there is a sandy bottom and when fish presumed to be lakers are spotted via sonar on the bottom in deep water (maybe 100 to 150 feet in summer) you can literally set your line by dropping the downrigger weight until it hits bottom, then raise it up a turn. The lead from weight to lure can be very short. Some bottom trollers like to use a banana-shaped downrigger weight for this, incidentally, dragging it right on the bottom.

Although trolling is the foremost method of lake trout fishing, jigging is also effective. Light jigs can provide exciting small lake trout action in north-country rivers, and for schools of small fish that prowl the shorelines of lakes in the evening. Large jigs are occasionally more effective than trolling spoons or plugs in places where lake trout are abundant. But it is best to limit jigging activites to known lake trout reefs, fishing for bottom-hugging trout that are spotted on sonar, or fishing in places where you've recently caught lakers. In north-country locales, it's worth jigging at river mouths, to the side of heavy current where a major tributary dumps into a large lake. You can also catch lake trout by casting and retrieving small spinners and spoons, streamer flies, and plugs, primarily in northern locales. In flies, try streamers when fishing in current and in the shallows, and possibly dry flies when small lakers are observed cruising shorelines for mosquitoes in the north.

Tackle runs the gamut from deep-trolling hardware to fly, spinning, and baitcasting equipment. Lakers give the best account of themselves on light line, which, because they inhabit open water, is very feasible.

WALLEYE

Walleye are one of the most popular fish in North America. Although not known as one of the spunkiest of fish on rod and reel, they are a challenging species to catch because they are not aggressive feeders, and are one of the finest tasting fish found in freshwater. Walleyes are especially prominent in the Midwest, the Great Lakes, the southern and eastern Canadian provinces, and major river systems. They are readily identified by their large glassy, opaque-like eyes and a white-tipped lower lobe on the tail fin. Recognized as a coolwater species (and called pickerel in many parts of Canada), they are a member of the perch clan; their smaller cousin, sauger, and the hybrid from these two fish, the saugeye, are less widely distributed but similar in behavior.

Like perch, walleyes are a schooling fish, so you can expect that when you catch one, more

The glassy-eyed walleye is a popular species of gamefish, found in schools and coveted for its tasty flesh.

are nearby. They also have somewhat light-sensitive eyes that make them most active in low-light and dark situations in many environments, although they do feed during daylight hours.

Walleyes relate to baitfish presence and to structure. Their prey, which is usually different species of minnows and small fish, varies with the body of water, often being whatever small fish are most prevalent. In some places that may be yellow perch. In others, it may be alewives.

The types of structure that they favor include rock reefs, sandbars, gravel bars, points, weeds, rocky or riprap causeways or shorelines, and creek channels. Walleyes are particularly known for congregating in or along the edges of vegetation. Walleye weeds, for the most part, are submerged, sometimes slightly visible on or near the surface, especially in shallow water, and often deeper and out of sight. Thick clumps of weeds are preferable to scattered weeds, because the former offer more cover. Clumped weeds is the easiest situation to fish. It may not be available, however, so scattered weeds become the second choice. Shorter weeds in moderately deep water are often preferred by walleyes than taller weeds in the same depth. Knowledgable walleye anglers always look for the weedline and its depth. An excellent situation to find, though not one as readily fished, is where the weeds are thick and the edge is

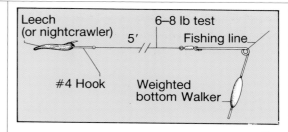

Various types of bait rigs are popular with walleye fishermen.

close to a sharp bottom dropoff. Working the edges of the weeds is particularly effective.

In some places, particularly large lakes, walleyes are also found in deep water, suspended or on the bottom where there are open, basin-like flats. In recent years, anglers have discovered that some walleyes, especially big ones and those that are likely to be feeding, are not holding to the traditional forms of structure that anglers have been working determinedly for so many years, but are in places that have been relatively neglected. They are there to take advantage of the migratory schools of baitfish that are prevalent in those waters, mainly smelt and alewives. So the walleyes relate to the presence of those fish and they may be in a few feet of water or in 20 or 30 feet, over a bottom that is much deeper.

Fishing presentations for walleyes run a gamut, but have largely centered on jigging, still-fishing or drifting with live bait, trolling with

Walleyes are abundant in both rivers and lakes, although the bigger fish generally come from lakes with large populations of baitfish.

migrate toward the upper end where a river comes in, or to a dam end. This is a good time to get bigger fish, incidentally.

In rivers, walleye fishing is a bit different in several respects. They spawn through the same temperature range, and they migrate after spawning, although they may not go very far in smaller systems. In both spring and fall they may be located off the mouths of tributaries; in spring, they are drawn by spawning needs, in fall, by baitfish. They do not suspend, however, and are almost always caught by making bottom-oriented presentations.

In large river systems, many walleyes are caught close to dams in winter and spring. At other times, work the deep water off wing dams, island channel cuts, deep-water bridge abutments, and center channel edges. Look for walleyes to locate along a river channel that has good depth as well, especially in midsummer.

Riprap is an especially favored walleye haunt in rivers, especially in the evening and if there is deep water nearby. Other prominent locales include cuts, where currents meet each other; eddies and slicks; along and behind islands; large rocks; and the head and tail of pools. River walleyes feed on assorted forage, including crayfish, hellgrammites, and minnows. They are caught by jigging, casting and trolling with spoons, spinners, and plugs, and fishing with live bait.

Jigs are the most effective river walleye lure, probably because they are worked close to the bottom and represent minnows or crayfish. Small and shallow rivers generally require 1/8- to 5/8-ounce jigs; in fast water you should increase weight.

Fish jigs with the current; there is no need to actually jig them, and a slow rolling action is best. In spring and fall, use white, yellow, chartreuse, and silver colors; in summer use brown, black, green, or orange-and-brown.

Live bait is also very effective. A live bait rig, 1/4- to 1-ounce weight, rigged with 20 inches of dropback leader and a No. 2 short-shanked hook, is used. Minnows, nightcrawlers, leeches, salamanders, waterdogs, and crayfish are used for bait, plus assorted minnows. Sinker style can be split shot, egg, Lindy, Baitwalker, or other bottom-bouncing type.

Tackle needs for walleyes in lakes and rivers are not very complicated. Spinning rods from 5 1/2 to 7 feet long in medium action, and reels filled with 8- to 12-pound line, are standard. For trolling, especially when planer boards are used, longer rods and stouter gear may be necessary. Bait casting tackle can be used, but is usually not necessary, and fly tackle is seldom appropriate in this context.

bait rigs, casting crankbaits, and trolling with plugs. Jigs are mostly used with bait (leeches, minnows, and worms) although hair- and grub-bodied jigs are used as well. Fixed and slip bobbers are used for live bait fishing, although sometimes a jig and worm is fished below a bobber. Trolling rigs include weight-forward or June-bug-style spinners, as well as spinner-and-worm/leech harnesses, and walking or bottom-bouncing sinkers. Many walleye anglers have employed a controlled wind drifting and boat movement technique called backtrolling – using a tiller-steered outboard motor or an electric motor – to keep the boat in proper position. Jigs and rigs are used and almost always fished very slowly.

Borrowing a page from salmon and trout fishermen, walleye anglers on big waters have recently gone to forward trolling more often. These fishermen are primarily using shallow to

deep-diving plugs (and sometimes spoons), trolling them on flatlines, in-line planers, large sideplaner boards, and even downriggers. Fishing is done at precise depths for suspended and mobile walleyes, and locating the fish, getting to the precise depth, and having good lure action are of paramount importance.

Walleyes spawn in early spring or late winter, usually when the water temperature is in the 42- to 50-degree range. They do this in rivers or other tributaries if they exist in a lake, and in shallow bays. Fishing, where legal, is relatively easy then, but becomes more difficult after spawning when the fish migrate out of rivers and bays into main lake structure and disperse. Through summer, various forms of structure, as well as deep water are worked. In the fall, walleyes become more concentrated again and are especially found on main lake points that are close to deep water. In large lakes they will

WHITEFISH

Whitefish are not as well known to American anglers as they are to Canadians. Three species of whitefish, round, mountain, and lake, are found in North America, with the latter being most abundant. They are generally found throughout Canada and Alaska and the extreme northern parts of the U. S., and are respected for game as well as gourmand values.

The average whitefish caught by anglers is in the 1- to 2-pound range. Fish of 4 or 5 pounds, and even larger, are sometimes caught. In lakes, whitefish are readily taken when schooled and when rising to flies, but are often hard to catch otherwise. Though many open-lake fishermen catch them accidentally while seeking other game, they are successfully pursued through the ice. In rivers where they are abundant, they are routinely caught by fly fishermen, sometimes being a nuisance rather than a pleasure, and they will be found in slow pools, beneath waterfalls, and along back-switching bank eddies.

Whitefish are principally an insect feeder, although they also eat mollusks, leeches, fish eggs, and the like. They are most likely to be caught on nymphs or dry flies, the latter especially in lakes when these fish rise to the surface in large schools which travel along the shores of a deep-water bay.

Whitefish rise gently when feeding upon floating insects, and often one sees the dorsal fin cutting through the surface momentarily. A dry fly presented slightly ahead of the cruising fish will usually be taken, but the hook-setting motion need not be vigorous. The whitefish has a soft mouth, so a smooth rod-lifting action will set the hook without tearing it from the fish.

These fish can be caught in other manners besides fly fishing, although not usually as reliably. Once in a while a whitefish will strike a spoon or small plug, though a jig is far more likely to be effective. A small dark jig is best; it can be fished plain or can be tipped with a small insect or grub, with the latter very popular when ice fishing.

Whitefish fight well, occasionally jumping and characteristically making a diving run and shaking near the surface. They are a fine light-tackle fish, with light or ultralight spinning rods equipped with 2- through 6-pound line very suitable, as well as light, medium-length fly rods for 5-through 7-weight fly lines.

Whitefish are found in rivers and lakes, generally being caught on flies or small jigs, but sometimes take a larger offering, like this plug.

EQUIPMENT

RODS AND REELS

There is no one rod or reel that will fill all angling needs. Yet there are hundreds of fishing rods and reels to choose from. A few of these are sold as matched combinations but the vast majority are available separately. Many different species of freshwater fish, special angling applications, and regional preferences has led to a proliferation in all types of tackle.

Today, fishing rods and reels come in a veritable host of types and sizes. The most popular

A bait casting reel sits on the top of the rod handle, and sports a level line winding mechanism.

and basic categories are bait casting, spin casting, spinning, and fly.

BAIT CASTING. Used with levelwind or bait casting reels, which sit on top of the rod handle and face the angler, this tackle provides excellent casting accuracy for the skillful user. For years, fishing with bait casting gear was a chore due to reel backlashes (line being fouled on the spool when casting). The situation is markedly changed now and bait casting tackle is arguably more functional for many fishing situations than other types of gear. It is especially preferred by anglers who use medium to heavy line strengths for large species.

Most bait casting rods are one-piece models,

This young lady is fishing with a hybrid spin casting outfit, featuring a reel that mounts below the rod but functions like a top-mounted spin casting reel.

though larger, heavier-duty products may have a telescoping butt, and are generally stiffer than spinning rods. Guides are usually small to medium in size, and newer models sport a blank that runs through the handle, which may be straight or with a pistol grip. Longer rods and straight handles are currently in vogue.

Many of the latest bait casting reels feature all- or partial-graphite construction, or graphite/titanium components that help decrease overall weight. Narrow spools with modest line capacity have become popular with anglers whose fishing circumstances don't dictate a lot of reserved line on the reel. A smooth sideplate also makes hand-palming more comfortable.

The cast control adjustment is an important feature on bait casting reels that serves to prevent backlashes caused by spool overruns. Essentially it is a spool-braking device. Nearly all bait casters now augment or override their standard centrifugal cast control operation with magnetic spool braking. Magnets on the sideplate of the reel are adjustable and allow a precise range of pressure on a reel. In theory you can take your thumb off the revolving spool and cast without applying thumb pressure and without incurring a backlash.

Older bait casting reels had a free-spool button on the side of the reel. Many newer reels have one-handed casting releases in the form of a bar between sideplates or a push button on the sideplate, and these will allow you to release the spool for casting by using the thumb on the hand that holds the reel. With other reels you have to use a finger on your non-casting hand to reach over and depress the spool-release button before casting.

Some newer bait casting reels sport a lever drag (drag is a tension feature that is used to affect the speed of line leaving the spool when a fish is running off or fighting particularly hard), a system that originated with big-game ocean reels. Lever drags have dual drag settings: locked-down strong for hook setting, and normal for fish playing.

Most of these features are standard on the more expensive and top-of-the-line bait casting reels, although less expensive mid-range models also have such features as high-speed retrieve, magnetic cast control, narrow spool, and one-handed casting.

Bait casting reels are often referred to as levelwind reels, incidentally, as are larger such reels which aren't suitable for casting, but used mainly for trolling, jigging, and bait fishing or for big and strong species of fish. The larger level-winds don't sport all of the features of their smaller brethren, but they do store more line, are very durable, and usually have smooth drag systems.

SPIN CASTING. While spin casting tackle is very popular, few avid or broadly experienced anglers use it. Although youths are primary users of spin casting tackle, beginning anglers of all ages as well as casual fishermen are also drawn to it because of simplicity of use, as well as relatively low cost.

Spin casting rods are similar to bait casting but have larger guides to accommodate the use of spin casting reels. Reels mount a little higher

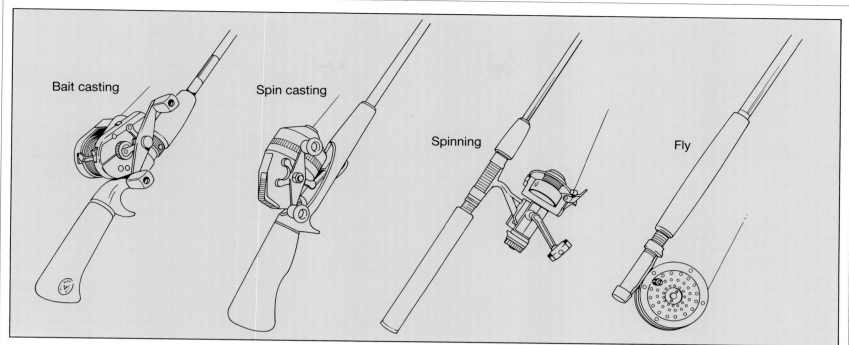

Above are bait casting, spin casting, spinning, and fly casting tackle.

on the top of the rod seat. Spin casting rods usually aren't as stiff, with a lighter action for use with light lines and lures.

The spin casting reel sports a nose cone through which line passes. There is no bail arm, as in spinning reels, but some type of internal pin (stationary or revolving) that picks up the line as it is retrieved through the hole in the nose cone and directed around a concealed spool. To cast, you depress a trigger or button at the base of the reel, and release the button when the lure or bait reaches its target.

There are some drawbacks to spin casting tackle that keep experienced fishermen from using it, as well as anglers in pursuit of hard-fighting, large fish. One of these is a generally low line capacity and the fact that with the spool

Spinning tackle, shown here, is most popular with freshwater anglers, and used in nearly all forms of fishing.

concealed under the cone (which is readily but not often removed) there is a tendency to let line get so low as to hinder the ability to play a fish that takes a lot of line or to having little left to cast. Line twist often builds up unseen on the spool, usually because the handle has been cranked while the drag is slipping.

The drag may slip when a decent fish is played because the reel lacks power. Lures that work best at high speeds of retrieve are often not compatible with spin casting reels because those reels usually have a relatively low gear ratio. Another drawback is the shorter casting range experienced with spin casting; this results from internal friction as the line comes off the spool and immediately passes through the hole in the cone. Accuracy suffers as well.

Nonetheless, many anglers do use spin casting tackle, primarily in situations where accuracy and distance is not critical, and where species of fish are usually small. The overwhelming usage is in freshwater.

Some spin casting reels are of better quality than others, of course, and sport features that make them suitable to achieving casting distance, eliminating line twist, or retrieving fast. Some even have interchangeable right- or left-hand retrieves, and some sit under the reel and feature a casting trigger on top of the reel.

SPINNING. Used with open-faced spinning reels that mount underneath the rod, this tackle is very popular for wide usage.

Spinning rod guides are big to accommodate the large spirals of line that come off the reel spool when casting. Handles are straight, with fixed or adjustable reel seats.

Modern spinning reels sport a skirted spool, which shrouds the shaft and slips over the gear housing, a feature that has successfully curbed the line tangling that previously existed with

spools that were encircled by that housing. Most spinning reels now feature pop-off (versus screw-type) spools, which aids spool changing without affecting the drag setting. And some now sport a bail-opening lever or trigger that permits one-handed casting.

The drag mechanism on spinning reels has

A fly reel is basically a spool for storing fly line and backing. It sits at the butt of a fly rod handle, and can generally be reversed for right- or left-hand retrieve.

changed significantly. The popularity of light monofilament line made it necessary to have a forgiving reel, one that would yield line when strong fish applied extreme pressure. Multiple-disc, spring-loaded systems that could be set reliably at various adjustments evolved.

There are two principal types of spinning reel drag systems: top mounted and stern mounted. Stern-mounted drag-adjustment knobs have been popular lately, though there are many fishermen who feel that a smoother operation is

There are a lot of fishing rods to choose from, and various things go into the selection process. Action, taper, weight, length, and other factors require consideration.

achieved with top-mounted models. The newest innovation in reel drags has been the pre-strike adjustable drag, which can be fixed at one level for setting the hook, and another for playing fish. This feature has existed in big-game saltwater reels for a long time, but it remains to be seen whether anglers casting for more diminutive game can adjust to this and find it functional.

Spinning reels have featured moderate- and high-speed retrieves for a long time. A high speed would be roughly 5.0 to 1 or greater, meaning that the rotor revolves five times for every turn of the handle. High-speed retrieves

are beneficial for reeling in a lure quickly to make another cast, or when playing strong fish.

FLY. Fly fishing tackle is unlike the other equipment systems mentioned in both appearance and function. It features the use of a large-diameter, heavy line to cast a nearly weightless object. The weight of the line carries the fly.

Fly rods are long and rather limber with small guides. Rod length varies from 7 feet to 12 or 14, although most fly rods used in North America are 7 1/2- to 10-footers. Fly rods are rated for casting a specific weight line; a fly reel usually sits at the bottom of the handle, but some rods have extension butts for leverage in fighting big fish. An 8- to 8 1/2-foot rod suited for a No. 7 line is probably the most popular all-rounder.

Fly reels primarily store line for fly casting and don't sport many features as other types of

reels do. Single-action and automatic fly reels usually have a modest drag, mainly to prevent fly line from bunching off when it is stripped quickly during casting. Small reels are used with light fly rods and have minimal line capacity. For big fish that take a lot of line, larger reels with sturdy drags and heavier rods are used.

OVERVIEW. Generally speaking, technological innovations in recent years have made fishing reels extremely sophisticated and functional. Trends toward lighter products, fast (as high as 7.0 to 1 in bait casting reels) retrieve ratios, quicker operation, and improved drag continue.

The list of reel advancements that has evolved includes one-handed casting options, levered drag adjustments, a flipping switch, direct drive control, higher retrieve ratios, convertible right- or left-hand retrieve, and lighter and more corrosion-resistant materials. Larger spools for spinning reels, to allow for greater casting distance, is a recent trend that will likely become more widespread.

Some anglers view these changes as mere bells and whistles, and not all such features are necessary for every angling situation. Many experienced anglers, in fact, are doing well with good-quality reels that are lacking many of the modern refinements. Some of the newer advancements are actually a hindrance to certain fishermen.

In rods, there aren't as many bells and whistles although nuances, such as exposed-blank handle construction and a mixture of linear and hoop fibers, which are currently trendy, do enter the picture.

Fishing rods are made of different materials as well as mergers of materials. The latter are known as composites. Fiberglass, graphite, boron, and kevlar are the principal materials that are used by major manufacturers in rod construction, with the latter two primarily relegated to composite use. There are several different grades of fiberglass and graphite. In general, fiberglass is an economical material and one that withstands a lot of abuse. Graphite is stronger and more sensitive. Graphite rods are preferred by most avid anglers for superior casting, hook-setting, and fish-playing attributes. Rods that are made mostly, or entirely (with the exception of resin) of graphite usually display the best attributes, but some graphite composite rods are good value.

There has been contention in the industry about the actual content of graphite that is contained in rods labeled as graphite, but no industry standard exists. IM6, until recently the latest high grade graphite, is now being used by most manufacturers in their premium rods.

There is curently an IM7 generation of graphite in limited use, but the real star in graphite is IMX, which is not currently available to most manufacturers but which has provided the lightest and strongest products yet, with prices that match, however.

The nomenclature of these products gets confusing, especially with graphite. IMX is simply a few letters that designate the top grade possible of strength-to-weight in graphite rods. IM7, therefore, is below it in the ladder, but one step above (and newer than) IM6, but still under IMX, which gets higher as the graphite manufacturers perfect the development of the raw material they supply to fishing rod manufacturers.

Most avid fishermen prefer one-piece rods because they have a better feel and transmit activity better than multi-piece rods, especially in the ferrule area (the place where sections join), and are less prone to breakage. But modern ferrules, which are designed to be part of the rod blank, make multi-piece rods less undesirable than in the past, especially where you must use such rods for storage, travel, etc.

PRACTICAL CONSIDERATIONS. Rods and reels ideally should be matched to each other, and this matching is referred to as "balanced tackle." This term means nothing more than that the rod and reel should complement each other and be suited for use together. You wouldn't use a small ultralight reel with a medium-action rod. Nor would you use a big reel capable of holding 200 yards of 10-pound line with a rod meant for 4- to 8-pound line. Filling that big reel with 6-pound line isn't a really a solution either, because it isn't so designed, and you'd still have a reel that is too large for comfortable use with that particular rod.

The length of rod to select is a matter of preference at times, of necessity at others. Longer rods are usually easier to cast, except in tight quarters; they help achieve long-distance casts; and they are helpful in hook-setting. Trolling, casting from shore, and fishing for large fish are circumstances that require long rods. The average length of a light to medium action spinning rod is 6 feet. Long rods are generally those over 6 1/2 feet long, except in fly fishing, where rod lengths virtually start at 7 feet.

When fishermen go into a store to look at rods and reels, they must determine what is suitable for their fishing needs. They should already have an idea what type of fishing they will be doing, with what line strengths and lures sizes, and under what conditions, in order to make an intelligent choice.

Assuming that you have some idea what your applications will be and what your needs are, you'll have to "try out" a prospective rod to the best of your ability. Don't judge by cosmetics or the composition of the reel handle. Wiggling the rod and flexing it is highly subjective and of dubious value, though you can check the action somewhat this way. By carefully putting the tip of the rod on a carpeted floor or up against the ceiling, you can flex it enough to see the shape of the rod when pressure is applied and know if it has uniform bending. The best option is to put a reel on the rod (preferably the one you're going to use with it) and tie a lure or practice casting plug or fly on. Now you can simulate the feel and casting performance. If it's possible, take the outfit outside where you can make a few casts (you may have to leave some collateral behind).

This is more likely to be possible in small service-oriented sport shops and fishing tackle dealers than in mass merchandisers and discount houses. The former usually have knowledgable sales help who can be of assistance in making selections and matching tackle, whereas the former seldom can provide that assistance. With mail order suppliers, you rely mostly on the printed literature in the catalog and on your estimation of the advertised equipment, unless you have seen or used the merchandise.

One of the most misunderstood aspects of rod selection is that of action, so you should pay attention to that point, as it will matter greatly in your intended uses.

Action refers to the point where a rod flexes along its length. The closer it flexes to the tip, the quicker the action. To determine action, take a fishing rod in your hand, hold it parallel to the floor and waist high, and snap it from side to side in a continuous motion. As you look at the rod you'll see a flexing point. If the flex is in the third of the rod closest to the butt, it's a slow-action product; in the middle third it's a medium action; in the tip third it's a fast action; close to the tip is an extra-fast action. Light, medium, and heavy are the primary actions, although there are ultralight and medium-heavy actions as well.

These terms also refer to the size of line and lures that rods are capable of handling properly. This, in turn, can be related to species of fish and their respective sizes and fighting abilities. A light spinning rod, for instance, would normally be used with 4- to 8-pound-test line and small lures. Such a rod could be used in fishing for white bass or bonefish, but not for stripers or tuna.

Action is also related to taper. In a "fast" taper rod, the diameter of the tip section is much thinner than that of the butt section. A "slow" taper signifies a gradual lessening in diameter from butt to tip. A fast taper rod has good hook-setting strength, exhibits more bend in the tip section than in the butt, and has more sensitivity. A slow taper rod has a more uniform bend throughout and is relatively limber.

Limberness is a quality that many anglers seek in a rod, yet this may not be good. A limber (meaning very pliable and soft), whippy rod can make the casting of light lures very easy. It is also a lot of fun to use for small, scrappy fish. But it can be a hindrance in the use of heavy lures, or such items as diving plugs and plastic worms, or for fighting large and strong fish. In many cases a stiff-tipped rod, though it doesn't cast as well, provides better strike detection and hook-setting performance than a limber rod. Some surface plugs and light floating-diving lures, however, are best worked on a soft-tipped rod (one that has strength in the mid section, but a soft tip). If you expect to use a rod for a variety of fishing applications, some compromise will inevitably be necessary.

Rods are also referred to in terms of power by some manufacturers, who use a numerical system to refer to power, with high numbers denoting greater power. Power describes how much effort is required to bend a rod. A light-power rod is one that requires little effort to bend. The more effort, the greater the power.

Power is not usually a word associated with reels, but it does enter the picture where gear ratio is concerned. The gear ratio on a reel is important in choosing tackle, particularly if specific types of fishing applications are intended.

Gear ratio refers to the number of times line is wrapped around the reel spool each time the handle is turned. A ratio of 5 to 1, for example, means that for each revolution of the handle, line is wrapped around the spool five times. On a bait casting reel this means how many times the spool revolves per handle revolution. On a spin casting reel it means how many times the head revolves around the stationary spool per handle revolution. On a spinning reel it means how many times the complete bail assembly revolves around the stationary spool per handle revolution.

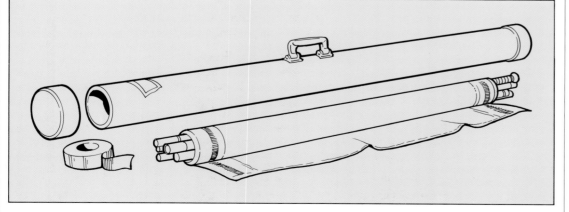

Tube cases protect rods when in transit; anglers can make their own out of PVC tubing, but commercially made models are available. Rods should be laid tip to butt and wrapped for protection.

LINE

Fishing line is one of the least expensive, least understood, and yet most important factors in angling. You can catch fish without a rod or without a reel, but you can't catch them without some form of line. Line not only makes all of your other basic tackle function, it plays the prominent role in the three most important factors of catching fish: presenting the lure or bait, hooking the fish, and landing it. Nevertheless, most fishermen know little more about line than what they have read in advertisements and the meager and insufficient information contained on product packaging. Worse yet, they do not exercise sufficient care in the handling and treatment of the one piece of equipment that is the most vital link between them and the fish. This does not make much of a difference when heavy tackle is used or when only small fish are caught, but otherwise, an understanding of the most important aspects of fishing line is very helpful for various fishing activities.

TYPES AND CHARACTERISTICS OF LINE.
Fishing line is becoming increasingly specialized, but today, for uses other than fly fishing, the types of fishing line include nylon monofilament, cofilament, braided Dacron, lead core, and wire.

Wire and lead core lines sink fast, are only applicable for trolling, and are used by relatively few fishermen. Braided Dacron, which is technically a multifilament line (strands are woven together), accounts for a very small percent of all line sold in North America.

Monofilament – which means a single strand of line but which has become synonymous with the word nylon – line sales account for most fishing line sold. Nylon monofilament has become extremely popular with anglers for all types of fishing since its refinement and premium introductions in the 1950s, and with advances in spinning and bait casting tackle. Nylon monofilaments can be separated into several classes, including co-polymer and tri-polymer blends.

Cofilament fishing line first became available in 1985. It is comprised of two filaments merged in the manufacturing process into one unit, and may include a sheath-core relationship.

Materials and manufacturing processes create the characteristics of fishing line and determine how it performs in fishing applications. The characteristics of any fishing line include some degree of the following: breaking strength, stretch, knot strength, memory, uniformity, and resistance to abrasion. Color is an additional feature, though not one that affects basic performance. It used to be thought that a good line was one that embodied the best of all of these features, and in a general sense, that is still true. However, in recent years, some line manufacturers have found ways to emphasize certain characteristics for specific angling applications.

It used to be that color and fluorescence were the most obvious differences in nylon monofilament lines, even more so than strength and limpness. Even now there is a potpourri of colors available, and one of the latest items is a line that has high visibility above water and low visibility below the surface. But specialty lines now go beyond cosmetics, having properties that are said to be suited for particular types of reels and/or fishing situations and which possess different attributes. Low-stretch and small-diameter nylon monofilament lines have been the most significant developments, the latter being a product that has the strength of a conventional line but is thinner. There are now oval (as opposed to round) copolymer lines strictly for levelwind reel use, and highly abrasion-resistant copolymer lines with low stretch. Some lines may be more of a marketing gimmick, aimed at cold weather use and certain fishing techniques, but many new wrinkles are certainly aimed at improving castability. Lets look at the specific features of all lines.

BREAKING STRENGTH. A new spool of a well-known brand of line I picked up recently bore a label which prominently signified that it was 8-pound-test, a very popular strength of line for freshwater anglers. In fine print underneath,

An important link between angler and fish, line is vastly superior today to its predecessors, and is available for specialized applications. Nylon monofilament, as shown here, is most popular.

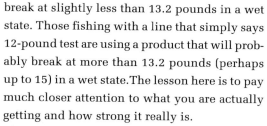

Light line, being employed on ultralight spinning gear by this angler, is capable of landing big fish in the hands of those who know how to use it properly.

however, was the stipulation "IGFA class 6 kg (12 lb.)." But it was neither of these.

It was, in fact, 13.2 pound line. That's what 6 kilograms is, 13.2 pounds. Someone who didn't realize that they were being deceived would have purchased what they thought was 8-pound line, thinking that it would have the breaking strength and stretch that is normal to a true 8-pound line. Instead, it was more than 50 percent stronger and having the greater diameter that is usually characteristic of a stronger line. This could adversely affect fishing in many ways, not to mention possibly disqualifying one for a line-class world record catch.

Ironically, the unknowing angler would have thought he had a pretty tough, durable 8-pound line because it would take more to break it than it would to break the usual 8-pound line.

Breaking strength refers to the amount (in pounds or kilograms) of pressure that can be applied to the line before it breaks. It is akin to durability in the minds of most anglers. Because nylon monofilament line absorbs water, its performance changes the moment it becomes wet. Here's the rub: wet breaking strength is always less than dry breaking strength; 15 percent less is about average.

You should realize that there are two classifications of line: "test" and "class". Class line is guaranteed to break under the labeled strength in a wet condition. Test lines generally break at or above (nearly always above) the labeled strength in a wet condition, and there can be great variation in how far above the labeled strength they actually break.

Anglers fishing with a class 6 kg. line (as in this case), for example, are using a line that will

break at slightly less than 13.2 pounds in a wet state. Those fishing with a line that simply says 12-pound test are using a product that will probably break at more than 13.2 pounds (perhaps up to 15) in a wet state. The lesson here is to pay much closer attention to what you are actually getting and how strong it really is.

KNOT STRENGTH. Line strength is affected by knots, incidentally, which generally weaken it. It is important to tie reliable fishing knots to get the maximum strength possible from fishing line. Knots that are tested in a wet condition are weaker than when in a dry condition.

Manufacturers claim that their technological processes produce molecular formations that result in specific knot strength abilities for their line. Since the same knots are tied with various levels of expertise by different individuals, this is hard to verify when comparing knots tied by one angler to those tied by another. Nonetheless, if you are tying known knots carefully and uniformly, and they are not holding, it could be because the knot strength of the line, meaning its ability to withstand weakening when knotted, is deficient.

ABRASION RESISTANCE. Another less obvious characteristic of fishing line is its abrasion resistance. Some lines endure abrasion much better than others, either due to greater diameter or to the molecular composition of the line itself. Lack of abrasion resistance is one of Dacron's shortcomings; Dacron doesn't compare favorably in this respect to even the poorest nylon monofilaments, and the poorest of these do not compare favorably to premium nylon monofilaments or to cofilament line.

STRETCH. Where Dacron shines is in its negligible stretch. Braided Dacron stretches a little simply by virtue of the fact that the braids have some give in them and pull tighter together when extreme tension is applied. Premium nylon monofilaments have between 15 and 25 percent stretch in a wet state. High-stretch lines cast well, but hinder hook setting (particularly in the case of an inattentive angler who forgets to keep all of the slack out of the line when setting the hook) and playing fish. The less stretch there is in a line the better the hook-setting ability and the more control you have over a fish, although you increase the chance of breaking the line. Having some amount of stretch allows for mistakes in fighting fish, inadequate drag setting, or countering sudden close-to-the-angler surges by strong fish.

Nylon monofilament manufacturers have long tried to develop a product that does not alter it's characteristics from a dry to a wet state and thus has comparably little stretch, or to

Line does take punishment when fishing, from hook setting to the stress of playing strong fish, and only good-quality lines will repeatedly perform up to expectations.

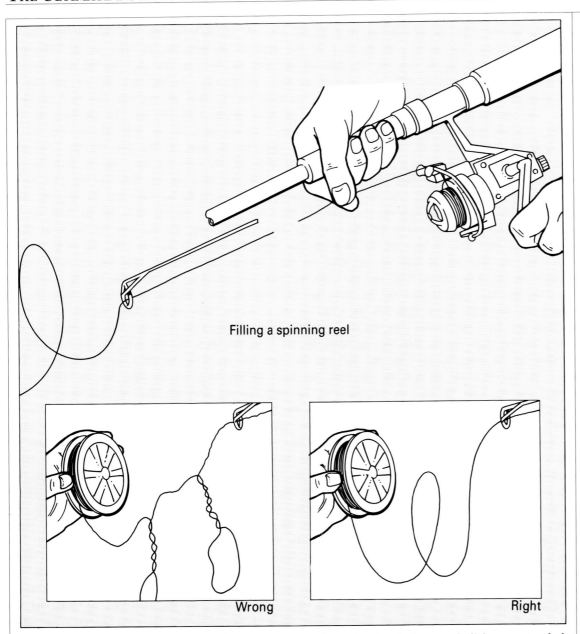

Filling a spinning reel

Wrong

Right

Because lines form a memory in the way in which they are set, and because spinning reels can actually instill line twist, it is important to put line onto a spinning reel as illustrated.

manufacture a line that has little stretch in a wet state without affecting other properties. The present cofilament lines and the new tripolymer monofilaments have much less wet-condition stretch than equivalent-strength nylon monofilament line. For experienced fishermen looking for top performance, these lines provide better hook-setting ability, more control in playing a fish, a better ability to feel what a lure or bait is doing, and to detect strikes, than other lines.

Good quality lines are capable of returning to their normal state after severe pressure (and stretching) is applied, and to maintain basic strength. Stretch should not be a permanent condition, although lines that have experienced particularly severe stress warrant close examination and possibly replacement.

MEMORY. Nylon monofilament and cofilament lines form a memory when placed in a certain

The purpose of fly line is to help cast a very light object, namely some type of fly; other line is carried by a lure or weight. This angler is using a floating fly line.

position (such as being spooled) for an extended period of time. Lines with less memory are said to be limp, and are more castable than stiff lines. This factor is important in light-line angling. Some lesser quality fishing lines tend to be stiff, contributing to spooling and casting problems. Castability is related to limpness (which engineers refer to as bending modulus). The most castable line would theoretically be one that was as limp as a noodle, but it couldn't possess the

other qualities necessary for a good fishing line. Castability is also affected by water absorption and line diameter. Wet lines cast better than dry lines. The greater the diameter of line the harder it is to cast.

UNIFORMITY. It is reasonable to expect that what you get at one end of a line spool you should get at every point along the spool to the end. With premium lines you generally do. Sometimes, however, the manufacturing processes may alter the diameter of the line in certain spots or in some way alter the characteristics in unidentified areas, which accounts for irregularities. It pays to check the line on your reel spool and on the service spool, although most of the time you will not be able to feel or visually spot irregularities.

FLY LINES AND LEADERS

Of the four standard types of fishing tackle – spinning, spin casting, bait casting, and fly casting – only fly casting stands out as being considerably differently from the others. In fly casting the object is to toss an extremely light lure, such as some type of fly, using a fairly heavy line. The line carries the fly, and is largely responsible for the depth and manner in which it is fished. Fly lines have to be matched to the rods that are used to cast them. Thus, fly lines take on an important dimension in fly fishing.

Fly lines are labeled according to size, function, and taper, all of which must be married to do the job required for the fishing circumstances. Size varies according to the density, or weight, of the line. The heavier the line, the more difficult it is for the average person to cast. Most heavy lines (sizes 10 through 14) are used to cast large, bulky objects, and when angling for big fish in fairly demanding conditions. Sizes 5 through 8 are most popular nationally.

Essentially there are floating, sinking, and floating/sinking lines. A floating line (designated by the letter F) is for surface or near-

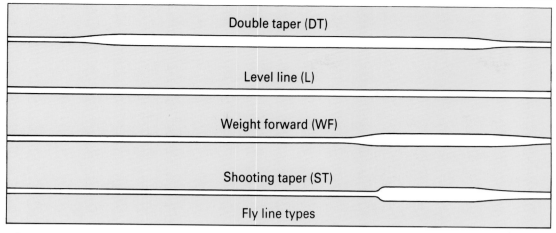

Double taper (DT)

Level line (L)

Weight forward (WF)

Shooting taper (ST)

Fly line types

Shown are several of the most common types of fly lines, with casting end to the right.

surface fishing, and is often the first line possessed by a fly fisherman, particularly a trout angler who uses dry flies.

A sinking line (S) is used only for fishing below the surface. There are different types of sinking lines, each of which varies according to how fast they sink. Their use is based upon fishing conditions (a slow-sinking line, for instance, might be used in shallow, gently-flowing water while a fast-sinking line would be necessary when to get your presentation down to fish near the bottom in a deep, swift-flowing river).

Floating/Sinking (F/S) lines possess a floating body and a sinking tip section. Most sinking lines are dark colored, and most floating lines are light colored. Dark green and white have traditionally been the favorites, but floating lines in yellow, orange, lime green, and fluorescent colors are available, mostly as an aid to angler visibility for casting and fishing control, and with no bearing on casting performance.

Fly lines are further characterized by their taper. A level line (signified by the letter L) is the same weight and diameter throughout, and essentially has no taper to it. A double taper (DT) line has the same taper at both ends, and is used primarily in short- to medium-range casting. A

weight-forward (WF) line, which is tapered only at the business end, is used in distance casting, and sports a lighter and smaller diameter back section that eases casting and aids distance.

There are also bass bug and saltwater tapers, which have a weight-forward portion that facilitates casting of large and wind-resistant flies and popping bugs; shooting tapers (ST), which are also meant for distance casting and which should be employed with a monofilament, rather than Dacron, reel backing (the line that is tied to the reel arbor, then to the back of the fly line); and special-purpose lines.

To determine fly line features simply read the letters and numbers on the outer packaging. A product labeled DT5F would be a double-tapered size 5 floating line. A line labeled WF8S would be a weight-forward size 8 sinking line.

In fly fishing, it is a necessity to use nylon monofilament leaders of varying lengths (up to 9 feet). These come in pre-manufactured knot-less tapered versions, or are constructed by the angler in knotted lengths of different strength line. The stronger, or butt, end of the leader is tied to the fly line, and the fly is attached to the light, or tippet, end. Lengths and strengths vary with fish and conditions.

Leaders may also be used in non-fly fishing situations, where either a lighter or heavier nylon monofilament line (the latter is called a "shock" tippet or leader) is attached to another fishing line, either to make a more subtle presentation (light leader) or to provide more near-the-lure strength (strong leader). The connecting knot must be strong enough to maintain the strength of the weaker line, and must also be able to pass through rod guides smoothly.

PRACTICAL USE

Knowing how to use and care for line is important to get the most out of it. Spinning tackle users and light line anglers experience a lot of difficulty with line, and often this is a result of improper use rather than poor line quality.

Properly filling a spool means that you'll get greater distance when casting. When line is too low, casting is more difficult and drag tension increases.

Probably the greatest problem that most fishermen experience in relation to line is twisting. Line twist can occur as a result of improper spooling, improperly playing a fish, having too loose a drag, using certain lures without a swivel, fishing in swift current, and using a lure that is not running properly.

Moderately twisted line is not difficult to cure if you are in a boat or near running water. Nylon monofilament and cofilament line will untwist itself if you let a long length of it out behind your boat or down current, with absolutely nothing attached to the end of it, and drag it along for a few minutes. Reel the line back in and you're ready to attach terminal gear and fish.

The best performance of your line and reel is achieved when that reel has been spooled to within 1/8- to 3/16-inch of the edge. This allows good casting distance and accuracy and permits better drag functioning.

You can put twist in the line by improperly spooling it, however. Nylon line has a memory factor, and it returns to its "memoried" state after being used. Line spooled onto bait casting, levelwind, or conventional reels is fairly free of twisting problems as a result of spooling. This is because the line is wound straight onto the reel arbor in a direct, level, overlapping manner.

Spinning reels and spin casting reels pose line spooling problems because these systems actually put a slight twist in the line as it rotates off the bail arm and onto the arbor. If the line is of poor quality, and/or if it already has a fair degree of manufacturer-instilled coiling, and the angler improperly spools it onto his spinning reel, the result can be twisting, curling, coiling line that will cause no end of trouble unless run out behind the boat and rewound.

The tricks to successful spooling are watching how the line comes off both sides of the manufacturer's spool; taking line off the side with the least apparent coiling; and applying moderate pressure on the line before it reaches the reel. After spooling new line on a reel, especially a spinning reel, it is also a good idea to soak the reel spool for a few minutes in warm water to help reduce the coiling tendency.

Fishing line on a reel should be checked and possibly replaced in time. The primary reasons for changing line are that it is too low on the spool, it's very old, or it has had such extensive, stressful use that a cautionary replacement seems warranted.

When line becomes too low it hampers casting and reduces effective drag settings, so it needs to be refilled. Many reels have large line capacities and yet, when a reel has too little left on it for good casting, it still has usually half of its capacity left. If the line has not been on the reel very long, it is still worth using. You should consider taking this off by tying the end to a tree or post in an open area and backing away so the line does not bunch up or become tangled. Take all the line off, put on a suitable amount of backing of stronger line, then take the end of the monofilament that you hitched to the the post and tie this to the backing. When your spool is full, you have fresh, unused back section of older line for fishing. If you have a large-capacity reel, but will only need a third or half of it for fishing, attach a backing to the spool before putting new line on. If you are going to replace all the line on a reel, strip it off and discard it in the garbage, not in the water or on land.

How long line may be used before being replaced is a question with no set answer. This depends on how much fishing you do, the strength of the line, how large and hard-fighting the fish are that you regularly catch, how much care or abuse your tackle receives, and the original quality of the line. An angler who fishes only a few times a year would be well advised to change his line at least once a year, preferably before the start of each season. A slightly more frequent angler should change it at least twice a year. And anglers who fish regularly should change their line every few weeks.

The type of fishing circumstance can also serve as a guide. Fishing in unobstructed water puts less demands on a line than does fishing around rocks, logs, timber, docks, and the like. In a week of fishing in heavy cover, you might change lines several times. Light line, because of its thin diameter, requires more frequent changing than heavy line.

You should also check your line periodically for abrasion. A nick, cut, or fray line can weaken it greatly. Periodically running your fingers over the first few feet (more if necessary) of line from the lure backward to detect nicks or frayed areas is a good idea. When you do find such spots, cut off the damaged section of line.

Abrasion usually results from underwater contact with objects and fish. Occasionally, imperfections in your rod or reel cause abrasion. A nick or burr on a rod guide, bail pickup arm, reel levelwind guide, or spool edge can be the culprit. Check for this.

Knots are another area in which anglers experience line problems; inferior or poorly tied knots may cause them to lose strong fish and terminal tackle. This can and should be addressed by following proper line tying procedures and by using first-rate fishing knots. (Knot tying instructions are found in Section III.)

Many fishermen are under the mistaken impression that their knots are good because those knots have never failed them. They don't realize, however, that they rarely test their tackle to its fullest or make the greatest demands on a knot. It's when you get to light tackle use, angling for very large and hard-fighting fish, and fishing under shock-loading circumstances, that you prove a knot, and these times are precisely when less-than-perfect knots fail.

Furthermore, even the best knots don't perform adequately unless they are tied properly and uniformly time after time. Fastidious attention to detail is rewarded with superior knot performance.

Frayed or nicked line will often give out under stress, especially when a strong-fighting fish surges at close quarters. This is also when good knots are especially important.

LURES

Recently a lure manufacturing executive was telling me how many different products his mid-sized company had. When specific models were taken into account, then multiplied by the various sizes in which the models were produced and the assorted colors in which they were produced, the number swelled to a staggering 1,500-plus. And this is just one of dozens of manufacturers making objects out of plastic, wood, and metal for the express purpose of fooling a fish into striking it.

Being that there are so many methods of fishing, so many different species of fish, and so many habitats in which to go fishing, it is perhaps understandable why there are so many lures to employ. In addition to that, fishermen have a deep fascination with the objects that they use to dupe fish, and there are extensive regional preferences in types and colors of lures to use for various fish species. The first thing that someone asks a successful fisherman is what type of lure he was using, which typifies the interest that people have in what items have, or will, catch fish. Some avid anglers possess so many lures that they could open up their own tackle emporium; many of these seldom get used, as anglers gravitate toward their favorite lures for the most part.

All lures are meant to imitate some form of natural food, either mimicking them closely, as in the case of flies or minnow-style plugs, or in a purely suggestive manner, as in the case of jigs or spinners or spoons. Fish strike lures for many reasons. Hunger is a prime motivation. Instinctive reflex, aggravation, competition, and protection are some others. They refuse to strike lures at times for many reasons, too.

No lure, no matter how appealing it is to the human eye, will catch fish of itself. How the angler uses it – in other words, where he puts it and how skillfully he retrieves it – are key factors in its success, although some lures are inherently better than others due to their design, swimming action, and appearance.

The angler who knows his quarry, and matches his lure selection to the habits of that fish and the prevailing conditions, is the one who is most consistently productive. The angler who is completely familiar with the characteristics of each lure he uses, and can make each work to its maximum designed ability, is the angler who will score consistently. The more

Spinners are among the most popular freshwater lures for various fish species.

There are many lures for different fishing situations and species of fish; how a fisherman uses a lure will largely determine his success.

you know about your lures and the fish you seek and the better you understand the conditions in which you seek them, the better prepared you will be to make a knowledgable lure selection.

There are several distinct lure categories and so many representatives within each category that there are enough lures to fill up an encyclopedia if writing about them all. All lures are designed to perform a specific function, however, and we can review lures in a general manner according to type or category.

SPINNERS

Probably no type of lure is sold in such quantity and with such international reception as the spinner. Essentially a spinner is a lure sporting a blade that revolves around a metal shaft, with a single or treble hook at the rear of the shaft. With standard spinners the blade is attached to the shaft via a U-shaped clevis or a hole in the top of the blade. These lures have flash, action, and vibration, are relatively simple to use, and imitate small fish or emerging aquatic insects.

A spinner may not be the best lure to use for all species, or to use in any circumstance, but in the right size and fished in the appropriate place, it is a lure that will catch most species of freshwater fish. The basic small spinner style is of foremost appeal in angling for trout and salmon, which probably see more spinners (in 1/30- to 1/4-ounce sizes) than all other species of fish combined. Smallmouth bass, panfish, pike, and muskies (large bucktail versions for the latter) are also favorite freshwater quarries for the spinner angler.

Variations of the standard spinner are incredibly popular in various places for different styles

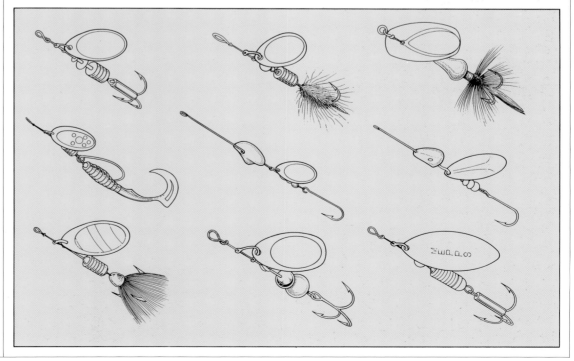

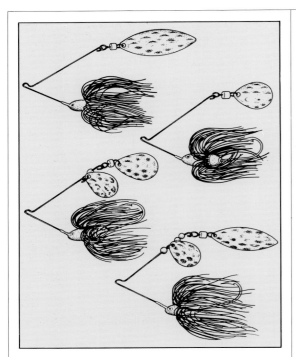

Spinnerbaits sport single or tandem blades and a jig-headed rubber-legged body.

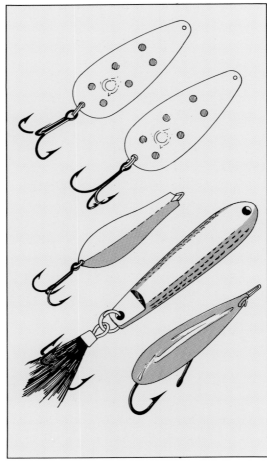

Spoons shown from the top are casting (two), trolling, jigging, and weedless versions.

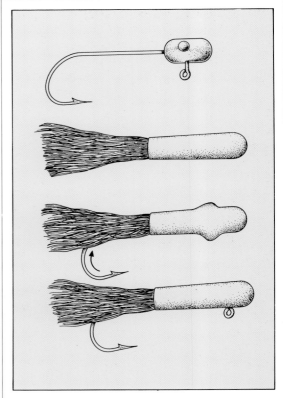

With tube bodies, a special jig is used and inserted in the tube to the head, with the eye poked out through the body.

of fishing. For instance, millions of long-shafted spinners, with a lead weight molded to the shaft and a single hook for impaling a live worm, are sold each year to walleye fishermen. These are called weight-forward spinners and are used for slow trolling, drifting, and casting. Simpler versions of these are known as June Bug spinners.

A fairly snag-free lure with one or two spinners attached to a lead-bodied hook and shaped in an open safety-pin arrangement is known as a spinnerbait, and is a very popular lure for largemouth and smallmouth bass, pickerel, northern pike, and muskellunge, all of which are cover-oriented species. A similar shape lure, but equipped with a large, cupped propeller-like blade made of metal or plastic, is known as a buzz bait, and is very popular for surface fishing for the same species of freshwater fish.

Spinning blades have been attached to plugs, plastic worms, jigs, and even to lead-bodied sinking lures (called "tailspinners"), and are found in varied shapes, materials, and colors. Sizes for all of these lures vary. Some sink faster than others, some blades revolve with more vibration, and some are often adorned with a trailer hook or curled-tail piece of soft plastic.

SPOONS

Spoons are extremely popular lures. Like spinners, they are international in appeal and at some time or another will likely catch nearly any species of fish, although they are more preferable for some species than for others and are predominantly used in freshwater.

Invented almost a hundred years ago by J. T. Buehl in New York, the spoon started as simply

Right: *Here are some large lures for pike fishing, including a spinner, far right, several spoons, and plugs.*

a utensil with hooks attached to it. Today, there are spoons of all sizes, shapes, and styles. Most spoons are metal and generally slender, with a slight curvature that provides swimming action when retrieved.

There is an assortment of thick-bodied spoons used in both casting and trolling. These range from tiny 1/32-ounce versions used for panfish and trout to objects 9 inches long weighing several ounces and used for large lake trout and muskies. Wafer-thin spoons which are too light to be cast are used in trolling where some device (weighted line, sinkers, downrigger, etc.) is

employed to get the lure down to the desired trolling depth.

Weedless versions are used for fishing in freshwater locales where there is vegetation and sport a weedguard wire protector over the hook. Weedless spoons usually have a single hook.

Jigging spoons are made of both metal and lead. The former are usually long and somewhat slender while the latter are usually short and broad. These are used for casting to (and rapidly retrieving through) schools of surface-breaking fish, since great casting distance can be achieved, and in vertically jigging in deep water. Varied species of fish are targets for vertical jigging, and these lures may range from 1/4-ounce in weight to many ounces, with 3/4- to 2-ounce sizes being most popular.

JIGS

If there's one type of lure that cuts across the species lines, it's a jig. Jigs are a pre-eminent North American style of lure, and do not enjoy quite the international use that spinners or spoons do. In fact, in some places, the technique of jigging is confused because of terminology with the act of deliberately snagging or foul-hooking a fish, which is generally illegal or unsporting.

There is no confusion about the basic jig, however. It is simply a piece of lead with a hook in it. The lead can be shaped in a host of ways, and is found in weights from 1/64 of an ounce to several ounces. It is useful for nearly every species of freshwater fish, and it is adorned with bait, rubber skirts, pork rind, plastic imitations of worms or fish or other food. Its successful use

There is a wide range of jig styles and shapes; note the soft plastic bodies on many of these jigs, and the rubber or hair bodies.

depends largely upon skillful manipulation by the angler.

There are so many good hair- or plastic-bodied jigs available today that there's really no good reason why fishermen don't have a decent selection of these lures, some or several of which can be pressed into duty at any time for a particular fish or angling circumstance. Many of the same 1/8-ounce marabou or soft-plastic curl-tail jigs that catch smallmouth bass, for example, can also be employed to catch walleye, bluegill, yellow perch, trout, and white bass, and they can contribute to the unintended catch of such fish as pike or pickerel. The same jigs that will catch big stripers will also catch large, deep lake trout. Maybe the preferred colors will differ;

Right: *This assortment of plugs for striped bass fishing includes minnow-imitating shallow runners (top), surface walkers or poppers (bottom), shallow divers, and a sonic vibrator (silver).*

Below: *Various sizes of plugs, with different bodies and diving abilities.*

sometimes they don't. But there is a lot of crossover value. When you consider this, plus the fact that jigs are also cheap enough that you don't fret much over losing one (which you do fairly often, especially using light tackle), it seems that carrying along a few jigs ought to be as routine as filling your fishing reel with line.

Just as there are many types of lead-headed jigs, so are there many body styles. Hair jigs, sporting bucktail or marabou, are old favorites; soft-plastic-bodied jigs, featuring curl-tail, grub, fishtail, and paddletail configurations are very popular. There are also various pork-rind or soft-plastic frog-like products that adorn the jigs used in casting and flipping by black bass anglers. Jigs tipped with natural or dead bait, like earthworms, minnows, leeches, or chunks of fish flesh, have merit for many freshwater fish.

PLUGS

There is some type of plug that will catch virtually every freshwater gamefish of importance to anglers (although it is usually out of character for carp, sturgeon, whitefish, and catfish to do so). Plugs come in all sizes, shapes, colors, and performance functions, in straight as well as in jointed versions, and are made of plastic, wood, and urethane foam. Floating/diving, sinking, and surface are the three categories into which plugs are divided.

Floating/diving plugs sit on the surface of the

Various double- and single-hooked flies for Atlantic salmon fishing.

water at rest and dive to various depths when retrieved or trolled. The extent to which they dive usually depends primarily upon the size and shape of their lip, and the location of the line-tie on the nose or lip of the plug.

Perhaps most popular among floating/diving plugs are minnow-shaped versions with small lips, which are designed to be fished very shallow, and which double as surface lures. Other floating/diving plugs are more bulbous or elongated (and referred to as crankbaits by

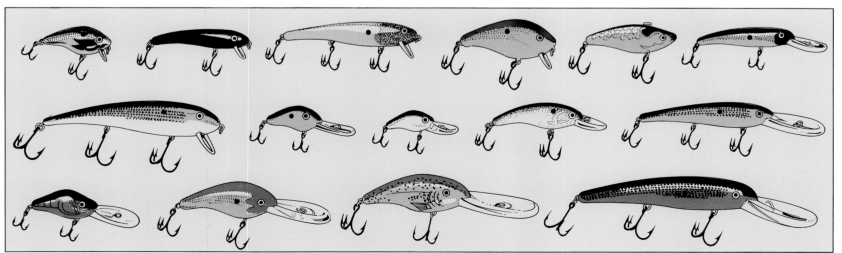

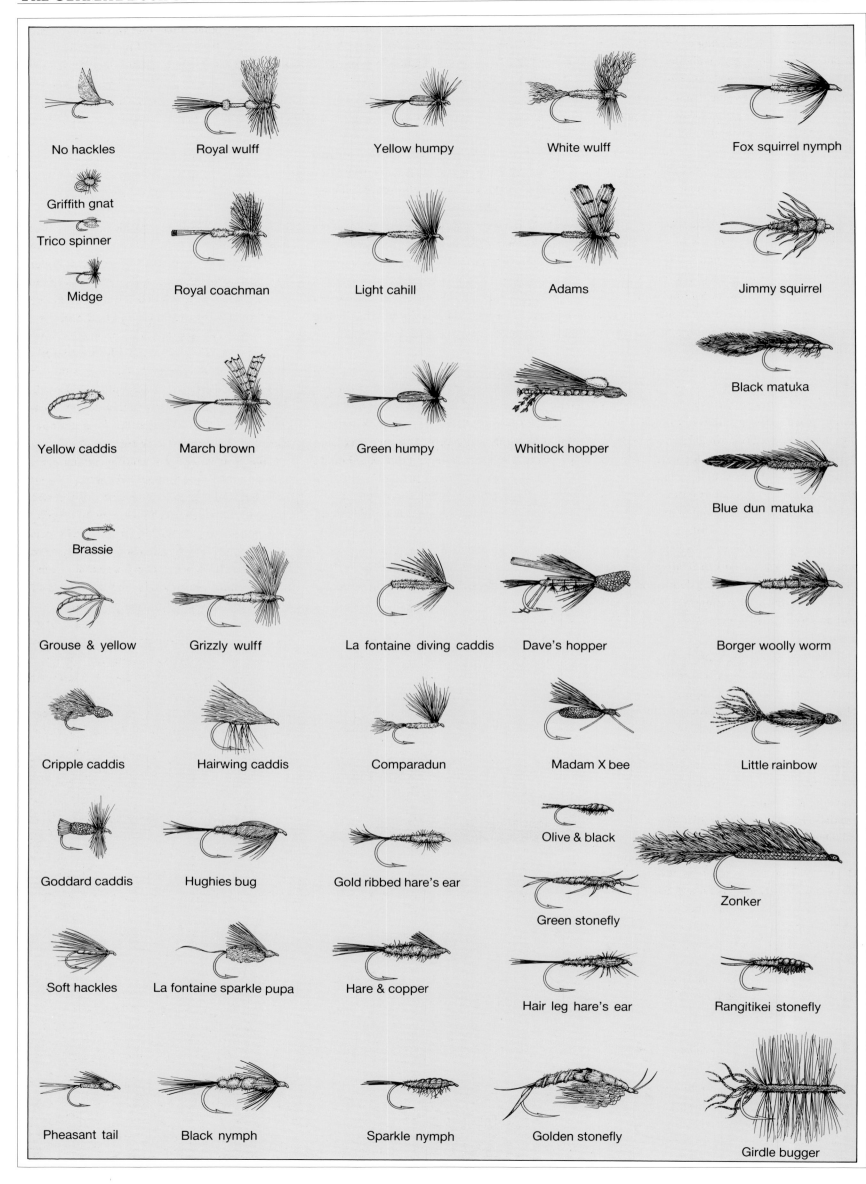

No hackles

Royal wulff

Yellow humpy

White wulff

Fox squirrel nymph

Griffith gnat

Trico spinner

Midge

Royal coachman

Light cahill

Adams

Jimmy squirrel

Black matuka

Yellow caddis

March brown

Green humpy

Whitlock hopper

Blue dun matuka

Brassie

Grouse & yellow

Grizzly wulff

La fontaine diving caddis

Dave's hopper

Borger woolly worm

Cripple caddis

Hairwing caddis

Comparadun

Madam X bee

Little rainbow

Goddard caddis

Hughies bug

Gold ribbed hare's ear

Olive & black

Green stonefly

Zonker

Soft hackles

La fontaine sparkle pupa

Hare & copper

Hair leg hare's ear

Rangitikei stonefly

Pheasant tail

Black nymph

Sparkle nymph

Golden stonefly

Girdle bugger

many freshwater anglers) and are strictly meant for below-surface retrieving or trolling duties. Some models have BBs inside that allow them to rattle when being retrieved and thus have a greater noise-making value. Their running depth may vary from 1 to 25 feet deep, and accordingly are classified as shallow, medium, or deep divers. The larger bodied plugs, which may be 6 to 9 inches long, are used for such large species as pike, musky, and striped bass. These lures generally reach greater depths when trolled, and are usually fished close to the bottom.

There is an exception to this, however. A popular trolling plug for salmon in the Great Lakes and West Coast waters is a plastic cut-plug lure that weaves wildly and is predominantly used in conjunction with a downrigger. This is a floating-diving lure, but one that attains very little depth on its own.

Sinking plugs are simply lures that do not float, but which are weighted to sink when they enter the water and will sink as far as the angler allows. These are often allowed to sink to a specific depth by counting roughly a foot of depth per second of descent, and then are retrieved. These are primarily used in bass fishing and are also referred to as sonic vibrators. There are metal, plastic, and wood-bodied models. Some of these, as well as some floating/diving plugs, are specially balanced to have a neutral buoyancy, so they will not sink or float upward once they have achieved a running depth, and which makes them appear to maintain a certain depth and be retrieved in a swim-stop motion like a natural baitfish.

Surface lures are perhaps the most popular plug in terms of preference, but generally the least regularly useful. Popping or chugging plugs, which feature a concave head, have many applications. They are primarily used for largemouth and smallmouth bass, as are wobbling surface plugs, which are characterized by their to-and-fro undulating action as the result of a wide lip or wings.

There are several types of lures of the so-called stick bait genre that are popularly used in freshwater. Certain types will walk enticingly on the surface from side to side if retrieved adroitly, while others are more like a jerk bait that gets repeatedly tugged forward. The noisier versions are those with a propellor on the rear or at both ends of the lure. These are primarily used for largemouth and smallmouth bass and sometimes stripers or white bass. With these lures, success is often proportionate to the retrieval skill of the fisherman.

FLIES

While there are many types of flies – or light objects that are cast with a fly rod and fly line but which may not technically represent a fly – they can roughly be separated into several categories: dry flies, wet flies, nymphs, streamers and bucktails, and poppers.

Dry flies are relatively diminutive objects that float on the surface and represent specific insects that are found floating on the surface of streams, rivers, ponds, and lakes. Stiff hackle and tail feathers are tied on a lightweight hook to float the fly. Wet flies are very much like dries; although they sink upon entering the water and represent drowned insects found in freshwater environs. The hackle on these flies is tied back and the body is dense to help sink the fly. Nymphs are also sinkers, but they are tied more precisely with wing cases and thorax to imitate the larval stage of aquatic insects. The choice of which type and then which pattern to use is dependent upon natural conditions and the kind of insect that fish (primarily trout) are feeding on at any given time.

Streamer flies and bucktails are meant to imitate baitfish and are tied on long-shanked hooks. Bucktails are tied with deer hair or other fur, streamers primarily with feathers. They are fished below the surface, and variations are used for different species of fish, with the longer and brighter versions used for larger fish such as pike and lake trout. Poppers, also called popping bugs, are primarily used for bass and panfish. They float and are made from balsa wood.

There are other "flies" that are cast by fly fishermen that don't quite fit into categorical peg holes. These include many steelhead and salmon flies, some of which are quasi-streamers and some egg sack imitations; foam-bodied spiders; mylar-bodied fish imitations; deer hair mice; and so forth, plus various creations from innovative fly tyers.

SOFT PLASTICS

Perhaps the single most popular one-species lure is the plastic worm, which is essentially used for largemouth bass. Immensely popular from late spring through fall in all areas of the country, the plastic worm is like a jig in that its effectiveness is directly related to the angler's fishing abilities, and unlike a spoon or spinner in that it doesn't look very much like a readily identifiable and prominent food item (although snakes are a bass food in some places). But it is the foremost artificial for largemouth bass, especially in southern states, and, like other popular lures, has proven itself through time.

Colors, sizes, and tail configurations vary. Some worms are impregnated and/or coated with flavoring elements. The most popular size is about 6 inches long. There are several rigging methods, with the Texas rig, in which a hook is embedded in the worm in such a manner as to make it weedless, being most prominent. Rigged in this manner, plastic worms are noted for their ability to be fished in all types of cover.

Besides worms, however, soft plastic baits include salamander, frog, crayfish, and minnow imitations, as well as an assortment of small to large bodies that are used to grace the hooks of other lures, primarily jigs. These come with a host of tail configurations, colors, etc., and are effectively used in freshwater for many species.

Left: *This smorgasbord of flies covers a broad range of fishing applications.*

Right: *Plastic worms are rigged in several ways: (1) weedless Texas style, with cone-shaped slip sinker; (2) Carolina rig, with sliding egg sinker above a barrel swivel; (3) do-nothing style with open tandem hooks and cone slip sinker above plastic bead and barrel swivel; (4) weightless spawning rig with hook close to midsection.*

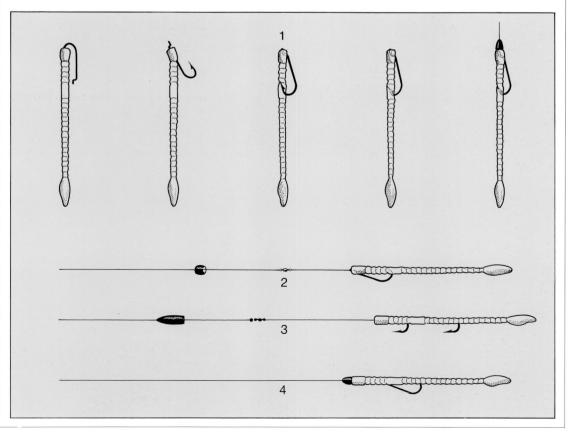

BAIT

Live and dead bait is used popularly in North American freshwater fishing, but not proportionately as much as in other areas of the world. Freshwater bait seldom tends to be in the form of small processed items, as in European angling. Such tidbits as maggots and larvae may be used to grace small jigs for ice fishing, but aren't used often by themselves, although corn kernels, baby marshmallows, and cheese are often fished for stocked trout. These are excep-

River drifting with earthworms produced this winter trout; note how the angler in foreground is keeping his styrofoam container of worms warm by tucking it inside his snowmobile suit.

tions, however, as bait generally tends to be natural, and larger, because the quarry are mostly all meat eaters and of larger size. There are, of course, many natural baits, used alive or dead. These include the following:

EARTHWORMS/NIGHTCRAWLERS. These are used in whole or in parts, on one or more bait hooks, and are tipped onto jig hooks, crawled behind spinner harnesses, and weighted and fished under a bobber. They are especially used in fishing for such panfish as bluegills and perch, as well as walleye, bullheads, stream trout, and river steelhead, primarily with No. 6 or 8 hooks. Nightcrawlers are generally preferred, but small and squirmy angle worms are also used, though primarily for panfishing.

CRAYFISH. Also known as crawfish or crawdads, and fished in both hardshell and softshell versions (the latter preferred but not always available), crayfish are hooked through the tail with a long-shanked hook. They are primarily used for smallmouth bass fishing. Tails and pieces of the tail are used for other fish, how-

ever, most notably for steelhead drift fishing.
MINNOWS/SHINERS. There are numerous species and sizes of baitfish (including fathead minnow, dace, Arkansas shiner, golden shiner, chub, and fathead minnow) used primarily as live bait for a host of large and small fish. Smaller bait may also be hooked through the lips to adorn the hook of a jig or jig/spinner combination. Small minnows are used for crappies, ice fishing, bass, walleye, and trout. Very large shiners are popularly used in Florida for big largemouth bass, and large baitfish (including suckers) are fished for species like pike, muskellunge, and trout.

LEECHES. These are more popular in the Midwest as a bait than elsewhere, and used whole primarily for walleyes and smallmouth bass. They are rigged similarly to worms, and when cast or trolled are hooked through the sucker with a No. 6 or 8 hook.

WATERDOGS. Also known as mud puppies, these salamanders are not available everywhere, but are used for a variety of gamefish.

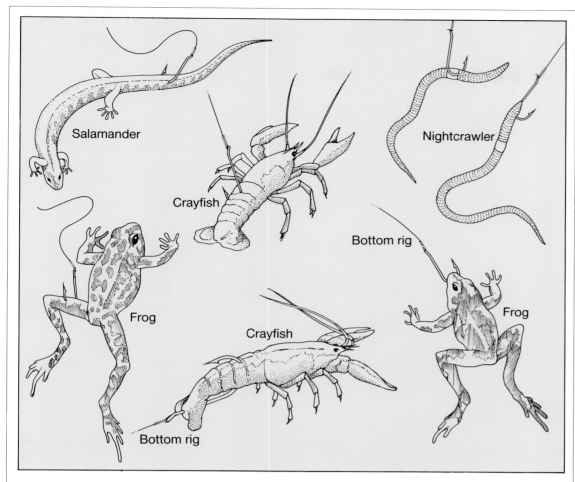

There are various methods of rigging live bait.

CRICKETS, GRASSHOPPERS, AND HELLGRAMMITES. These delectables are used for many small fish. Hellgrammites attract stream trout and smallmouth bass; grasshoppers and crickets are good for various panfish species as well as crappie and stream trout. Hellgrammites should be hooked under the collar with a No. 6 or 8 hook, and the others through the body with a long-shanked light-wire hook.

FROGS. Live frogs are quite popular in some Canadian and northern U. S. locales and rather ignored most everywhere else. The prime quarry is bass, followed by pike. They can be hooked through the lips or thigh of the leg.

SALMON EGGS. Salmon eggs are very popularly used for drift fishing for trout and salmon. Rainbow trout and steelhead, in particular, are major quarries. These are fished singly with small salmon egg hooks, as a group in an unwrapped cluster or in a nylon mesh spawn bag (called a spawn sack). Imitation eggs and egg sacks are quite popular as well. The natural eggs are cured and then preserved for fishing applications.

HERRING. Included here are such fragile baitfish species as alewives, which are also called sawbellies and found in northern climes where they are popularly used alive for trout in lakes; shad (primarily gizzard but also the threadfin variety), which are found in southern U. S. climes and fished live or as dead or cut-up bait; and herring, which are coastal, river-run fish used alive or dead for stripers and various catfishes on the East Coast and for salmon (via lift-and-drop mooching) on the West Coast.

OTHERS. There are other morsels used as bait for various freshwater fish. Where catfish are concerned, the list of items practically knows no bounds, and includes numerous stink bait concoctions as well as chicken liver (many prefer to use frozen liver). Some miscellaneous baits include: doughballs, for carp; caddis larvae, for stream trout; mayflies, for trout, crappies, etc.; bluegills, for striped bass (which is illegal in some states); grass shrimp, for panfish; perch eyes, for tipping on a jig when ice fishing for yellow perch; ciscoes, whitefish, and other large species fished alive for northern pike; and chunks or strips of fish meat, for tipping on a jig, especially for lake trout, or behind a spoon for pickerel or pike, or in some instances deadbait bottom fishing for assorted species (pike, lake trout, catfish, sturgeon).

Most live baits are hooked through the head or lips (tail for crayfish) for casting and free-lining, but through the midsection for stillfishing with or without a bobber.

Bait has to be presented properly to be effective. Where live bait is used, liveliness is vital. Many fish aren't interested in inactive or dead bait, so it's important to keep your bait as fresh and vigorous as possible. Change live bait whenever the current offering seems to be losing its vitality, and make sure that it acts naturally. A crayfish that rolls instead of crawls, for example, or a minnow that doesn't swim, lessens your chance of success. The water that bait is kept in ideally should be oxygenated or changed periodically to keep it healthy for the fish. Some bait, such as alewives and herring, can only be kept in circular or oval bait wells; they bunch into the corners of other wells and die, so the method of retaining them is important.

It is helpful to hold your line when live-lining bait. When fishing with a float or bobber it's easy to tell if a fish is mouthing your live offering. But that isn't the case when letting bait run freely. Then, it is often difficult to know if a fish has picked up your offering or if your bait is hung on brush, rock, or grass. Keep a light hold on your line to detect gentle strikes, and when in doubt, pull ever-so-softly on the line. If it moves off vigorously, you've got a fish.

Unless a fish has savagely attacked your bait offering and run off with it, wait to set the hook. Don't be in a rush to set the hook when live bait angling. A fish needs time to consume its quarry. Often it takes the bait cross-wise in its mouth and swims a short distance away before swallowing the fish. By waiting a short time, and by not putting tension on the line, you stand a better chance of hooking the fish.

One of the inherent problems of fishing with bait, however, is that fish tend to be deeply hooked and hard to release in good condition if it is necessary to release them (which, because of tighter management and increased size limits, it is often necessary to do). There is a good chance that a fish released with a hook in it will survive. Clip the line off above the hook. In freshwater the hook will deteriorate within a few weeks if it is not stainless steel or cadmium-tin. If the fish is not bleeding profusely, and if you have been careful to handle it as little as possible, it should survive.

This double-hooked herring with the angled head cut is ready for slow trolling, or mooching, for salmon.

TERMINAL GEAR

HOOKS

While much ado is made over lures, rods, reels, and line, terminal tackle is an overlooked yet essential component of fishing equipment. Hooks, for example, whether used on lures, with flies, or alone for baitfishing, are not as well understood by anglers as they ought to be. Not any hook will satisfy every fishing situation.

Although the integral parts of a hook are essentially the same, styles are determined by the way in which their features vary, which in turn influences use. Variations in features include forging for extra strength; turned up or down eyes (the former is preferred on short-shanked heavily dressed flies while the latter is preferred by some for its line of hook penetration); and sliced (used to retain bait or plastic worms and keep them from sliding down the hook), keel (used with some plastic worm rigs and with large streamer flies), and humped (for cork-bodied popping plugs) shanks.

Hook sizes range from as large as 14/0, which are used in saltwater, to as low as 28 for freshwater fly fishing. Size is determined by the gap, which is the distance between the hook point and the shank. Gap width may differ, however, between families of hooks.

It takes some study to discern the various discrepancies between hook patterns. Differences include the shape and angle of the point, curvature of the bend, length of the shank, and depth of the bite. Popular styles include:

SPROAT: has a straight point; popular with flies and lures

KIRBY: point offset to the right helps prevent hook from slipping out; good for bait fishing

O'SHAUGHNESSEY: outward bend to point; heavy wire; many applications

ABERDEEN: light wire, round bend good for use with minnows; will bend before breaking

CARLISLE: stronger than Aberdeen; used with

bait; long shank prevents the fish from swallowing the hook

SIWASH: heavy wire; extra long point offers good retention; used for big, active fish

SALMON EGG: has a short shank; concealed by small bait

EAGLE CLAW: point is offset and curved inward to aid penetration; used often with bait

LIMERICK: long shank, wide bend provide extra hooking space

BEAK: similar to Eagle Claw

A basic aspect of good hooks is strength, which is resistance to bending up to a stage where the hook almost would break, preferably bending instead of breaking. Resistance to pressure is influenced by hook style and size and is substantially aided by forging.

The ability of hooks to withstand corrosion varies, particularly in saltwater, and is an important aspect of selection. No finish or design of hook is completely rustproof. Carbon-steel hooks are significantly less resistant to corrosion than stainless steel or cadmium-tin, and freshwater fishermen seldom use the latter in ordinary fishing activities. If a hook sits in a wet tackle box tray for a long period of time, it will corrode; however, the most important aspect of corrosion applies to hooks that are left in fish that are to be released (a common occurrence, especially when using bait).

Bronzed, blued, nickel, and gold hooks, which are most common in freshwater, will breakdown (be well corroded, brittle, and unusable though not totally decomposed) in two three weeks of freshwater immersion, compared to 48 to 54 hours in saltwater. Stainless steel and cadmium tin hooks take an indeterminate time to breakdown in freshwater. The more that a hook is used, meaning that it is sharpened and comes into contact with rocks, sand, and even the teeth of fish, the more its resistance to corrosion is decreased.

Fly tyers are especially attentive to hook selection; the box in front of this tyer has various size and styles of hooks in it.

Angling is such a broad endeavor that there are many styles and patterns of hooks to suit specific needs. Nonetheless, every good hook should have a sharp point, which can be made sharper by honing and which may be short for quick penetration or long for greater retention. Hooks are not necessarily as sharp as they can be when new. Once used, hooks become dull quite fast. The sharper the hook, the better the chance of hooking and landing fish. You can tell when your hook is sharp enough if it digs in as you scrape it over your fingernail. The ideal is to sharpen all new and used hooks before fishing with them. Barbs should be sharpened as well as points, and points should be triangulated. The object is not to get a point that is long and thin (which will lack strength), but to keep it short and sharp without having a rounded tip. The cutting edges of the hook should taper to a true point, and the barb should be touched up to help hook penetration. It is better to sharpen from the point back toward the barb than to sharpen in the other direction, which may cause the point of the hook to bend and thereby be less of a penetrating factor. Hold the hook so that the point faces you and file the point and barb in a motion that extends back toward the bend of the hook. Make it a practice to triangulate the point so that there are three cutting edges, rather than to simply file one side or just the top and bottom. Work back to the sides of the barb as well. (For more on hook sharpening, see Section II.)

Most hooks have barbs but some don't and a

The size and strength of hook to use varies with fishing application.

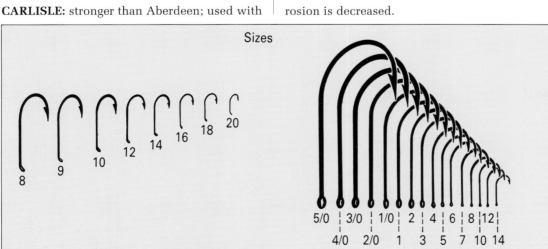

Sizes

8 9 10 12 14 16 18 20

5/0 3/0 1/0 2 4 6 8 12
4/0 2/0 1 3 5 7 10 14

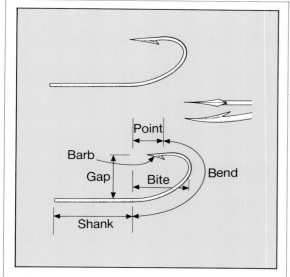

When the point of a hook is properly sharpened, it should be triangulated.

few anglers file the barbs down on their hooks to render them useless. This may afford better hook penetration but has the primary benefit of making it easier and less damaging to remove a hook from a fish that is to be released. An increasing number of remote fishing lodges mandate the use of barbless (and sometimes single) hooks on all lures used in their waters. Using barbless hooks is especially useful when you are catching and releasing lots of fish, and when using multi-hooked plugs for pike fishing.

There are barbless hooks on the market, but you often can't find them in your local tackle shop in the wide range of styles and sizes that you may want. Some fly fishermen use barbless hooks, and places that cater to this branch of

sport fishing may have a selection of barbless fly hooks or dressed barbless flies.

You can make your own hooks barbless simply by filing the barb off or by pinching it down. Filing works best with small light-diameter wire hooks. To pinch the barb down, use a pair of pliers, place the blunt end over the barb, and squeeze tightly to flatten the barb. It is a good idea to sharpen the point well afterward. Remember to maintain a constant tight line on a fish when using barbless hooks, as the hooks can become dislodged easier if there is even momentary slack in the line.

SINKERS

Like hooks, there are many different types of sinkers. These lead objects, which are used to bring lures or bait down to certain levels, come in many shapes, sizes, and applications.

Trolling sinkers include the torpedo sinker, which has minimal drag or water resistance because of shape; a torpedo style bead chain sinker, which swivels and prevents line twist; a keel style, which tracks well with little swaying motion; a planing sinker, which dives to achieve depth; a clinch sinker, which is simple to add to or remove from fishing line; and a rubber core sinker, which is simple to use and has no abrasion. Many sizes and weights are available. These are all fastened in-line, either being affixed on the main fishing line, or tied to a leader. The bead chain styles are especially good for preventing line twist and, with

Barbless, single-hooked lures are particularly beneficial for toothy species, such as this pike; note the wire leader that has been used with this spinnerbait to prevent line cutting.

a snap, aid leader and lure changing.

Sliding or slip sinkers include ball, egg or barrel, cone or bullet, and walking. Egg and ball sinkers slide freely on the line, are often stopped by a small split shot or a barrel swivel, and are preferred for open water. Cone-shaped sinkers provide minimal drag, are relatively weedless and are used with plastic worms, but may be pegged with a toothpick to keep from sliding in heavy cover. Walking sinkers are used with a stopper when casting or trolling with bait along the bottom; they remain upright when a fish runs with the bait.

Bottom-fishing sinkers include pyramid, bank, dipsey, and split shot. Choice depends on fishing conditions, including the species you seek, the depth to be fished, and such factors as current and wave action. Pyramid sinkers hold bottom especially well where there is much current or wave action and are especially useful where there is an undertow current. Bank sinkers are good in deep water and cast well. Split shot are preferred for light tackle. Dipsey sinkers are also used with light to medium tackle

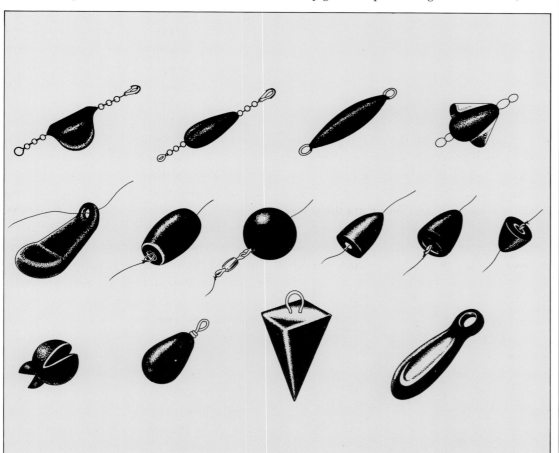

Top row: *Trolling sinkers include keel bead chain, standard bead chain, torpedo, and planing.*
Middle row: *Sliding sinkers include walking, barrel, ball, and cone (three types).*
Bottom row: *Bottom sinkers include split shot, bell, pyramid, and bank.*

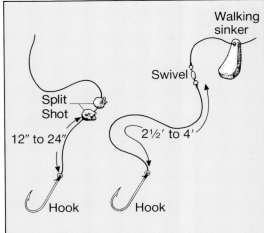

Bottom bait fishermen can use split shot above the hook, or use a barrel swivel/walking sinker combination, as illustrated.

The rig used to catch this chum salmon features a barely discernible three-way swivel, ball sinker, and beaded leader extending to a plug that is belly-wrapped with bait.

and where bait is suspended off the bottom above the sinker.

Sinkers can be fixed on the main line or on a dropper line. Split shot is usually clamped firmly ahead of a hook and is primarily used for suspended bait and light line. A rubber core sinker is fastened by turning the rubber core around the line ahead of the hook or lure. Clinch sinkers are affixed like split shot. Split shot, egg, and pencil sinkers can be fixed to a dropper leader via a three-way swivel, which lessens hangups when fishing bait in fast water and facilitates unsnagging without losing the rig.

BAIT RIGS

There are also a number of pre-formed bait rigs that are used where bait must be weighted to be fished. A spinner rig, for example, is a popular freshwater bait fishing rig used with worm or minnow. A fixed sinker or sliding sinker stopped by a barrel swivel will be used with it. Derivatives of this are the spinner and worm harness rig, with two or three hooks, and a spinner rig on a leader attached to a bead chain sinker. A walking sinker rig uses a snap swivel to stop the sinker and hold the leader. A spreader rig is especially useful for bottom fishing although rarely used in freshwater; a springy wire is used for the horizontal section, with a nylon leader to the hooks, and fishing line extending from above. Another multi-bait bottom rig is one with two or three three-way swivels spaced well apart. A popular bottom fishing rig features a three-way swivel attached to a bell sinker and a leadered hook. The Baitwalker rig can be used in appropriate sizes for trolling and casting, and is relatively snagless. An 18- to 36-inch leader connects bait or lure to rig.

SNAPS, SWIVELS, RINGS

Have you ever heard an angler say that he fought and lost a fish that broke his snap or snap swivel? That shouldn't happen. If it does, it's due to a weakened or defective snap that should no longer have been used, or to using a snap that was too light for the strength of line being employed. Snaps and snap swivels lead to more tackle problems than all other terminal gear together.

It would be worthwhile to take a few different snaps some time, clip them around a firm object, attach a reliable scale to the clips, and then pull on them until the clip breaks, noting how much pressure it takes to do so.

The amount of force that it takes to break or separate a snap is a key to its usage. If it takes, for example, 15 pounds of force to do that, and you use the snap with 20-pound line, then it's easy to see how the snap would yield before the line if you hooked a fish large enough to require the utmost fishing pressure. Poor-quality snaps, or light snaps used with too-heavy tackle, are

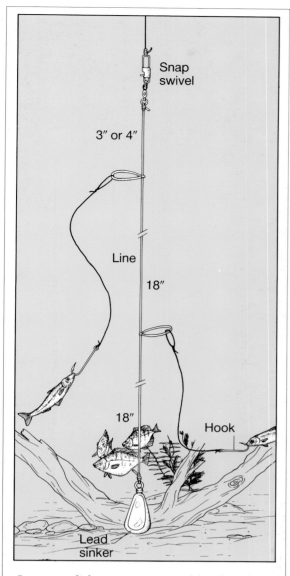

Some panfishermen use a rig like this above that has several dropper hooks on leaders, with a bell sinker for weight.

the main causes of problems.

There is a difference between a snap and a snap swivel. In addition to being a snap, the latter has a rotating swivel. The principal reason to use a snap is because it facilitates lure changing. A snap also makes some lures work better (rounded snaps are preferred over vee-notched snaps). Snap swivels are used for the same reason, but also to avoid line twist when using certain lures. When you use a lure that doesn't invite line twist, and that runs well by itself, you don't need either of these devices. It's best to tie your line directly to a lure if you can, and to change knots when putting new lures on. However, use a snap swivel when trolling with spoons or spinners, and when fishing with these lures in current.

Ball-bearing swivels, incidentally, are far superior to brass swivels, albeit far more expensive, too. These swivels rotate freely, while brass swivels, especially cheap versions, frequently do not perform properly, thereby negating their effectiveness. The manner of locking is also important.

Cross-locking (sometimes also called inter-locking), which is found in the newer breed of many snaps, has more holding power than the clipping version.

Except for color, these are identical cross-locking ball bearing snap swivels.

Other swivels include barrel versions, which have rings at both ends that rotate freely to reduce line twist, and are used to connect two lines; and three-way swivels, which have three connectors that rotate and which are used to separate bait or lure from sinker via separate leaders.

A general rule with snaps and swivels is to use the smallest size that is compatible with the size of lure, strength of lure, and type of fishing to be done. Too large a snap is as much an impediment to successful fishing as one that is too small and weak. As for color, some anglers prefer flat black, but many anglers think the silver and gold colors help attract fish.

O-rings are another terminal connector, and one that is used primarily with lures. Lures that do not incur twist may have improved action with the addition of an O-ring to the line-tie area

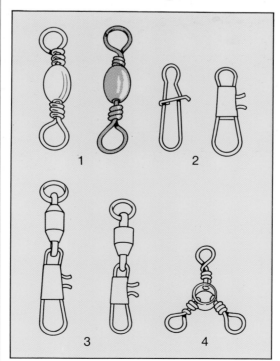

Shown are (1) barrel swivels, (2) snaps, (3) snap swivels, and (4) a three-way swivel.

of the lure. Some lures come with rings. Like snaps, they should be strong and large enough for the lure, fishing line, and conditions.

BOBBERS

There are a number of bobbers used by bait anglers. Also known as floats or corks, bobbers are usually brightly colored for visibility in water, although clear bobbers are used in some situations.

When used with light baits and weights, bobbers help achieve greater casting distance when using lightweight baits, but they are primarily used to suspend bait and to signal a bite. Different sizes are needed for use with different sizes of bait.

Bobbers can be categorized as either fixed or sliding (sliders are also referred to as slip bobbers). Fixed bobbers set the depth of bait at a predetermined level, which is usually no deeper than the length of the rod used. Clip-on plastic bobbers (red/white or red/yellow) are most popular. Sliding bobbers are usually fished quite close to the angler and in a lot deeper water, and line slides freely through the bobber for deeper presentation.

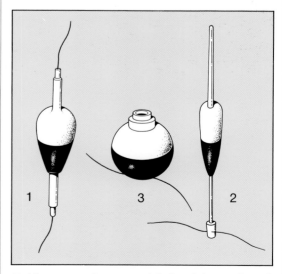

Bobber types shown are (1) slip, (2) pencil, and (3) button.

BOATS

A boat is a vital tool for freshwater anglers who want to be highly mobile and find fish that are not (or not as) accessible from the bank, pier, or by wading. There are many factors that influence the type of boat that is desirable or necessary to use; these include water conditions (size and tendency to get rough), the distance to be traveled on the water while fishing or to get to the appropriate places to fish, the type of fishing to be done, and the equipment needed. Boats run larger in big bodies of water because of the influence of current, waves, and weather. The

The so-called bass boat, seen here, is simply a fishing machine designed for use on fairly large waters and for anglers who primarily cast and use an electric motor when actually fishing.

biggest boats used in freshwater angling resemble ocean sportfishermen, being in the 25- to 35-foot range; these are used for trolling on the Great Lakes or large rivers, usually by charter boat skippers.

A vee-hulled fiberglass boat is especially suitable for large lakes, ponds, and rivers, where rough water dictates sturdy craft and where a big boat with a lot of engine muscle can help cover a lot of distance quickly. Aluminum boats can also be used under these conditions, although flat-bottomed models (johnboats) simply do not handle rough water well. The vee-hulled aluminum boats take rough water a little better, but still not as good as fiberglass boats; they sit up higher in the water and, because they are lighter, are more susceptible to being blown around in the wind. Sixteen- to 25-foot boats, aluminum and fiberglass, fill the bill for a wide range of freshwater fishing.

A smaller aluminum or flat-bottom boat is very functional for fishing on small lakes, rivers, and ponds, where it is not necessary to cover a lot of territory and where adverse conditions are seldom present. Small aluminum vee-bottomed

boats can be used in the same manner, except that they are less suitable for small river fishing and more suitable to moderate-size lakes owing to their deeper-draft design. Canoes are popular in small lakes and ponds and in flowing water, although they are an unsteady craft and are highly susceptible to positioning problems.

Whatever boat you have, or find interesting, it should be thought of as a fishing tool. It has to get you where the fish are. It must weather the best and the worst water conditions. It must be reasonably comfortable to allow you to put in long hours. It must be versatile to handle a variety of angling pursuits. It must be designed and/or modified to allow you to fight and land fish (especially big fish). And it should have readily available accessories.

Unfortunately, there is no one ideal boat that will suit all fishing needs and interests. Let's take a look at key factors to consider when thinking of purchasing a new or used boat that is trailered and which is capable of handling several anglers, since this is where the bulk of the market is in freshwater nowadays.

Storage is one of the most important items to

consider. There is tackle storage and incidental storage, of course, and while some boats look great off the water, they suffer from a lack of proper storage area when in use. Anglers tend to clutter a boat up quickly with fishing paraphernalia and accessory items, so pay attention to the storage that a boat has. Look for dry storage if you will be needing to keep various things under cover.

As for tackle storage, first consider rods. Good rods today are expensive and they should not be left to bounce or tangle in a heap; be sure that they can be properly restrained both when the boat is running on the water and when being trailered. Check that rod storage areas will hold the length and style of rod that you use most often, or can at least be customized to adapt to your own special needs, and that they are easy to get into.

As for tackle boxes, only you know what storage you need in this regard, though most avid fishermen carry more than they need or can use in any event. However, tripping over tackle boxes, having them slide around when the boat is on plane or bouncing through waves, and not

A boat is an important piece of equipment for many freshwater anglers; these salmon anglers are primarily fishing from small aluminium craft that are very suitable to the size of this river and to the need for mobility.

being able to get them out of the way for fishing action, are common troubles that can be avoided. Look for a boat that will meet your needs in this area while actually fishing, and while not.

Do you keep fish or bait alive while angling? If so, you'll need a livewell of some sort. Long term storage and boating great distances usually demand built-in systems, with adequate aer-

ation. A system that brings water in from outside, rather than recirculating the same water, is infinitely better. Recirculation is especially undesirable when the water is warm.

Of course, you will have to consider usable fishing space, and this may be one of the key points in your selection process. It is surprising how many people try to adapt a runabout or ski boat to serious fishing, although the usable space for gear and mobility within such boats is seriously lacking. Check the layout of the boats you review for uncluttered and usable inside space, and be attentive to the possibility that you will want to add some accessories, such as downriggers, to the boat, and need appropriate and accessible places to do so.

In new boats, packages have become the rule rather than the exception, due to the consolidation of motor and boat manufacturers and the desire to market ready-to-go items. The majority of these are targeted at sportfishermen. Whether you are thinking new or used, pre-packaged or mix-and-match, you should be taking a critical look at the boat you buy for fishing, and not be swayed by appearance.

MOTORS

Most boats have motors and motors thus are an essential part of the freshwater fishing scene. There are electric- and gas-powered motors, the former being more important in a strictly fishing functionality sense. Nevertheless, outboard motors are important in a general sense and some are extremely important for specific fishing applications (like backtrolling). Many features have been incorporated into them in recent years that make them more functional for angling use. This is especially true of the smaller

Many big-boat walleye anglers rely on a small outboard motor as not only auxiliary power in case of a main-engine problem, but also for slow trolling and boat maneuvering.

horsepower models, many of which are used for trolling and slow boat-positioning efforts.

More freshwater fishermen these days are using 9 to 15 horsepower outboards as auxiliary or "kicker" motors becuase they use minimal gasoline, make less noise, and are preferable for maneuvering a boat by hand. Hand operation, or tiller steering, is even being used on boats up to the 200 horsepower size these days, although in the mid-80s, tiller steering could only be found in small and mid-range motors. Fishermen who need to use their outboards a lot while fishing (as opposed to using them mostly to get to the places where they will be fishing) prefer tiller steering because of the quicker response they get while directing the boat, and also becuase this frees up more space in the interior of the boat for anglers and gear

by not requiring a console for a steering wheel and cables. Shallow-water tilt-up positions, electric start, one-hand throttle and shift controls, and many other features have made it easier for anglers to fish and run an outboard at the same time.

An electric motor is truly one of the most important pieces of fishing equipment that many anglers can possess. Those who strictly troll out of large boats, fish from shore, do no casting, or who don't fish on lakes where outboard engines are prohibited, probably have no need for an electric motor. As for the rest of the angling fraternity, an electric motor is one of the best products to come along for fishing in this millenium.

Commonly referred to as "trolling motors" (although only a few people actually troll with them), these products shine for their ability to quietly maneuver a fisherman into places to make proper fishing presentations. Many small-lake fishermen, and those with small boats used for a variety of fishing applications, possess electric motors. Electric motors essentially take the place of oars and sculling paddles, but are quieter and interfere less with fishing activities.

All electric motors are battery-powered. Some are powered by just a single 12-volt battery; others use 24 volts, requiring two 12-volt batteries; and some have the capability of running off either one or two 12-volt batteries. Some produce considerably more thrust than others, which means they are basically more powerful.

However, there are such things as sustained thrust and initial thrust, the former being the power generated while under ay and the latter being the initial startup power. Initial thrust is greater than sustained thrust. The amount of energy (designated as amperes, or amp) consumed per hour by electric motors varies, and this figure, when known, will tell you how many hours of continuous use you can get out of a battery at varied motor speeds.

Check the specifications of these products and determine how much power you need and for how long you need that power in normal fishing circumstances. Generally, the heavier your boat and load, the more thrust needed. Another factor is how much fishing you do in areas of substantial current, or wind, which drains the reserves of a battery quicker than calm-condition operation. An electric motor does not automatically recharge the power source, and in the course of a full day's fishing you will likely drain the energy of a battery down considerably, so you need a charger to re-energize the battery.

One of the features you ought to look for in an electric motor is silence. Shallow-water anglers who use electric motors can conceivably get much closer to fish than boaters with far noisier gas outboard engines. Not spooking fish is obviously advantageous. Some electrics are considerably noisier than others, however.

On most fiberglass and many aluminum bass boats an electric motor is mounted permanently on the bow, with the bracket support installed on the port to help put a little weight on that side and counterbalance the console and driver weight on the starboard side. On many small boats, electric motors can be mounted on the front or back, but for convenience and best boat control, transom mounting is preferable, as is manual operation. Some boaters, especially walleye anglers, have both a bow-mounted electric motor on an 18-foot big-water boat and a transom-mounted tiller-steered electric on the back; the latter is used when slowly trolling or positioning the boat for precise bait presentation in fairly calm water conditions.

Permanent-mount electrics are used on conventional bass boats and large craft and can be operated manually or in remote fashion, depending upon the unit. Remote units are primarily operated via a foot-control pedal that is on the bow deck; some newer units have no wire foot control cable but an electronic cable that sends signals from anywhere in the boat. Manual models do not have a foot control pedal or cable running to the motor, and are steered by using your foot or hand at the head of the motor to direct it.

A lot of changes have been occurring in the electric motor field, and fishermen can expect these products to become more sophisticated as time passes. One of the newest innovations as of this writing is a seeing-eye-dog type of electric motor which features a photo-optic electronic compass that senses the slightest deviations in course and triggers the steering mechanism to compensate and maintain a selected heading. It is like an autopilot electric motor. Another innovation is a motor with a low-profiled, highly sensitive, turntable-design foot control that provides electronic steering with awesome ease. Only 90-degree movement with the foot provides 380-degree motor rotation and it also sports auto return and auto park features that place the motor in the proper position.

Better propellors have been the focus of manufacturing attention in recent years, too, not only for propulsion, but for cutting through vegetation. Many electric motors are used by anglers who fish for bass, pike, walleye, and musky in and around weedy habitat, and an electric motor that is constantly gathering weeds and becoming fouled is an irritant. Multi-bladed electric motor propellors now exist that provide quiet operation, low cavitation, improved steerage, and superior weedless operation, and come standard on some newer products.

Many mid-size boats that are used for casting feature a bow-mounted electric motor for positioning and quiet movement. Note the sonar unit at this angler's feet, where he can look at it while maneuvering the boat and fishing.

SONAR/ELECTRONICS

Most fishermen simply use the term "depthfinder" when referring to what is actually sonar equipment. Certainly, transmitting depth is the foremost function of sportfishing sonar, but defining bottom types and contours and locating fish are also important functions.

An outgrowth of sonar (short for sound navigation and ranging) applied by the military in World Wars I and II, today's electronic depth-finding and fish-locating equipment is helping anglers enjoy their sport and become more learned and proficient. In some circumstances it is viewed as being virtually indispensable. This is because sportfishing sonar is the boat angler's underwater eyes. With it he can find concentrations of migratory, suspended, schooling, and nomadic fish, plus he can locate unseen habitat that may be attractive to fish. With sportfishing sonar devices he can become accurately acquainted with the beneath-the-sur-

Sonar is useful for navigational purposes in some freshwater environments, but also for such fishing activities as trolling, as this angler is doing.

face environment of a body of water in significantly less time than without it. Additionally, the use of sportfishing sonar allows an angler to navigate better, more safely, and quicker than he might otherwise. Locating fish with sonar, however, is no guarantee that they are the kind of fish you are looking for, or that you'll be able to catch them.

Sonar instruments employ transducers that swiftly send out pulses in a three-dimensional cone-shaped wave. Cone angles range from 8 (most narrow) to 50 degrees (extremely wide), and this in turn influences how much underwater detail will be viewed. Trollers usually prefer the widest cone and extremely deep water anglers the narrowest cone.

Sportfishing sonar falls into several categories: graph recorders, flashers, video recorders, and liquid crystal recorders (LCRs). Graph recorders make a chart paper printout of readings. The best graph recorders exceed all of the other types of sonar in the quality of detail that they provide; the cost of paper, and the need for frequent changing, are prominent drawbacks. Flashers were once the mainstay of the sonar

field, but have fallen out of general favor in recent years due to the emergence of LCRs; flashers have excellent detail but require some practice to learn to properly interpret their signals. Video recorders are the most expensive sonar and least preferred by serious fishermen, although their multi-color TV-like appearance is entertaining.

LCRs have become the dominant force in sportfishing sonar, partly because of their simplicity and relatively economical cost. LCRs are getting better but are sometimes difficult to read because of the nature of the window and the number of pixels on their screen; most anglers leave them in the automatic mode, which is often inadequate.

With LCRs, signals appear at one side of the screen as you go over them, cross the screen and disappear at the other end. Some of the better models have a screen update to recall a full screen's worth of information; a zoom feature that narrows down the area being observed; an automatic depth-determining mode; forward and reverse displays; positive fish identification modes; fish and bottom depth alarms; split screens; target-separating grayline; and other microprocessor-controlled features.

Changes are taking place rapidly in the sonar realm, and new generations of equipment have come fairly rapidly of late as technology races to provide anglers with equipment that will visually enhance the electronic interpetation of the underwater world so anglers can better under-

stand it. Three-dimensional LCR displays is the newest innovation. These sport multiple or scanning transducer beams and display a three-dimensional composite image of bottom contours and fish. The bottom is depicted like an LCD contour relief map, minus color but with a constantly changing scene as the transducer records new information. Some units have a wide viewing area and a reverse viewing feature to see side images, as well as a two-dimensional display, plus other characteristics.

Three-dimensional sonar has the potential of being the new wave in sportfishing sonar. Neither this, nor any other sonar presently available, however, will tell you what species or weight of fish is depicted. Someday we may have that. There is at least one sonar product, however, that allows anglers to target specific types of fish based upon the environment they are angling in; the fisherman selects the type of fish he is seeking and the environment he is in, and then lets the pre-programmed sonar take over and it will make necessary adjustments. Fish that are displayed, in theory, are likely to be those that are sought, as the device is said to filter out the signals that would indicate other, non-target, species.

The other latest trend in electronic equipment for freshwater anglers has been more usage of loran, and the interfacing of loran with sonar.

A liquid crystal recorder being used by an angler in shallow water.

Some sportfishing sonar possesses loran features, but many anglers are purchasing separate loran equipment. Long used in saltwater, loran is primarily useful on big bodies of fresh water, especially the Great Lakes, for pinpointing locales where concentrations of open-water nomadic fish (salmon and walleyes in particular) are found and where it is hard (but necessary) to return to a hot spot or re-locate fish that are on the move. They also serve navigational purposes, especially in big water where fog may be encountered or for night-time boating.

ACCESSORIES

When you boil sportfishing down to the barest of essentials equipment-wise, you have line, hook or lure, rod or pole, and perhaps bait or reel. But there is almost no angler whose inventory includes just that, and some have enough paraphernalia to fill a garage. That paraphernalia, known as accessories, ranges from items that many anglers would consider to be virtually essential, if not basic, to products so specialized that few possess them. Fishermen are notorious gadget and equipment-laden folks, so there is much in the accessory field to attract their interest. The following review of this field has been distilled down to the most widely used and most functional items.

This electric downrigger is set at 22 feet; it is programmable for automatic oscillation at various depths.

DOWNRIGGERS

Downriggers won't help the stream trout fly caster, the heavy-cover bass angler, the crappie minnow dunker, and certain others, but they will benefit just about anyone who trolls, and are becoming almost as common on fishing boats as sonar and electric motors. They are the best thing to hit the trolling scene since outboard motors were invented. They not only revolutionized trolling techniques in recent decades, but they have made trolling a more sporting, fruitful, and fun endeavor.

The reason for the growth in usage is because downriggers leave less to chance. Downriggers put your offering in the right place, time after time. It's a snap to raise or lower a lure; you don't have to fight a fish encumbered by burdensome tackle; you can change offerings quickly; you can easily run more than one fishing line on the same downrigger; you can maneuver in tight quarters if your lures aren't set too far back; you can fish just about any kind of lure or bait;

and they are simple to use.

Downrigger trolling basically takes the place of running an object on a weighted or unweighted nylon monofilament, braided Dacron, or fly line; behind a lead-core or wire line; or behind a diving planer or releaseable weight. Each of these systems can suffer from imprecise depth control because you often don't know exactly how deep you're fishing. When you do know, you may have an extreme amount of line out, or you're using tackle that could subdue a submarine.

Downriggers overcome these problems because they take the burden of getting a lure to a specific depth away from your fishing line and put it on an accessory product. They offer controlled depth presentation, and can be used with light as well as heavy tackle.

Downriggers consist of a reel, cranking handle, boom, wire cable, and pulley that are part of the basic product; a heavy lead weight (8 to 12 pounds) that attaches to the end of the downrigger cable; and a line release mechanism that may be located on or near the weight or at anywhere on the cable.

In use, a lure that is attached to your fishing line is placed in the water and set at whatever distance you want it to run behind your boat. Then the fishing line attached to that lure is placed in the release. Fishing line and downrigger weight are lowered simultaneously to the depth you want to fish. When a fish strikes your lure, the fishing line pops out of the release and you play the fish on your fishing line, unencumbered by a heavy weight or strong cable. In sum, you piggyback your fishing line to a heavily weighted non-fishing line, and the two separate when a fish strikes.

Downriggers come in manual or electric models. Many small-boat fishermen have manual downriggers or started with manual models and worked up to electrics. Manuals come in small versions that clamp onto the transom or gunwales of boats or even fit into the oarlock receptacle, and some are available in either right- or left-hand-crank versions; electrics are generally made for permanent and sturdy mounting locations and some manuals are similarly mounted.

Electrics are more expensive than manual downriggers, require a power source, and are more prone to malfunction, but are preferred because of their ease of use. Some electrics are slower than others at raising and lowering the weight, and it is often desirable to have a unit

that will quickly perform these tasks. Electric downriggers are raised and lowered by flicking a switch, while manuals are always hand-cranked up and in some models are also cranked down (on some you can release clutch tension to lower a downrigger weight instead of handle-cranking it down).

Although you can often raise or lower a weight faster with a manual model than with an electric, with most electrics you can hit an automatic up switch that retrieves the downrigger while you are tending to other chores. This is very useful when using several downriggers on a large boat.

The length of the boom, which carries the cable from the reel over the side of the boat, varies from short 1-foot arms to 8-footers, depending on boat size and location and the need to spread out weights to cover the greatest possible horizontal range of water. Most downriggers also have a line counter that measures the amount of cable that reels off the spool, indicating the depth of the weight. Some downriggers sport one or two rod holders that attach to the frame or base of the unit. Rod holders are critical to downrigging, and whether they are on the downrigger or situated nearby, they are needed to hold the rod that is employed with the downrigger.

PLANERS

There are two types of planers, both of which are used for trolling: diving planers and sideplaners. Diving planers attach to fishing line a few feet ahead of a lure and dive deeply. They are used with a stout rod and heavy line, and remain on the fishing line while playing a fish. There are no weights used to get the lure down; the resistance of the planer makes it dive. When a fish strikes, it trips a release mechanism that allows the diver to offer minimal water resistance as the fish is played. These planers offer a deep-trolling alternative to fishermen without downriggers and to those who wish to avoid wire or lead core line or the use of heavy weights. They are primarily used in fishing for salmon in the Great Lakes and on the West Coast, and to a lesser extent for lake trout.

The term "sideplaner" is used to refer to two types of devices that are employed on the surface and which do not dive below it; they are also called simply "boards". The more popular devices are sideplaner boards, which are long plastic or wooden surface-running planers that evolved on the Great Lakes for trout and salmon trolling, and which have caught on wildly in environs where trolling—especially in shallow water—is a necessity. These devices solve many of the difficulties of shallow trolling, and make presentations much more versatile than merely running a flat line out behind the boat.

Sideplaner boards work something like a

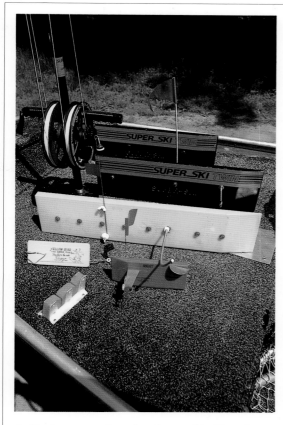

In the foreground are two types of in-line planer boards; behind them are single- and double-runner sideplaners, plus a dual-reel sideplaner standpole.

downrigger on the surface. A non-fishing line or cable tethers the planer to the boat, and allows it to run at varied distances off to the side. One or more fishing lines are attached to the planer or tow line via release clips; you are free to fight a fish unencumbered when it strikes your lure and releases the fishing line from the clip.

Sideplaners can be used in trolling for many kinds of fish. They vastly increase presentation capabilities because they allow lures to pass near fish that may have been spooked by the passage of a boat (or would be spooked if a boat was run near them) or are in areas where you can't or don't want to take a boat.

How far you set the sideplaners out depends on how close you want your boat to shore, how far apart you want to spread your lures, how much room you have to fish, and how much boat traffic there is in the area, among other factors.

To use large sideplaners you must have a method of tethering them to your boat and retrieving them. You can use manual downriggers for that, though this limits your outward range. A few companies are making sideplaner reels, but you can fashion your own retrieval system with an old high-capacity level-wind reel or other reel-like storage mechanism, spooled with 150- to 200-pound-test monofilament or Dacron, and attached to a stand pole with a swiveling pulley at the top.

You can run lures any length behind a sideplaner that seems feasible. Because the lures are trolled well off to the side of the boat, and behind a relatively unobtrusive planer, they often don't have to be run very far back.

Obviously, a host of fishing combinations are possible.

The drawbacks to using sideplaners are that they require a little more equipment and cash outlay, it takes some practice to get used to them, it can be tough to work everything if you're alone in the boat, and they pose logistical problems at times. However they'll put you over a lot of fish that you couldn't otherwise reach.

The other type of sideplaner, which is smaller, attaches directly to your fishing line, and pops free when a fish strikes. This sideplaner has a calm-water fishing advantage, but must be retrieved after a fish is caught, and makes hooking fish a little difficult. It is worked in a very similar manner, except that a fisherman employs one planer per rod, instead of using several fishing lines per planer. The rods must be fairly stout, and be placed in holders while trolling.

Some anglers rig these small boards in such a way that the planer does not trip free of the fishing line when a fish strikes, but remains attached to it. When a fish is on, they reel their line in until the planer comes to the boat, then unhook it and continue landing the fish. Sometimes this is a two-man operation, sometimes it is done by one angler. This permits them to continue fishing and to keep the other lines (and planers) out if desired, without having to return to retrieve a floating board. The larger and harder fighting the fish, the harder this is to accomplish. However, these boards alleviate the need to have equipment for towing and retrieving boards. Many species of fish can be caught with these, but they are most popular with walleye anglers.

TACKLE STORAGE METHODS

The traditional tackle box was a metal container, but the realm of items in which to hold tackle has vastly expanded to a potpourri of systems, many suited to specialized applications. Plastic boxes are by far the most popular these days,

This doubled-sided tackle box with see-through lid and movable compartments is a very popular tackle storage system for freshwater anglers who use small- to medium-sized lures.

for ease of care and also because plastic can be molded into a great range of designs, yet there are still a few metal boxes, particularly small aluminum models used by fly fishermen, and even some wooden ones, to be found. Leather and cloth tackle satchels are also in use, as well as flexible, foldable tackle systems made of dense sailcloth, with compartments covered by vinyl.

The traditional style of tackle box comes in trunk, hip roof, and drawer configurations. A trunk box has one or more trays that pivot up together to reveal a large open compartment at the bottom of the box. Hip roof boxes are similar, though they have two sets of trays facing each other. The drawer box has trays that slide out, and usually has the most compartments for storage.

The type of box to use largely depends on the amount and size of objects that you need to store. Typically most fishermen outgrow their boxes and purchase more or larger ones as they accumulate tackle and/or their fishing interests expand. Tackle boxes with movable dividers allow you to fashion the number and size of storage compartments to suit your needs.

Many fishermen who do a lot of angling and/or who fish for various species keep several boxes, often organized by lure types or tackle-by-species. Single- and double-sided plastic tackle boxes with see-through lids are particularly favored by avid anglers. They have movable compartments, hold a surprising amount of gear, and can be readily stowed or stacked on top of one another. Some boxes are geared toward specific types of storage needs, such as big lures (for musky fishermen), and possess features (a rack to hold spinnerbaits, for example) that acccommodate this.

When considering purchasing a tackle box, check to see if it is watertight, if there is channeling that will prevent water from entering the interior, and if the latches are strong and allow snug closure. Some boxes are designed to prevent accidental spillage (even tipping) in case the latch is left open and the box picked up. Look for a good-quality hinge-pin arrangement in the back rather than one that is part of the molded box; the hinge-pin will last longer. A good handle is critical, too. Large handles aid carrying and exchanging, but if they stick out too much from the box they may get in the way. A recessed handle is desirable where boxes will be stacked or objects placed on top of them.

Not all storage is as formal as a box or satchel, of course. Wading anglers who are mobile need something that can be worn instead of toted. A fishing vest is a multi-pocketed and compartmented tackle storage system that is worn over

Following pages: A large float tube is suitable for most any size of water, and with fin propulsion will allow an angler considerable mobility.

shirt or jacket and predominantly used by fly casters and river and stream fishermen. Full-length versions are standard, but shorter models are used by deep-water waders and float tube anglers. Both have many pockets, some designed especially to hold specific items (reel spool or sunglasses), and are designed for the storage of many small items, and even include a pouch in the back for small fish.

NETS

Landing nets are an important and regularly used accessory with freshwater anglers, from stream trout anglers to boaters. Naturally, nets should be suited to the kind of angling being done and the fish anticipated. Stream nets have a short handle and small hoop diameter (12 to 14 inches) for small fish while boat nets have longer handles (perhaps collapsible) and larger hoops. The further one has to reach (from boat or pier), the longer the handle needed. Pier and bridge fishermen use a large, handle-less net that is lowered and raised on a rope. There are a few nets available that incorporate a scale into the handle in order to weigh a fish that has been netted.

With all nets, the larger the fish, the bigger the hoop and the deeper the bag. While it seems foolish to net small fish with big nets, it's worse to be caught with a net that can't fit the fish. For small-boat fishing a net that is at least 4 feet long from net rim to handle butt, with a wide rim and a deep net bag, is a popular choice. Most nets feature aluminum handles and frames. Mesh bags are rubber, nylon, plastic, or cotton, although cotton tends to rot. All nets should be rinsed after use to increase their longevity.

Alternatives to netting fish include the use of a gaff, mesh bag, or tailer. Tailers are mainly used on Atlantic salmon. Mesh bags with wooden side handles have been used by fisheries technicians to support fish without handling, but they are cumbersome, difficult for a lone angler to use, and have not been popular with sportfishermen. Gaffs, which are sharp hooks attached to a handle, are seldom used in freshwater because the size of fish does not warrant them, but also because they are often used on fish to be killed (impaling them in the side and back). A short-handled gaff, however, might be used to snare a fish in the lip; the fish can then be released without harm.

WADERS

Anglers who fish from the bank, who wade, or who get in and out of boats during the course of fishing (such as river drifters), need waders or hip boots to keep them dry and to help provide good footing. There are several types of waders. Boot foots are probably most popular and feature one-piece construction with a boot that is permanently attached to a chest-high upper section and is firm enough to walk on. Stocking foot waders are also chest-high, but have a soft foot section that is worn inside a pair of wading shoes (or sneakers in warm water). Boot foot and stocking foot waders are worn with suspenders and should be used with a waist-level outer belt to help keep water out and trap air inside in the event of a spill.

Hippers are short waders that are very similar to the lower section of boot foot waders in construction, but they have separated legs which reach only to the hip and are held up by a strap that loops onto the wearer's belt. Though they are often referred to by fishermen as "hip boots", they are slightly different; hip boots cover the same area, but technically they are made from heavier material from top to bottom.

Hippers or hip boots are meant for wading in relatively shallow water. It is easier to get in and out of a boat or car in hip-length products, and they are easiest to take off or put on. They are also cooler to wear in warm weather, and good for long-distance walking on land.

The biggest advantage of chest-high waders is that they get you to deeper fishing holes, either by allowing you to wade deeper to cast or to ford deep places to get to locales you can't access otherwise. They are a bit heavy and bulky, however, which provides more warmth but makes for more difficult distance walking or climbing. Boot foots are easier to take off or put on because of their one-piece construction, but generally are not as comfortable and are heavier than stocking foot waders with wading shoes. Stocking foot waders fit the body closer, which can mean less drag in the water and easier climbing, and the wading shoes worn with them often provide better foot support and traction.

The materials used in the construction of waders and hip boots has come a long way. Stocking foot waders have undergone the greatest transformation, with many ultra-lightweight products available. Closed-cell neoprene, a material akin to that of wetsuits for skin-diving, has become very popular for both stocking foot and boot foot waders. Products made from neoprene are light, very flexible, and more form-fitting than waders of old. This synthetic rubber material is very stretchy, meaning that neoprene waders do not impair mobility or climbing. They are time-consuming to put on, however, and they are warm – too warm for long-distance walking and for warm-water or warm-weather use – though very good for cold weather and cold water.

The soles of many waders are equipped with felt, which enhances traction in slippery bottoms. Felt wear out and has to be replaced or at least re-glued from time to time. Gripping cleats, which are metal studs of various shapes, are worn over standard rubber boats where walking is extremely slippery.

FLOAT TUBES

Float tubes for fishing purposes are becoming more popular. Fishing from a float tube is not generally as effective as fishing from a boat, but it is a good way for anglers who don't have a boat and other boating-related accessories to reach spots they might not be able to get to otherwise, and it is simply a different and very pleasurable experience. Float tubes are conducive to a slower, more thorough pace of fishing, and, though used on large and small waters alike, are particularly favored for ponds and small lakes, including hard-to-access remote bodies of water.

Most float tube users wear chest-high waders when fishing. Neoprene waders or insulated rubber waders are used where the water is cold, and lightweight models in warmer water. Footwear is the key, because you need some method of propelling yourself around. This is done either by the use of swim fins or paddle pushers. The latter are a device that strap around the boot heel and have a paddle that allows you to go forward by moving your legs as if you were walking. Swim fins are preferred by many because they provide quicker movement from point to point if your leg muscles are in good shape. However, you must move backward in them virtually all the time to get anywhere, and they are tough to walk in on land or on a murky lake bottom.

The better float tubes are lightweight and don't actually use a truck tire inner tube (earlier models did), but are self-contained products made of sturdy material that is blown up via some type of pump. Some have two or three inflatable compartments, and some have accesible storage compartments. All have an apron that sits over the front of the tube, to be used as a place to rest tackle or to drape fly line while casting.

Tackle selection has to be conservative. You generally only have one rod with you, and can't take a full tackle box full of equipment, though with a fishing vest or suitable storage compartments on the float tube, you can still bring a fair amount along.

ROD HOLDERS

A rod holder is an essential tool for boat fishermen. Rod holders come in many forms and are made by many manufacturers. Open boats, center-consoles, and cabin craft often sport through-the-gunwale or flush-mounted holders that keep the rods upright for storage. This isn't practical for many small boats; for those, horizontal mounting is preferable. The decks of many boats are often cluttered with rods, and some anglers leave these to bounce freely when the boat is moving at high speeds. A flush-mounted holder placed on the deck securely

retains them. Holders such as these can also be used on the seats or sides of aluminum boats.

A deluxe arrangement of rod holders and other fishing paraphernalia is typical on many boats where trolling is a way of life, and where many boaters erect a board that goes across the transom. Two downriggers are usually mounted on the boards, with another two on the gunwales. Ample rod holders are placed on the board to allow rods in use to be within a narrow scope of vision and also to keep the lines clear of the motor to avoid cutoffs when turning sharply.

FISH STORAGE DEVICES

Something to put fish in is another highly useful accessory, as taking proper care of the fish you want to keep is important for consumptive purposes. That item might be a stringer, creel, cooler, livewell, or wire mesh bag. Small-boat fishermen who don't have a livewell or a cooler with ice to keep fish in will employ a stringer, which is attached to the boat and holds fish in the water. Rope stringers are the simplest and cheapest, but fish get bunched together on these. Metal or plastic clip-on stringers, with individual clips for securing fish, are a better alternative as long as they are sturdy enough to withstand the weight of fish being contained.

Canvas or basket creels are used by some mobile stream fishermen. Metal mesh bags, with a foam collar to keep them afloat, are favored by some boat and dock panfishermen, who find it easy to slip a fish through the top door and keep the catch alive. Livewells in many boats have eliminated the need for these devices, especially stringers, and have allowed anglers to keep their catch alive and fresh for long periods of time, especially if the water in those livewells is cool and recirculated regularly. Livewells are

nice to have if you want, or need, to keep fish alive during the fishing day, or to keep large bait alive. They are not practical in many small boats, however, because they take up a lot of room and, when full of water and fish, add a lot of weight. You can utilize a 48- or 64-quart cooler with an aeration pump as a livewell, however, as long as you have a battery to power the pump. In panfishing, it's popular to use wire mesh bags that float in the water to contain the day's catch of relatively small fish.

BAIT CONTAINERS

Bait containers rank high on the accessory charts, too. For baitfish, steel or plastic buckets, including some with a perforated insert pail, which contains the bait and which can be easily removed to facilitate water changing, or floating plastic buckets with spring-loaded door, are the primary models. The latter can be kept in the water and is especially useful for slow trolling. Both can be used for other bait, such as leeches, crayfish, or salamanders. Worms, however, are usually kept in small plastic or fiber containers, or simply in the styrofoam container that small quantities are sold in. Larger bait, especially that used in saltwater, are kept in boat baitwells or large storage containers. For some species, particularly herring, the containers must be round.

CLOTHING

More and more fishermen are finding that they enjoy their sport more when they are comfortable, and that sometimes translates into being warm and dry. You wouldn't ordinarily think of clothing as being a fishing accessory, but it certainly is where foul weather gear is concerned. Moreover, there is currently a trend toward supplying fishermen with general-use garments that

This angler is using hip waders, which are looped to his belt; note the sunglasses and brimmed cap to improve visibility, and the short rain jacket that doubles as a fishing vest.

have style and function. Many of these fairweather garments are made of Supplex, a strong highly abrasion-resistant nylon material, and Cool Max, a fast-wicking fabric that resists water absorption and does not retain body oils and odors. The result is light, cool, machine-washable garments, many of which have assorted functional styling features.

In raingear, the advent of Gore Tex in the 80s heralded a new wave in lightweight rainwear, although Gore Tex has failed many users in the water-repellancy arena. There is a lot of rainwear that is specifically designed for fishermen today, meaning that it will allow the casting and motion activities that occur in fishing without hindrance while doing its water protection duties. Waist-length, windproof, waterproof casting jackets are now more common, for example. Some have an outer shell of Supplex or Vent-X, the latter being nonporous yet able to wick perspiration out. Chest-high bibs or waist-level pants are standard as part of rainsuits, with many frequent anglers preferring the chest-high version for extra back warmth and water protection.

A step up for cold weather anglers is antiexposure coveralls that are U. S. Coast Guardapproved as flotation devices, but which provide warmth, protection from wind and rain, anti-hypothermia protection, and are also designed for cold weather boating and fishing action. The better ones sport a mobility system that allows one to cast, raise arms, and bend over without the garment binding under the arm/collar/crotch, without a frontal bunched-up effect, and without cuffs creeping up.

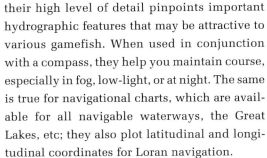

A good rainsuit, preferably one with a large hood and bib overalls, is almost an indispensable item for anglers.

ICE FISHING GEAR

In northern areas, ice fishing is quite popular with anglers, some of whom are very productive by fishing with bait or jigs through the ice- and snow-covered lakes and ponds. Walleye, pike, perch, and pickerel are the main quarries, and though it is possible to use standard rods and reels for jigging through holes in the ice, there is some specialized tackle that is used for this endeavor.

Most importantly, for bait fishing, is a tip-up, which is a device that sports a spool filled with line, to which a baited hook is attached, and which sprouts a highly visible flag when the bait has been struck. Fish are retrieved by hand-lining. Short rods, in the 18- to 24-inch range, are used for jigging through the ice, and assorted jigs are the lures used, some tipped with bait.

In addition to these items, ice fishermen need an auger, manual or gas-powered, or a spud or chisel, for making holes; a scoop to clear the hole of ice fragments; and a styrofoam-insulated minnow bucket. Portable or permanent shacks are used in some locales, although many ice fishermen like to be mobile and move from place to place to fish and to search for schools of fish.

MAPS

Maps that detail underwater contours and hydrographic features help in navigation and in finding locales that may provide good fishing. Most preferred are underwater contour (hydrographic) maps and navigational charts, which are distinguished from topographic maps. The latter seldom denote water depth or the location of reefs, rocks, shallows, and such, while the former do. Underwater contour maps are available for many natural and manmade lakes, and these can be particularly useful because their high level of detail pinpoints important hydrographic features that may be attractive to various gamefish. When used in conjunction with a compass, they help you maintain course, especially in fog, low-light, or at night. The same is true for navigational charts, which are available for all navigable waterways, the Great Lakes, etc; they also plot latitudinal and longitudinal coordinates for Loran navigation.

Navigational charts are produced by American and Canadian federal agencies and are available at some sporting goods stores, tackle shops, marinas, and major-city map stores, and cost a few dollars apiece. Dealers usually stock local area maps and can order others. The larger the scale, the more detail there is.Other maps of big freshwater lakes may be available from jurisdictional agencies such as the Corps of Engineers or TVA, although their maps are rarely detailed enough to provide more than general information. Maps for freshwater lakes supplied by private firms, however, are often geared to fishermen's interests and provide a great deal of underwater contour information. Their size and scale level will determine how helpful they are as boating and fishing aids.

INCIDENTALS

Among the other practical and oft-used simple accessories for anglers are pliers, either needle-nosed for hook removal or blunt-nosed with wire cutting edges; nail clippers, to cut line and knots; a spring scale, including those with a tape measure (useful where length limits are employed); a fillet knife, preferably with a thin and somewhat flexible blade ranging from 6 to 10 inches long; a hook sharpener and a knife sharpener; a surface temperature gauge, which is especially useful in spring and early summer; a trolling speed indicator, which is predominantly used on the Great Lakes to define slow boat speeds; marker buoys, for use with sonar to identify open-water angling locations; polarized sunglasses, for eye protection and enhanced visibility; and sunscreen lotion, which, though it plays no part in fishing per se, does protect the skin from possibly harmful exposure to the sun. It should be noted also that fishing scents are used by many anglers, and that there are a potpourri of sprays, rub-ons, mold-ons, etc. available; some fishermen swear by the use of these items, while others scoff at their use and have good success irregardless.

Left: *Flagged tip-ups dot the ice, accompanied by gas-powered augers and assorted other ice fishing paraphernalia.*

Right: *This winter steelhead fisherman is wearing this colorful insulated flotation suit for warmth as well as safety, plus a pair of neoprene fishing gloves.*

Skills, Savvy, and Techniques

FINDING FISH

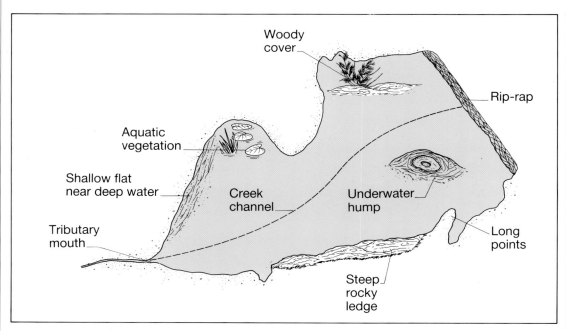

Lakes may have a wide variety of features; the type of species sought and the time of year will govern where to look for fish.

Successful fishing is the result of many activities, one of the foremost of which is finding fish. The act of finding fish to present your lures, flies, or bait to involves a combination of things, including visual observation, intensive searching, understanding the habits of fish and the habitat in which they are found (this varies from species to species), and using savvy to realize how these elements relate to one another and then be able to take advantage of that.

Visual observation is one factor in selecting places to fish and in looking for signs that indicate the presence of fish (see intangibles, observation). Most often, however, anglers don't observe fish but search for them, which frequently means that they need to watch water conditions to determine where fish may lie and how to present lures to them. This is referred to as "reading water", and is done in all types of environments. It is sometimes more obvious in rivers than in stillwaters (ponds, lakes, reservoirs). The latter especially pose problems for many freshwater fishermen, particularly in places that they do not know well.

Every year, thousands of freshwater anglers confront the question of where to find fish in a new, or unfamiliar, body of water. Some people are mainly interested in catching "anything that bites." They may just dunk bait, prop their feet on the gunwale, and catch some rays, or simply tie on a popular lure and troll hither and yon. But the angler whose main objective is to catch fish needs a more thoughtful approach.

In the past three decades, the desire and need to learn more about the places being fished spurred the creation and increasing sophistication and usage of various electronic equipment. Some have become important, if not almost indispensable, to many ardent modern-day anglers. Sonar devices and temperature-sensing units are chief among these and they truly are instrumental in helping any boat angler unlock

Below: *Finding fish can seem like a formidable task, especially on large bodies of water, and particularly when you are unfamiliar with the*

Often it is beneficial to take the time to look for fish with sonar equipment prior to angling, in part to locate them but also to study underwater features. This angler has a paper graph recorder on his console, and an LCR nearby.

This rocky island point, and the rocky shoal in the background, are easily spotted visually, but sometimes it takes closer scouring with sonar to find the features that are attractive to fish.

the secrets of the places he fishes.

Lakes, ponds, and impoundments are all quite different, so the type and size of body of water plays a role in what you do and how you do it. The species available and/or desired is another consideration; obviously the more you know about fish behavior and habitat the better. Gamefish are usually found in certain places for specific reasons and the better you understand the relationship between their depth, cover, temperature, food needs, and so forth, the better you are able to put the pieces of the underwater puzzle together while employing electronic equipment.

The picture of that puzzle can be flushed out a bit by some work that you do before you get on the water. Obtaining and studying lake maps, particularly those with underwater contours and depth and channel markings, is a key factor. At the very least, these will familiarize you with the general lay of the lake and its characteristics, but perhaps also detail some very specific structures (such as rock reefs, old roadbeds and culverts, sunken weeds, etc.) that may be important to fish. Such maps are not available for all waters, unfortunately, or the ones that are available may not be as detailed as you'd like; in any event, you still have to put your boat in the water and wet a hook.

Picking a spot to fish and immediately wetting a hook, however, is often not such a good idea. Sure, everyone wants to get fishing right away, but it is often wise to do some cruising first, looking over the water with your electronics as you go. Sonar study is especially important, but at certain seasons, temperature evaluation may be equally so.

Let's assume that we're on an unfamiliar lake for the first time. We leave the ramp or dock and the first thing we do is check for surface water temperature. This is a matter of habit, like making the bed in the morning, and something that is more important at some times than at others. Spring is a season when evaluating sur-

Some fish may hold off a point while others may be inside a bay along the edge of the weeds.

face water temperature is of utmost value.

If it is the spring, we may want to seek the warmest locales on the lake first. Often that is along the north or northwest shores, where tributaries enter (especially after a warm rain), or in coves, bays, and sloughs. Many freshwater gamefish, and/or baitfish, spawn sometime in spring, often near shore or in and near tributaries, and water temperature is a triggering factor. By finding spots that have favorable temperatures, or temperatures warmer than other areas in the lake, you may locate either the places where fish are congregated, or the places where fish are most likely to be active.

As fulltime guides and charter boat captains can attest, angling for inactive fish is very tough; obviously, fishing where they aren't is a waste of time. Therefore, monitoring a surface temperature gauge (these are found as self-functioning units but are also increasingly being offered as concurrent options with sonar instruments) in the spring is an important adjunct to the business of casting or trolling.

As we start out on this lake, we also watch

our sonar instrument. That, again out of habit, was turned on right after we started the motor and will stay on until we stop fishing (unless it is a portable, battery-operated unit). For the moment, let's assume that we're trying to unlock the secrets of this lake in the summer. What we will look for depends to a large extent on the species of fish we intend to catch, but let's say we have an interest in all gamefish and thus need to consider all of the variables.

We could start out simply by looking for fish on the sonar unit. When you know your quarry well, it is possible to be able to identify the species you see on a sonar unit, but most of the time specific identification is uncertain. Knowing the habits and types of locales preferred by certain species of fish makes it easier to identify those species on sonar, but there is a lot of gray area here.

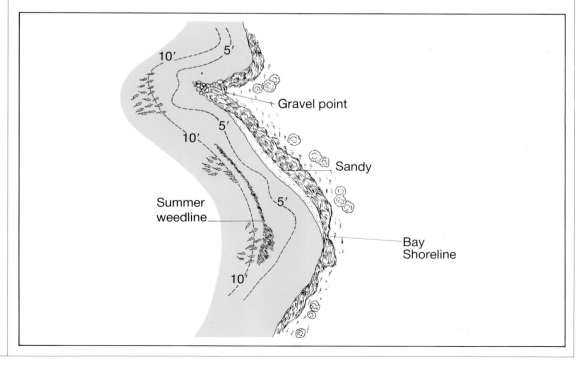

Points often extend underwater and are among the best places to look for various species of freshwater fish.

In some cases it will be important to look for the level at which concentrations of fish, especially large ones, are found, because it will give you an important clue to the depth to be fishing. This is especially pertinent in mid-lake open-water situations, for trolling, and when seeking such species as trout, salmon, suspended walleyes, and striped bass. In other cases, it can be helpful to find schools of bait and to know where or at what depths they are found. This can also point you to the depth to fish.

Looking for fish is something that we want to do, but it is generally best done while at the same time learning the lake and looking for suitable places to cast or troll for our targeted species.

Observing general depths and underwater contours is something we should be doing as we move around the lake, too. In certain waters, this is one of the most interesting things that will be done while unlocking the secrets of a lake. People who don't use sonar often have no idea how deep the water is in many of the places that they stop, meaning that they often fish it less efficiently than possible.

One of the things we want to pay attention to is the slope of the shoreline, how deep it gets near shore and as we move away from shore, especially if there is rock, wood, or vegetative cover. This can be gauged to some extent by

visual observation of the land formation onshore (a gradual slope on land usually indicates a flat and gently sloping terrain under adjacent water whereas a sharp slope onshore indicates a quick dropoff underwater), but the particulars aren't as readily discerned without sonar. In the spring, certain species of fish, such as bass, might be more attracted to a shallower shoreline area (which would warm up quicker) than to one that dropped off quickly. The reverse could be true later in the year, especially if the steep shoreline was protected from late-day sun.

If we will be fishing in open water (well away from shore), we will not only be checking for basic depth, but for the presence of such features as shoals, submerged timber, and old creek beds or channels. Many types of warmwater and coldwater fish are attracted to a shoal because of the proximity to deep water and the ability to find prey there. When we find a shoal (or hump, mound, or reef), we'll glue our eyes to the sonar and motor all around it; we'll watch the conformation on all sides, how quickly it drops off, and especially if there is bait or larger fish hanging along the dropoff to deeper water. We'll scour it with our underwater eyes first; we won't just motor over the shoal, stop at the shallowest spot, and start fishing. We'll use the sonar to learn about the shoal; it only takes a moments.

Where there is timber, it is often important to fish the tops of submerged trees, but where those are 30 or more feet below the surface it's impossible to stay in just the right place without

having sonar as a guide.

Clearly we need to study the sonar to know about the timber before fishing as well as watching it closely while fishing. We also should be looking for fish (in many cases this will be striped or white bass). It might be a good idea to use buoy markers to define the edges, channels, and such.

One of the key things that we will do to learn about this lake is to check out points. A point is a place where the land juts out in the water away from the shore and where the bottom terrain underwater continues to taper down and off. Some points are very obvious, some are subtle; some taper very gradually and extend (almost like a bar) a long way out into the lake, while others end abruptly and drop quickly to deep water.

Points are important lake features for many

This back bay could be a good springtime place to locate bass; it's shallow, it has stumps, and it appears to have a small creek entering.

species of fish, so we will use the sonar to do several things: look for fish on the breaklines (the distinguishable drops to greater depths) and in the immediate vicinity of well-defined points; establish the contours of points in order to fish them most effectively; and look for less obvious points while otherwise fishing or cruising.

Some of the best places I've fished in many freshwater environments are points that are not readily detected by looking at the shore, but which are found either by accident while fishing along a shoreline and watching sonar, or because someone else took me to them, usually saying something like, "very few people know that there's a small rocky point here, because it looks like any other stretch of shore." They found it originally on their sonar.

Another very important lake feature, especially for walleye, bass, pike, and musky, is vegetation. This may be lily pads, cabbage weeds, milfoil, hyacinths, or some other aquatic plant. We are going to look these over carefully, with and without sonar, if we seek the aforementioned species.

If vegetation appears in shallow water and we are fishing for largemouth bass or pike, we will use our sonar mostly to monitor depth while casting, since we can visually find the places that we should fish. But when the vegetation is in deeper water, tapers from shallow to deeper water, and/or is submerged, we are going to use our sonar for precise positioning as well as for monitoring depth, and it becomes much more important to our fishing.

In our initial efforts, we'll slowly cruise along the edges of the vegetation, trying to define its contour, establishing the depth at which it

This angler has stopped trolling to cast around a tributary, hoping that trout or salmon might be attracted because of warmer water or bait.

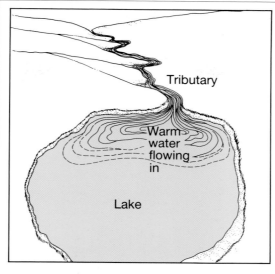

In the spring, the area near a tributary is first to be influenced by warm rains or runoff.

ceases growing (which is the weedline and which often appears in 12 to 14 feet of water in northern lakes), looking for clusters of isolated weeds or for open patches amidst thick weeds, and generally getting to know what lies below.

Because fish are often close to the bottom in the weeds or deep in the vegetation, we often don't see fish on the sonar while scrutinizing the weed edges. But it is possible to see fish amidst scattered weeds and sometimes we will do so. Primarily, however, we are trying to establish an underwater picture of what we might see with our eyes if the weeds were on the surface. This will point us to the places (edge, irregular features, pockets) to concentrate our efforts.

There are a few other things that we will try to discern as we use our electronics to learn about a body of water. The bottom composition – soft as in sandy or hard as in rocky – in specific places may be noteworthy and clue us in to whether the species of fish we seek may be in that area. The thermocline, which can be a summertime clue to locating certain fish, is

identifiable on some high-quality sonar units, provided they are used correctly (see sonar use).

Once we have become familiar with a body of water – and this needn't take a great deal of time as long as we don't try to survey the whole lake at one shot – or with select locales, we can stop to fish them. How we will do so depends, of course, on what species we seek, the time of year, and the depths or techniques involved. But, as a brief illustration, suppose our sonar shows that there are fish at 30 feet along the dropoff of a point. Now we know that it won't pay to cast a crankbait into shallow water and crank it back; a better move would probably be slow-trolling with a bottom-bouncing sinker rig or with a lure behind a downrigger or it would be jigging.

We also might employ buoy markers, incidentally, to help identify the places we've checked on sonar, and to act as reference points. These are used, for example, to mark the deep sides of shoals, the breaklines on either side of a long point, the location of a cluster of fish, pile of brush or a road bridge, the meandering of a submerged weedline, or the course of a channel.

While I have emphasized in this example the use of electronics to aid in exploring and learning waters, with or without that there is much that can be learned simply by observing the shoreline and surrounding topographical features. If the shore is sandy or rocky, it's likely that the bottom of the body of water nearby will have a similar characteristic. When the land declines steeply down to the water level, the lake there will drop off sharply into deep water, but where the shore is of a gradual slope, the lake near shore will be likewise. This is particularly true in manmade bodies of water and in times of high water.

Points are an important landform for anglers to be aware of. Many points extend underwater

well out into a lake before dropping off abruptly into deep water. This can attract both migratory and nonmigratory species of fish and can be worth exploring, although by looking strictly at the water's surface you seldom have a clue that there is something unusual below and near the point.

Perhaps a little more obvious are such features as rock walls, fence posts, and roadbeds, which are typically found in manmade or man-enlarged bodies of water, and which extend from shore into the water and provide cover for some species of fish.

Even more obvious, of course, is vegetation, stumps, timber, docks, and the like, which provide cover and attract bait and smaller prey fish. Some species of fish are especially attracted to various forms of cover and fishermen want to look for emerged and submerged cover, especially if it is near deep water, because it may hold the type of fish they seek. By judiciously casting to these objects, and in the case of vegetation, seeking the pockets and edges within, they can enhance their opportunities for catching fish.

For many anglers it is comforting to fish in streams, ponds, rivers, inlets, marshes, and small lakes because of the relative small size of those waters, not only from an accessibility or boating standpoint, but because the options are narrower. But when one leaves the launch ramp and heads out to face a lake with miles and miles of shoreline or a maze of islands, the big water can be inhibiting.

Big waters have abundant populations of major gamefish, in many cases species and sizes of fish unknown to, or infrequently found in, small waters. To enjoy these bounties you have to solve the problems posed by fishing big water, and not be overwhelmed by them.

This cover-laden bay proved to be a good spot to find a large northern pike.

There's little doubt that in big lakes and river systems, tributaries play a critical role in game-fish behavior and therefore fishing success. This is especially true in the spring, when many predator and prey species enter tributaries to spawn, or come into the near-shore areas influenced by tributaries because of the presence of food and more comfortable conditions.

Tributaries, whether they are major rivers, small streams, the outlet of upstream dams, etc., are the lifeblood of big water. In the spring they bear the rain and snow-melt runoff that helps open up the lake, then the warm water that ultimately raises the temperature of the cold main lake. A warm rain is a blessing for a big body of water that is influenced by a major tributary, because it will stimulate activity, feeding, and possibly spawning, though it sometimes takes two or three days for a heavy warm rain to have an impact on a big lake system. This phenomenon is most evident in large mid-South impoundments hosting stripers, white bass, black bass, and walleyes.

However, the area where a tributary intersects a lake is an edge that attracts bait and major game fish. Water that is a few degrees warmer than the main lake temperature flows into the lake and mixes with it, encouraging fish activity. There is often a distinct mudline created around tributary mouths, which results from stained or muddy spring runoff. On some waters, this attracts gamefish because there is usually a thermal break here as well, with the inner edge being warmer and the mudline itself being attractive to bait and prey species.

Water temperature is certainly a key to gamefish behavior. In the Great Lakes, for example, early-season fishing primarily occurs in fairly shallow water close to shore. Trout and salmon seek warm water there, as do the alewife and smelt that they feed on. Sometimes the way to get action is to find the warmest water along the shore (use a pool thermometer or surface

temperature gauge).

Elsewhere, however, the upper layer of water may be warmed up a bit on a mild sunny spring day, and act as an attracting edge. This might cause fish to be caught very shallow. This is especially so for bass, for example, which will eventually make nests in warm shallow water, or for trout or salmon, which will be attracted to pockets of warm water or vertical separations of different temperature water away from immediate tributary areas. This may be in the vicinity of a warmwater discharge, or it may simply be the phenomenon of water movement and mixing. Nonetheless, surface temperature variants can be edges.

Perhaps the most extraordinary example of this phenomenon is that of the so-called thermal bar that exists in mid to late spring on the Great Lakes, where there is a sharp surface distinction between temperatures offshore at a time when near-shore environs are relatively warm and theoretically in a temperature range that should attract trout and salmon. Nevertheless, colder offshore water on a distinct surface thermal break is the better place to be looking for fish, particularly salmon and steelhead.

Temperature remains a factor after spring for many fish species. Water stratification sends cold- and coolwater fish to deeper freshwater locales in the summer, meaning that when you fish open-water areas you have to know the preferred temperature of the species you seek, attempt to find out the depth that this temperature is found, and try to relate this to prominent areas that would attract your quarry (such as long sloping underwater points, submerged creek channels, sharp dropoffs, and so forth).

The thermocline is usually a fairly narrow band of water, but it is found where temperature drops off sharply, often averaging a drop of one-half to one degree every foot. Sometimes it is only 10 feet wide and 15 to 20 feet below the surface; usually it is a bit wider and begins deeper. To locate the thermocline you should lower a thermometer down on a rope or fishing line, checking it every 5 feet or so. Give the thermometer enough time at checked depths to register the proper reading.

Most lakes that stratify like this have a good deal of deep water. Shallow lakes don't stratify, as they become uniformly warm with too little variation from top to bottom. Fewer southern lakes stratify than northern ones, but in many generally the same patterns hold year to year.

In lakes with clearly defined thermoclines it is possible to identify the thermocline on a good sonar instrument, primarily with paper graph recorders and LCRs. Where there is a

Right: In rivers and creeks, pools hold the deeper water and are often the places to look for fish; the outside bends are also good because they have undercut banks and deep water.

This long pool on a salmon river allows several anglers an opportunity to work their way downstream through it at a time.

thermocline it's important to fish in and around it because that is where there is the best combination of food, oxygen, and temperature. But keep in mind the temperature preferences of the fish you seek, because the actual temperature of the thermocline will vary by locale and fish may be just above or below it.

A thermocline usually lasts until the fall, or when there is a trend toward cool air temperatures. When the surface water cools off enough, a body of water mixes and the thermocline dissipates. This is often referred to as the "fall turnover."

Big waters are slow to warm up in the spring, and slow to cool off in the fall. This can mean that small bodies of water may be better to fish in the earliest part of the season, till the larger

waters warm up, and that big waters may sustain good fishing for a longer period in the fall.

Other places offering warmth are bays and coves, especially if they are shallow and contain the type of cover preferred by the species you seek. Bays are especially good places to fish in the spring on natural lakes that are not fed by major tributaries, and may also be productive in sprawling manmade lakes that do have tributaries. Bays with a north and northwest exposure (or sections of a bay with such an exposure) get the most sun in the day. They also benefit from southerly winds, which stack warm surface water up on their shores. Thus, they tend to warm up fast and may attract certain species if the habitat is right.

Grass, weed beds, and other forms of vegetation may also be important fishing areas of big lakes, but this habitat may not be readily observable, or may not be found in all sectors of a lake. Bays, coves, islands, and shoals are usually good

places to start the search for vegetation, which is as likely to be submerged in moderate depth water as it is visible and close to shore.

A good tactic for anglers apprehensive about where to begin fishing is to approach big water as if it were several smaller bodies of water, and focus on one section at a time. Some anglers become familiar with big lakes by zeroing in on prominent points. Some fish use points as full-time domiciles, because they offer frequent opportunities to ambush prey. Others migrate by them often, or leave deep-water haunts to visit points temporarily to feed.

There's no doubt that knowledge of fish habits and habitat requirements through the seasons is one of your greatest allies when solving the mysteries of where to fish and what to look for in a big body of water. In freshwater, for instance, if lake trout are your quarry you should be looking for rocky shoals, reefs, and islands near deep water, as lakers are prone to come in from deeper water to such areas, feed, then leave. Open-water salmon don't orient much to underwater features, so when they aren't close to shore in spring or fall, you have to fish specific temperature zones (mostly in deep water), and aggressively search for them and for baitfish. Stripers, too, are often nomadic and follow schools of bait, but in many impoundments where they are found, the tops of submerged timber, old river channels, and other identifiable underwater terrain give them a place to find food. Largemouth bass and pike orient strongly toward various forms of cover, usually near shore, so they present different demands upon the angler. Use your knowledge of a species when deciding where to go and what to do.

Also, think in terms of edges. Fish, like most animals, are attracted to some type of edge, be it structure or temperature, and anglers may find it helpful to be thinking of what type of edge— such as a long sloping underwater point, a reef or shoal, or even a rocky versus sandy bottom— may appeal to the fish they seek because of comfort, security, or feeding reasons.

A prominent edge lair might be a shoal or reef; an underwater mound or island, sand bars, and gravel bars, are similar. These locations may be rocky or boulder-strewn, or they may be sandy with moderate weed growth, but they attract small baitfish, which in turn attracts predators. Often, there is deep water on one side.

How you fish such places is almost as important as the fact that you do fish them. When trolling the perimeter of weeds, sand bars, shoals, and so forth, for example, you might have a shallower running lure on the side of the boat nearest the edge, and your deepest running lure on the opposite side. If fishing two lures off the same gunwale, put a deep runner on the inside rod on a short to medium length line and a shallow runner on the outside position but on a longer length of line (it might get as deep as the

Judging from the bank, there is a gradual and relatively unobstructed slope to the water here, which would make it a good spot for a brush-pile, especially at the point where it broke off to deeper water.

other lure but be further back to avoid tangling and also aid fish playing and hook setting). Or, use a lure on a short line behind a downrigger and a diving lure on a longer flatline. The deep-water/shallow-water interface near islands can be similarly thought of as an edge, incidentally, as can a sharply sloping shoreline. These are places where bait migrates naturally by, and logically present feeding opportunities. Current is also a factor. A locale where strong current can bring bait washing by, or which retards the movement of weak, crippled, or wounded fish, is another. Back eddies, slicks, tidal rips, and current edges are more good spots. In rivers, where a secondary tributary meets a major flow is also a promising intersection, especially in summer when the secondary tributary may be dumping cooler and more oxygenated water into the main flow.

Knowing what types of edges appeal to which species of fish makes a difference in fishing in current. For example, the inside bend of major tributaries is often a hotspot to troll or cast for stripers in the spring. Stripers like a point where water rushes by, so they hold on the inside bend of a channel and use this spot to ambush whatever comes around. Walleyes are a fish that are particularly known for locating along an edge, particularly along a deep-water breakline. It is common, for instance, for walleyes to move shallower in the evening to the fringes of a bar or a rock or gravel point that breaks sharply to deep

water. One successful fishing tactic here is to use plugs that dive to 8 or 10 feet deep and troll from deep water to the point, then go along one side and work along the edge.

Some fish are particularly known for congregating in or along the edges of vegetation. Weeds attract small baitfish and larger fish in the food chain, and they also offer protective cover. Working submerged weed lines, where the weeds end and the bottom begins to drop off to deeper water, is not only possible, but an especially effective fishing method.

Many fish use the edges of vegetative cover or other structures to hide and to ambush prey. They lurk in or by places where food is abundant and where they can lie relatively concealed to pounce on appropriate-sized forage. Some anglers refer to such feeding stations as ambush points, and, often, the closer they are to deep water, dropoffs, shelves, ledges, creek beds, channels, and the like, the better. Whether you angle for fish that prefer the confines of cover

These seagulls are in a frenzy, as the striped bass under the water are tearing through schools of shad and slashing along the surface. Anglers can cast to such activity with great expectations for getting a strike.

or the vastness of open water, be aware of the subtle borders and margins of these habitats and seek and fish those places.

Get to know the waters you fish by studying navigation, hydrographic, or underwater contour maps, if available; by studying your sonar readings diligently; and through observant on-the-water fishing experience. It takes a combination of all three. Even the best maps often fail to pinpoint a certain underwater feature that attracts gamefish. That might be a trough, for instance, near shore and created by wave action. Or it might be a slight pinnacle or mound or hump that rises off the lake or ocean floor enough to attract baitfish and thus predators, but not enough to be highlighted between charted depth sounding information.

You can, and should, get a head start on learning about a new or unfamiliar lake by simply talking to those who know something about it. Visit local tackle shops (several if possible) and talk to the people there as you purchase bait, license, lures, etc. Talk to people at the launching ramp, marina, and so forth as well. Ask specific questions and be observant. You don't have to do this, but it sure can't hurt, and it may lead you to a spot, technique, or lure you wouldn't have considered otherwise. This is all part of the information-gathering process that leads you to finding, and catching, fish.

While we have focused a lot on non-river environments, much of this information is also applicable to flowing water, especially large rivers. The reading of water is most obviously practiced by anglers who fish in smaller rivers and creeks, where some boating is done, but most fishing is by wading or angling from the bank. Current in rivers and creeks is a premier

influence on where and how fish are situated, both for resting and feeding purposes. Fish face flowing water, so lures must generally come downcurrent toward them in a natural manner.

In flowing water it is the deeper places that often hold fish and which are sought by anglers. Slow-moving water is a sign of depth. Water is deepest where the current comes against the bank; years of this have gouged the bank and bottom, resulting in deeper water. Shallow water is found on the inside of a bend. In many places the bank is much steeper on the outside of a bend than on the inside, and this is another clue to the location of the deeper and shallower portions. This is not only important from a standpoint of angling, but also for the purposes of navigating a boat or wading safely.

When current strikes an object it may cause less turbulence in front of, or behind, that object. This may be a place where fish locate because they don't have to work as hard to resist the flow, and also because it may be a good place to find food. Boulders are the most common object in currents, but small islands or shoals also exist, and in high water, stumps and fallen trees are also objects that can attract fish.

FISH ATTRACTORS

Many fish are found close to structural objects of some kind, be they natural or manmade. The construction and planting of artificial habitat has become a very popular activity over the last decade, by groups and individuals as well as by state agencies, specifically to attract fish for anglers. These structures, called attractors, provide shade, shelter, and food. They concentrate small plant and animal life that attracts the intermediate-size fish that larger fish prey upon. Thus, they make good places to angle throughout the year, and especially in the summer months.

In freshwater, through the planting of brushpiles in some lakes, ponds, and reservoirs that are largely devoid of cover, individual fishermen have created habitat that attracts fish and offers open-water angling opportunities. Channel catfish, bluegill, largemouth bass, and crappie are particularly concentrated by the existence of brush and tire attractors.

In some freshwater locales, large attractor structures planted by fisheries agencies or sportsmens clubs are well-marked and known to the general public. But many individuals plant their own. Private and commercial dock owners, for example, often plant brushpiles to provide fish habitat at arm's length. Some guides and avid fishermen plant their own brushpiles to have "secret" fishing holes that often are very

Having just landed a walleye, which is a fish usually found in groups, an angler can expect to find more such fish in this area.

productive. These are unmarked and located at sites known only to those who do the planting.

If you have a notion to create your own hotspot, check first to make sure that it is legal to do so. Some states prohibit them, though many don't. In some bodies of water you must first check with the controlling agency (municipal water supply, Corps of Engineers, etc.); a permit may be required.

Shallow flat areas, large sandy bars, and ledges adjacent to dropoffs are popular sites for planting attractors. Small trees and an accumulation of brush and limbs are the most favored attractors for individual planting. Hardwood trees last longest, though discarded Christmas trees (which are softwoods), because of their abundance, are widely used, especially for crappie shelters. Trees can be planted singly or in clusters; they must be weighted and tied down. Cinder blocks work well for weights. Tying should be done with nylon rope or nylon coated wire.

In northern areas, brushpiles can be constructed on the ice and left to sink when the ice melts. Elsewhere, you must put the brush or trees on a boat (pontoon boats can be good for this), bring them to the site and then plant them. On lakes where the water level is lowered in the winter, you may be able to affix an attractor to a stump or rock which is exposed and which will be well-covered by spring. Don't plant in places where navigation may be impeded or where motors may strike the structure. Attractors are usually planted 3 to 20 feet deep.

On large bodies of water, you should use the sonar on your boat to precisely pinpoint the place to set the attractor, and use permanent landmarks as reference points to line you up when you want to return unerringly to the attractor without having to do a great deal of searching. As for fishing the attractor sites, use minnows, jigs, and plastic worms; light wire jigs are best because the hook can be bent to work free when it is hung.

When Fish School

Although we have eluded to it in other places, the phenomena of schooling fish is also something to be reckoned with in freshwater; however it does not occur everywhere and with all species. This is an aspect of finding fish that seems to be quite obvious. But not always. In some places people actually depend on schooling fish behavior for the bulk of their deliberate angling activities. In many locales in the fall, striped bass, hybrid stripers, and white bass chase and consume pods of baitfish (usually threadfin or gizzard shad) and roam over a wide area as they keep up with the bait and maraud them.

Often this phenomenon is best observed in early and late daylight hours. With white bass,

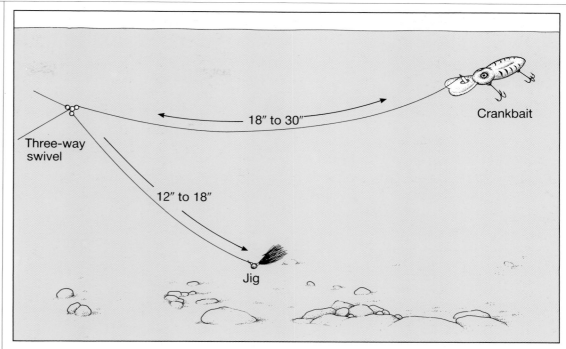

it happens on points and along rocky shores as well as in open water, but with stripers it may happen anywhere. The key is observation.

Striper anglers usually motor to places where schooling fish are frequently observed or were seen the morning or evening before. They shut the outboard motor off, and watch and wait. When a sudden splashing occurs in the distance, and/or a flock of seagulls is seen hovering expectantly and diving to the water, that's a giveaway and also the signal to shift into breakneck gear.

The tactic is to race to the site of the commotion, glide to the outer edge of it, cut the motor, and cast into the melee. Sometimes nearly any lure will do; sometimes it must be close in size and shape to the baitfish being pummeled. Two or three anglers may get into fish this way, and if the school moves on you try to move with it, being careful not to put the fish down (which often happens anyway, due to the fish you catch or the intrusion of your boat or that of others) and trying not to lose their direction.

Some species of fish are known as "schooling" fish because they tend to be found in groups. Walleye, yellow perch, and crappie are popular species that are usually clustered, and it is commonly realized that in nearly any place that you catch one of these fish, there are surely others around. Panfishermen well know that they can locate a school of fish, especially crappie, and catch them by the score with jigs or live bait as long as they are fishing at the proper depth. Crappies school heavily in deep locales in summer and fall and stay in one particular area. They require a presentation with some finesse, rather than the slam-bang action that is associated with the frenzied behavior of other species. But at least with these fish, once you've found a concentration, you don't have to work to keep locating them.

There may be reason to think that clustering occurs with more species of freshwater fish than we tend to think. And in places where there is little or no fishing pressure, this is more likely

When stripers are in a schooling situation, a troller can work the edges of the school with a double-lure rig such as this and catch one or two fish on a pass.

to be observed, the difference being that fish in highly pressured waters are wary and more likely to be spooked while those in virgin or lightly pressured waters are more tolerant.

Northern pike (and their chain pickerel cousins) are great examples of fish that can be deceptively abundant, although not actually schooled per se. In northern Canada waters I've seen schools of 2- to 5-pound lake trout cruise shallow rocky shorelines in the evening feeding on bugs, and have had great catch-and-release fishing with flies and small jigs on light tackle just by casting to wandering pods of fish. If you're patient, you can sit and wait for these trout to come by; if not, you can intercept them by boat, shutting the motor off before getting to the fish, then casting to their midst as they cruise by. These fish are in no way behaving like surface-busting striped bass would, yet they are cruising in packs and they are aggressive. In these shallow clear waters, you can actually stalk the school. Often several fish will charge your lure, and it's a kick.

Walleye, char, and lake trout may be found in heavy concentrations in those northern locales where there is a large inlet to a lake at various times of the season, and the fish seem to be secure because of the depth and heavy current present. Such a place can provide fast fishing for a while, but it may need to be rested when the action slows, perhaps for 30 to 60 minutes before returning and getting into more fish. This seems to be more likely for char and lakers than it is for walleye, but it also seems to be because the fish come in to feed and then leave, rather than taking up permanent local residence. In any event, finding these types of situations can result in the kind of fishing action that dreams are made of.

SONAR USE

Sportfishing sonar is extremely sophisticated and advanced nowadays, and is becoming more so. Not all types and brands of sonar are created equal, however, just as with fishing rods, reels, and line. Even the best sonar is not magic equipment. It is seldom enough to just turn this device on, and expect it to lead you to the fish, or to expect that simply by helping you find the fish, it will assure the catching of them. Sonar use can be equated with lure use. A lure is often only as good as the person using it. How you use it is as important as the fact that you use it.

If you do not spend time learning to use your equipment and learning to interpret the information that it provides, then you might as well not have it. When you get a new piece of sonar equipment, go out on the water with instruction book in hand, and go over it page by page, working the machine so that you are fully versed in its use, and hopefully have a good understanding of what its display is telling you. Then go out and fish.

Fishermen have to develop confidence in their units and in interpreting them before they seriously use them for fishing. After you've digested the instruction manual and know the functions of the machine, take the time to experiment with it over known terrain. Bring your boat over shallow water near shore, where you know the depth, and check to see that the sonar

This paper graph recorder is marking a thin cluster of weeds growing in relatively shallow water on a fairly soft (probably mud) bottom.

reads accurately. Find a stump several feet down and see how it registers on your machine. Go over a sandy bottom, a mud bottom, a rocky bottom, and so forth.

Below: *An angler diligently watches his bow-mounted sonar while maneuvering his boat and working his lure.*

Some fishermen have a good deal of trouble learning to use their sonar well, whether it be flashers, liquid crystal displays (LCDs), graph recorders, or video sonar. Difficulties often center around the control functions, particularly sensitivity. The sensitivity control (also called gain) is akin to volume. Many inexperienced sonar users keep this turned down too low. When the sensitivity is too low, sonar may fail to register key bait, fish, or bottom readings. When extremely low, only an indistinct bottom may be registered. On some units, a high sensitivity setting prompts a lot of false signals and distorted images.

On a flasher-style depthfinder, the sensitivity should first be turned up just enough to indicate bottom depth. Then it should be increased till a second reading, double the depth of the bottom, is recorded. Adjust the sensitivity control so the echo signal is faintly distinguishable. As you move into deeper or shallower water you'll have to respectively increase or decrease sensitivity.

With a graph recorder it is best to turn the sensitivity up high, usually at a two-thirds to three-quarter setting. Increase it till you have a strong, well-defined bottom marking. If you turn it too high you may get black marks all over the paper or interference signals; turn the sensitivity down slightly to avoid this. If you are getting no marks (good machines can detect algae, debris, tiny baitfish, and severe water temperature changes) between the bottom and the surface, or the bottom is indistinct, the sensitivity setting is too low. As you increase or decrease depth, or if water conditions change markedly, you may have to alter the sensitivity slightly. Sensitivity is adjusted automatically on LCRs, but it is sometimes necessary to switch to the manual mode and adjust the sensitivity setting to get finer details on the screen; you usually sacrifice some other functions, however, when you do this.

Flashers are harder to read than graph or liquid crystal recorders because signals disappear quickly, and at times flashers produce so many signals that you cannot digest the information quickly enough to interpret it. A flasher can reveal almost as much as a graph recorder, but you have to watch it virtually all the time and need practice to confidently determine what every signal is. Depth is gauged by watching the innermost part of the signal band. A hard bottom typically gives off a wide signal. A soft bottom produces a weaker signal and a narrow band. A dropoff will appear as a wide series of signals, which is actually the transducer receiving several signals of varying depths at one time. A rocky bottom appears choppy and broken up, while a sandy bottom is solid. Even a sandy bottom can appear choppy if the boat is moving through substantial waves, which cause the boat to bob up and down. Weeds return a thin, pale

These trollers closely watch their sonar unit, which is located on the inside port gunwale, in order to maintain a slow troll over a certain depth, and also to locate concentrations of fish.

signal; fish in weeds show up as brighter signals. A school of baitfish produces a flurry of short-duration signals.

On recorders the bottom is easily distinguished. Trees, stumps, boulders, dropoffs, and the like, are all readily observed, without having to watch the monitor continuously. A grayline feature, which issues a light band below the bottom that helps distinguish bottom terrain features is helpful in identifying targets.

While you seldom can be sure of size or species, you can tell if fish are active or not, and thus potentially susceptible to angling. With some species, suspended fish are likely to be inactive, while others, situated on top of a stump or edge of a drop, may be waiting in ambush. At times you can watch fish hit a jig worked vertically below the boat, or see fish follow a lure. It is possible to watch fish come off the bottom, follow a trolled lure, strike it, then be played out of the cone angle up to the surface.

Some fishermen turn their sonar on (especially the LCDs) and let it run like it was a one-channel one-volume-setting television. Wrong. LCD users, for example, may complain that they never see the thermocline on their units, but they usually won't unless they put it in manual mode and increase the sensitivity. Paper graph recorder users could get more out of their units,

for example, by turning the sensitivity control up and running the paper at a very high speed; many run the paper so slow that important information is so tightly compressed as to be uninterpretable. These are just simple examples of how people do not become familiar enough with their sonar to be able to diversify their use of it.

Besides becoming familiar with all aspects of your sonar, you should also be attentive to how you use it in regard to the techniques that you are employing while fishing, or to the habitats and habits of the fish you seek. Again there is an analogy to be made to television.

Everyone knows of people who sit "glued" to the TV watching mindless sitcoms; it takes virtually no brainwork on the part of the viewer, hence the couch potato syndrome. Sonar is like a mini-TV screen (one of the main reasons why some charter boat captains have fancy color videosonar is that their customers will be entertained by watching it) and you can plod along and just watch it. Or, you can use it by thinking about what it is displaying and how you can adapt your fishing tactics to what it is (and is not) telling you. The real issue is using your sonar in conjunction with your brain, your general fishing savvy, and your knowledge of angling.

Of the many good anglers that I've had an opportunity to fish with, some of the most impressive have been those who spent the first part of the day looking for fish by boating around and watching their sonar intently. This is a reversal of the shoot-first-act-later mentality; it does not apply to fishing for largemouths or pike in weeds, of course, but it can apply to many typical fishing situations. Some species of fish, such as walleyes, are schooling fish, and when seeking them you are usually looking for concentrations, especially when they are suspended over deep water. Trollers can best capitalize on this by using a wide-angle transducer to take in a broad view of the water below their boat, not looking for the occasional fish here and there, but for many fish in a single area, because the chances of getting one of those many fish to strike your offering is much greater than of getting the stragglers to do so. In a smaller body of water, however, you might never find really big concentrations of those fish, so you have to scale down your expectations.

With some species of fish, if you are not "marking" them – seeing them on the display – while fishing, then you are simply in the wrong spot. And probably wasting your time. When trolling the Great Lakes for trout and salmon in the summer, when the fish are deep and you must have your baits at the right level on a downrigger, why spend hours trolling over water that does not show any fish? But some people do that.

Sure, those fish, especially salmon, are nomadic, and wander in search of bait. Stripers are the same way. If you don't even see schools of baitfish on your sonar, you will probably surely not see their predators. In this case, if you find the bait, you'll stand a much better chance of finding the fish you want to catch. That doesn't necessarily mean that you will catch them; it just means that at least you are in the right place.

Remember the old saw about 90 percent of the fish being in 10 percent of the water? Whether it is true or not is immaterial; but you certainly can't catch the fish where they're not. Once you locate them, then you have to start figuring out what the proper presentation method will be. And you have to keep staying

with the fish, because the bait will move and the fish will move.

Ironically, sonar is ineffective as a fish-locating device in shallow water, a fact that many inexperienced anglers tend to overlook. The reason is simple. Most fish will not stay beneath a moving boat – especially one under outboard motor power and maybe even under electric motor power – in under 10 feet of water unless there is heavy cover (vegetation or stumps) below. Most good sonar users will tell you that they never see gamefish on their sonar in less than 10 feet of water, and I personally seldom see them in less than 15 feet on most open bodies of water, especially if it is clear.

The fish may be there, but they scatter and move off to the sides as the boat passes over. You have to know your quarry in terms of the season, its habits, etc., to determine if the shallow fish are around and then you have to actually work the shallows to be certain. (Keep in mind that "shallow" may mean water that is from 10 to 15 feet deep overall, or the top 10 to 15 feet of the water column where the overall depth is substantially greater.)

The exception to this, of course, is species like bass and crappie, which cluster around some forms of cover in shallow water. Usually you would not be boating in the places where those fish are caught because it is impractical or because the motor disturbance would put the fish down anyway.

Another exception is salmon that are in rivers at spawning time or near tributaries prior to spawning where they are so focused on the mission ahead, and so thick in numbers, and the boat traffic is so intense daily, that the fish may well be observed shallow on sonar irregardless. But that is not the norm.

It is important to realize that in some circumstances you will not be using your sonar to actually locate fish, but to find structure, maintain a precise depth for boat positioning, define the boundaries of some type of underwater terrain, and so forth. You might look for certain structure in order to find fish on it (such as flats that hold suspended walleyes), or you might look for variations in underwater terrain that might attract fish while you are angling them (such as humps for largemouth bass or stripers or reefs for lake trout or smallmouth bass). Fish move in and out of some areas, and while you may not spot fish on them, you have to find them and be fishing them at the right times.

Defining the edges of underwater structure is a very important practical aspect of sonar use. It is especially vital where there is submerged vegetation. The breakline where the deep edge of the weeds ends and the bottom drops off is important to locate for pike, musky, and walleye fishing. Following the contour of a long sloping point to where it drops off to deeper water is important for fishing various species.

Many people who cast all the time, such as bass, pike, and musky anglers, primarily use their sonar to watch the depth and to look for sudden changes, which indicate dropoffs or ledges and such. That's why there is usually a sonar instrument located near the boat operator – whether that is the person running an electric motor from the bow of the boat or running an electric or small outboard motor from the stern.

The newest breed of sonar is three-dimensional in display, offering a very different view of the underwater scene from what most anglers are accustomed to.

CASTING

In many types of freshwater fishing, the ability to cast, and to cast well enough to place a lure in a specific place, is a fundamental and critical aspect of angling technique. In many cases, without mastering this skill, there would be little or no success. Most anglers have basic casting procedures down adequately, though more practice wouldn't hurt, and the finer points could use sharpening.

Although accuracy is an important part of the casting game, attaining distance has lately taken a more acute position in the minds of many

The advent of ever better equipment has allowed anglers to cast more effortlessly now than ever before.

fishermen, especially with the use of spinning, spin casting, and bait casting tackle. This is partly because many tackle suppliers are touting products whose chief virtue is being beneficial for achieving distance.

This is especially prevalent in spinning reels where spool design, line wrapping systems, and spool rim materials have been modified to make it easier for line to flow off the spool. Rods, too, have gotten some attention in respect to enhancing distance, particularly guides and products that are part of a matched system. Bait casting tackle manufacturers started producing longer rods in the late 80s (most at the prompting of bass anglers), partially because longer rods help anglers cast greater distances.

In recent years the advent of thin-diameter/conventional-strength lines, which are increasing in popularity, has intertwined with the distance-casting game. The better quality conventional-strength lines with thinner-than-conventional diameters are proving to be slick, limp, and eminently castable; one of the results is an improved ability to achieve distance.

Although these are the primary influences, the trend toward truly deep-diving plugs was also a factor in the evolution of freshwater anglers toward routinely casting further. In order to take advantage of the diving capabilities of the newer plugs, fishermen want to make long casts so their lures run at the desired depths for the greatest amount of time possible in a cast-and-retrieve situation. Thin-yet-strong lines let lures dive deep; combined with long rods and improvements in reels, they help the caster toss a lure almost as far as a good quarterback can throw a football. And that's a long way.

So casting a great distance is now easier to accomplish than ever. But is it necessary? There is no correct answer because of all the variables that influence fishing success and all the different situations/waters/lures/etc. that one encounters. Many fishermen tend to think only in terms of the main advantage to casting greater distances: they can get their lures to fish they wouldn't have reached, or they can cover more ground than otherwise possible and thus be able to attract more fish.

Long-distance casts are attractive to many anglers, but this produces added difficulty in setting the hook; many fish that strike at long distances, such as this fish, are not landed.

That is, of course, possible, though perhaps not necessary. With some species of freshwater fish, and in some types of water, there is seldom a need to cast great distances. Most walleye, largemouth bass, pike, and panfish anglers, for example, do not need to make long casts because of the nature of the fish, the cover they inhabit, and the fishing techniques used.

The clarity of the water is one criteria for distance. Generally, fish in clear water are spookier than those in turbid water. The harder it is to see your lure as you drop it in the water, the murkier the water is; this is an indication that you can probably get fairly close to your quarry.

A prime benefit of getting close is simply the ease with which you can achieve accuracy. This is especially true for bait casters, who use educated thumb spool contact to control the placement of their lure. It is especially true when fishing in heavy cover, such as timber, or in places where it is difficult to cast, such as a small brushy creek. The effect of wind is minimized at shorter distances and (with bait casting) the chance of getting a backlash is lessened.

Backlashes occur in bait casting reels when the spool turns faster than the line departs the spool; they happen to even highly experienced casters when they give extra punch to their forward casting stroke in order to get a lure farther out. This even occurs when using the best mag-

netic spool braking reels, which are supposed to prevent such misfortune.

With practice and with continued long-distance casting in actual fishing conditions, you can lessen the chance of backlash and also increase accuracy. If you start long-distance casting efforts by not shooting for the moon at the start, but building up to greater distances gradually (which is hard to do when a fish breaks water just a bit beyond your normal range), then you will overcome this problem.

One of the drawbacks to long-distance casting is the loss of fish; more fish that strike and get hooked at long distances are lost before being landed than fish that strike and are hooked at shorter ranges. What percentage more? I don't know. My gut feeling is quite a bit more. There is a good reason for this occurrence, though, one that many anglers don't realize but can do something about.

The key here is hook setting. Fishermen are more effective at setting the hook at short and mid-range distances than they are at long distances. Most people simply do not set the hook well when a fish takes their lure a long distance away. Sometimes this is because they don't detect strikes as well, which may be a function of their attentiveness, their savvy, or the tackle they are using. After all, not all rods are the same. Certain types of lures are still hard to fish when cast long distances. "Feel" baits, those that you have to know what they are doing as you fish them and which are generally made of soft plastic, such as light jigs and plastic worms, are examples, and it is quite hard, even with the

best tackle, to be fully tuned into a long-distance strike when using them.

Softness has something to do with that, but not everything. One of the fishing films done by noted cinematographer Glen Lau showed a largemouth bass swimming up behind a quickly moving diving plug, engulfing it, and then expelling it all while the lure kept swimming forward. The angler working that lure, which had two sets of treble hooks, reported that he never felt the strike. Perhaps the rod wasn't sensitive enough. Perhaps his line was too elastic. Elasticity in line is commonly referred to as stretch, and it is this element that works against fishermen as much as any other where long-distance strike detection and hook setting is concerned. You can generate more force and be more efficient at setting the hook at short distances, and are less efficient at long distances.

Rather than casting long distances as a matter of habit, you might try making a more stealthy approach to fish. Wading river fishermen know that it is possible to get fairly close to rising trout or to salmon in their lie by going slowly and as unobtrusively as possible, by not making excessive above-water motions and keeping movement in the fish's direct viewing window down to the barest minimum, and by being patient and not casting until they are in the most advantageous position for the best presentation.

Pond and lake fishermen, be they boaters or bank casters, should do likewise. Most lake and pond fishermen are impatient; they want to cover lots of water and in doing so they often don't make the best possible presentation.

THE CASTS

The types of casts made with spinning, spin casting, and bait casting tackle are very similar, but fly casting is not because a different principle is at work. In the former, a weighted object propels a light line (usually nylon monofilament). In fly casting, a weighted line propels a virtually weightless object (the fly).

CASTING STYLES

With spinning, spincasting, and baitcasting tackle, the basic casts are the overhead, sidearm, and underhand. The overhead cast is employed by far the most, while the other casts are infrequently employed. In some situations, however, either because of the nature of the cover in which some species are found or because of the necessity of accurate lure placement, there is a regular need to utilize all three of these casts and perhaps some others.

In the overhead cast, the wrist and forearm do all the work, using the top section of the rod for thrust. The cast begins with the rod low and pointed at the target. Bring the rod up crisply to a point slightly beyond vertical position, where flex in the rod tip will carry it back; then, without hesitating, start the forward motion sharply, releasing the lure halfway between the rod's vertical and horizontal positions. The entire casting action should be a smooth, flowing motion; you are doing more than just hauling back and heaving.

The sidearm cast is essentially similar in motion to the overhead, except for horizontal, rather than vertical, movement. The sidearm cast can be dangerous if performed next to another angler in a small boat, so you must be mindful of the position of your companions at all times. To cast underhand, hold the rod waist-high, angled halfway between vertical and horizontal positions. The rod must be flexed up, then down, then up again to gain momentum for the lure through the flex of the rod. Many rods, incidentally, are too stiff to permit this kind of casting. There are a few other casts used in special situations. One, employed in tight quarters or for short ranges, is a flip cast, which is something of a cross between the sidearm and underhand cast (different from flipping). It starts with the rod horizontal to your side, but you only bring it backward a short distance and then make a loop with the tip so that the tip springs around in a 270-degree arc and flips the lure straight out and low. This cast is used for short-distance (under 20 feet) work in areas where you can't bring your rod up or back for a conventional cast. It is also almost impossible to accomplish while sitting down in a boat.

Another is the bow-and-arrow cast, which is a short-distance cast used with a limber rod in tight quarters in which you hold a lure by its rear hook in one hand and simultaneously release the hook and line from a freespooled reel. This cast is rarely used currently in actual angling situations.

A popular casting technique, however, is flipping, which is done primarily with bait casting tackle, but also with spinning. This is essentially a controlled short-distance technique used by standing anglers in close quarters for presenting

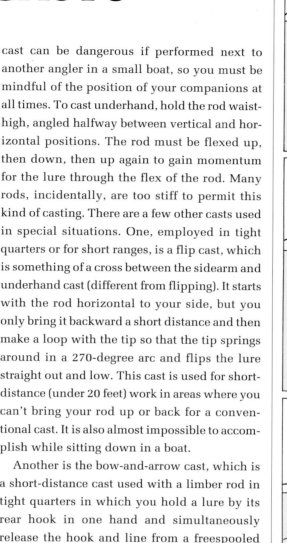
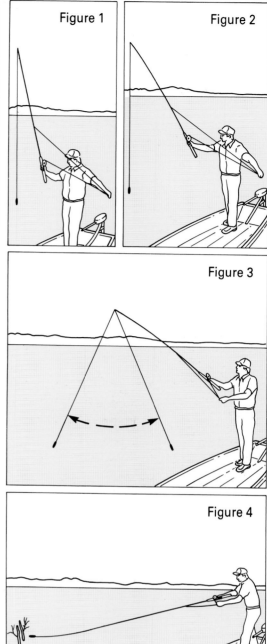

Flipping is a specialized method of making a close-quarters, silent presentation of a jig or plastic worm.

a moderately heavy jig or plastic worm in a quiet, accurate manner to cover that cannot be properly worked by a lure cast from a long distance away. A long stiff rod and fairly heavy line are customarily used in heavy cover, although the principle can be adapted to other situations. Steelhead anglers, for example, use long, light rods and light line to flip small lures or bait into midriver pools for drift fishing.

To flip, let out about 7 to 9 feet of line from rod tip to lure. Strip line off the reel until your free hand and rod hand are fully extended away from each other; this will give you 5 to 7 feet of line in your free hand. Raise the rod tip and swing the lure back toward you under the rod. The motion utilizes wrist action, not elbow or

Left: *A salmon angler lays out a long cast to work the tail of a run. Notice how the line is unfurling to present the fly softly.*

shoulder movement. The bait swings back toward you and when it reaches the top of its pendulum-like swing, flick your rod-holding wrist to direct the lure toward its target. Lower the rod tip, and let line flow through your free hand. Extend your rod arm if necessary to reach the target, and keep the line in your hand until the lure enters the water. When you retrieve the lure to move it to another spot, lower the rod tip and point it toward the lure, grab the line between reel and first guide with your free hand and strip it back while lifting up on your rod (similar to the double hauling technique used by fly casters). Swing the lure out and back and send it forward again to the next object.

Fly casting has the aura of being difficult but it needn't be. It does require an adroit combination of coordinated wrist and forearm movement, but brute strength isn't necessary, nor is a lot of wrist action or quick, whippy rod movements. There are two primary casts: the overhead and the roll, with the former predominant.

The overhead cast has both forward and backward movements and you can't present the fly ahead of you properly without having made an adequate back cast. Beginning with the fly line and leader extended straight out in front of you and the rod in an approximate 2 o'clock position, raise the rod decisively to the 12 o'clock position and flick your wrist sharply, allowing the rod to go no further than an 11 o'clock position. This action brings the fly line and leader off the water and sends it in the air behind you. Pause for an instant to let the line straighten out, and just as it does, bring the rod forward to the

2 o'clock position again. A tight loop should unfurl and, as the line straightens and the fly reaches its destination, follow-through by lowering the rod tip. The forward casting movement is akin to that of hammering a nail into the wall, and it is a matter of timing to know when the rod is loaded properly to provide the optimum forward impetus.

This overhead cast is used for short and long distances, although as distance to be cast increases, there is a tendency for many anglers to try to push at the end of the forward cast, or wait too long for line to unfurl on the back cast. Shooting tapers help achieve distance, as does employing coils of line in one hand for shooting or using the double-haul technique.

In the double haul, the angler uses his non-rod hand to give some speed to the pickup and forward momentum of the fly line. It is a technique that takes practice to master, as the motions have to be blended properly together. Assuming that you cast with the right hand and hold fly line in your left, you would accomplish this as follows: hold the line firmly in your left hand ahead of the reel, and a moment before bringing the rod up (in the overhead casting maneuver) to lift line off the water, pull sharply on the line, bringing it down to your hip in your left hand as the line flows backward; as the line straightens out, bring the left hand up to the reel and, at the same time as your right hand begins to power the rod forward, pull sharply on the line with your left hand; as the rod comes forward, release the line to shoot extra line forward through the guides.

Exhibiting good technique, a fly fisherman halts his backcast momentarily before bringing the rod forward.

The roll cast is a very practical cast for both making fly presentations at a distance of up to 40 to 50 feet and also as a means of laying out line to pick it up for a standard overhead or double-haul cast. In a roll cast there is no back casting motion per se, and the line is not lifted off the water as in an overhead cast. To roll cast, lift the rod tip up steadily but not quickly until it is just past a vertical position and at a point where there is a curved bow of line extending from the rod tip behind you, and then bring the rod sharply forward and downward. The last motion brings the line rolling forward with leader and fly following.

Although not actually a casting function, the technique of mending fly line is used in flowing water to give the fly a natural drift, and is something not done with other lines. Mending is a method of lifting and flipping the belly of fly line upstream so that the fly does not drag in the current.

Knowing the mechanics is the most basic part of casting, but one has to also develop the skill of being accurate (even in adverse conditions, such as wind). Getting the right length of line out and placing it properly is the key with all tackle. With spinning tackle you should use your index finger to control the cast and water entry. With bait casting gear you do the same via delicate thumb control on the reel spool. Raising your rod tip at the last moment helps

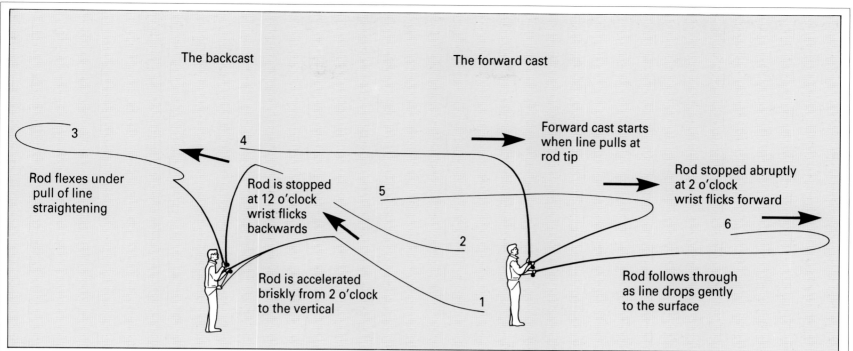

The backcast

3

Rod flexes under pull of line straightening

4

Rod is stopped at 12 o'clock wrist flicks backwards

5

Rod is accelerated briskly from 2 o'clock to the vertical

The forward cast

Forward cast starts when line pulls at rod tip

Rod stopped abruptly at 2 o'clock wrist flicks forward

6

2

1

Rod follows through as line drops gently to the surface

Above: *Basic fly casting incorporates timing between backward and forward motions.*

soften lure impact, but is not reliable as a means of controlling accuracy. In many situations, especially in freshwater, the first cast to a prospective fish lair is often the most important one, so it pays to make each cast count.

People who have difficulty being accurate or achieving proper distance when using spinning or bait casting gear might try using two hands.

Below: *To achieve proper wrist alignment when using bait casting tackle (1), depress freespool button, and with casting thumb on the spool, rotate the reel so the handle faces up. Begin with the rod low and pointed toward the target (2). Bring the rod up crisply to a point slightly beyond the vertical (3), and without hesitating start the forward motion sharply, releasing the lure roughly halfway down.*

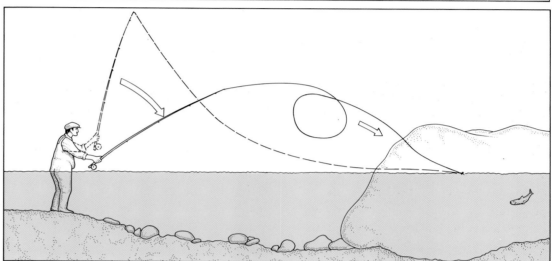

This is especially true for youngsters and women, and it is not a sign of wimpiness on the part of fishermen. I do a lot of two-handed casting, partly as a carryover from learning days and partly for ease of use. Two hands are especially beneficial when making an overhead cast.

The purpose of the roll cast is to get the main belly of the line off the water to re-present the fly, as well as to make short casts in tight areas.

You have more strength and control, and both your distance and accuracy are improved.

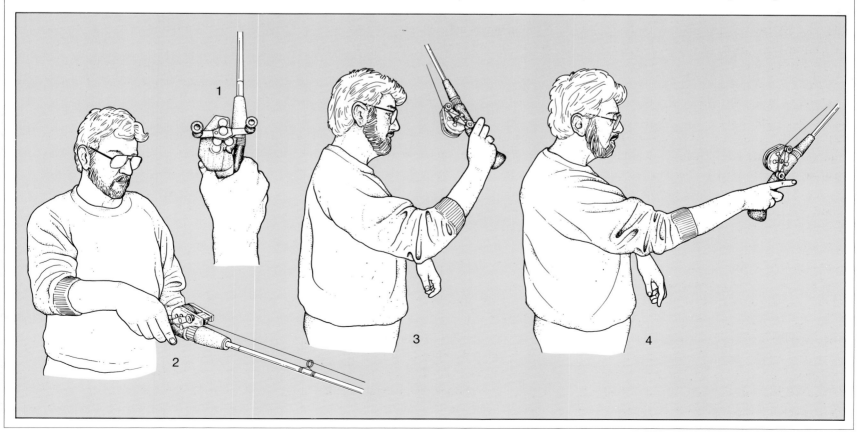

1

2

3

4

Preceding pages: *With a little line between lure and rod tip, an angler prepares to make a cast with his spinning rod.*

Here's how to cast with both hands, assuming that you are naturally right-handed:

1. Dangle the lure a few inches from the rod tip and hold the rod in front of you and level with the ground.

2. Place your right hand on the rod handle and around the reel seat, grasping the line with your right forefinger.

3. Put your left hand on the rod handle. Keep hands together, face the target, and point the rod directly at it.

4. Start to cast by raising the rod up sharply with your wrists and forearms rather than by moving your whole arms. Bring your hands up quickly to the right side of your face and about level with your chin.

5. Without hesitating, make your forward motion toward the target, releasing the line with your finger as the rod comes forward. Use the lower hand to put some snap into the forward

Accurate casting is important in many freshwater fishing situations; this angler wants his first cast to this stump to land close but a little beyond one side of it.

casting motion, turning your wrist over sharply to give the cast momentum.

Keep the rod on a straight path overhead. Do not let it drift to the side. Continue to face the target and do not twist your body. You must practice. This is how to perfect your timing. If you don't make the rod movement sharp you will be lobbing instead of casting, making it more difficult to achieve distance or accuracy.

A final point about all casting is a practical and safety concern: Always glance behind you before casting so you will not strike anyone or anything when making your cast.

SPECIAL NOTE ABOUT BAIT CASTING

The hallmark of bait casting tackle was, and still is, accurate lure placement and control over strong-fighting fish. The black mark was casting control, as this gear was notorious for being difficult to learn to cast without incurring a so-called "backlash" or spool overrun, in which a bird's nest of line needed to be painstakingly untangled from the spool. Just as the era of hand cranking an automobile has passed, the day of backlashes is largely over.

But can you just pick up a bait casting reel and start fishing, like you can get in a car and

start driving? Not if you haven't done it before. Just as those who have only driven a car with automatic transmission need to learn and make certain adjustments when getting into a car with a stick shift, anglers who have previously only used fly or spinning gear need to adapt to bait casting tackle. Fortunately, that isn't hard now.

Since pure casting technique does not differ that much between bait casting and spinning or spin casting gear, and since achieving accuracy is mostly a function of practice and on-the-water experience, the real key to bait casting proficiency is in setting up the spool braking system.

Until fairly recently, bait casting reels featured only a centrifugal spool brake. The way to use that was, and still is, as follows:

Assemble rod and reel; spool reel with line; tie lure to line and reel lure to within a few inches of the rod tip. Locate the centrifugal brake knob (round, about one-half-inch in diameter, located below handle) and turn it tightly clockwise. Depress freespool button or bar; the lure should not descend. Turn brake knob slowly counterclockwise until the lure starts to fall. Reel the lure up and fine-tune the knob adjustment so that when you take your thumb off the spool, the lure falls downward slowly without having to jiggle the rod. Note that this adjustment needs to be made again whenever the

weight of lure used changes significantly.

You are now ready to cast, but must learn to exercise judicious thumb pressure on the spool while the lure is in the air in order to control the spool and prevent it from turning faster than the lure is traveling (which produces a backlash). Learning to do this has caused headaches for many anglers.

Magnetic spool braking is an innovation of the past decade. Virtually all new bait casting reels for freshwater use have this feature, and although different systems are used, the end result is that magnets on the non-handle sideplate of the reel exert pressure on the spool in proportion to the speed that the spool revolves, with more pressure being applied automatically the greater the speed, and less pressure as speed tapers (such as at the end of a cast).

Magnetic spool controls feature a range of tension settings, but before a setting is selected for casting, you must make the centrifugal spool brake adjustment outlined earlier. With that done, turn the magnetic control to a desired setting and cast.

The higher the magnetic setting selected, the greater the spool-braking force exerted. For beginning bait casters, a high, or maximum, setting is desirable to prevent backlashes while getting casting mechanics in order. As more proficiency is achieved, the setting can be relaxed and greater casting distance will be possible. Experienced casters use a low setting (20 to 30 percent), but change this when conditions dictate. Casting into the wind, for example, often requires increasing magnetic pressure.

In theory the magnetic spool braking feature is supposed to prevent backlashes and it actually does so at the highest settings, where it is often possible to cast without exerting any thumb pressure on the spool. However, modest thumb pressure is still desirable when magnetic force is decreased, and it takes a little practice to develop that light touch and a feel for when it is needed and when it is not.

It's surprising how many anglers attempt to use bait casting gear without realizing that you don't cast it with the reel facing you as it rests atop the rod handle. Instead, do this: depress the freespool button or bar and, with casting thumb on the spool, turn the reel sideways so the handle is facing upward. Your wrist will be in the same position as if you were writing with a pen or tossing a dart. It stays this way throughout the cast. Release thumb pressure on the spool as the rod arcs forward and you're in business.

Making a well executed cast and getting the lure precisely on target is often not the end of the casting action. When angling in some places and using lures that sink, for example, you have to be able to start fishing them the instant they hit the water, or they'll get tangled or snagged on objects in the water. A spinnerbait worked very

Adjusting the magnetic cast control of a bait casting reel increases or decreases spool tension to affect casting distance and backlashing potential.

shallow is an example of a lure that should "hit the ground running."

Left-handed bait casters who retrieve with their right hand, and right-handed bait casters who retrieve with their left hand will have little trouble if they thumb the spool properly and get cranking the instant the lure touches down, but such fishermen are in the minority and most bait casters are right-handed casters who retrieve with their right hand as well, meaning that they have to switch the rod and reel from right to left hand at some point.

Most good casters become adept at making this transfer while the lure is in flight, taking their right thumb off the spool just as the lure touches the water and then quickly grabbing the reel handle and cranking before the lure has a chance to get deep. This takes fine timing and is an oft-overlooked aspect of bait casting technique. You must master this (or learn to cast with your other hand) in order to effect the best possible retrieve under certain circumstances.

If you sort of lob or toss a lure with bait casting gear you're not really casting and you are inviting backlash trouble (although this can be desirable when casting some forms of bait so it doesn't tear off the hook). You can make this soft type of presentation more readily with a spinning reel, but in bait casting with lures, you really want to make the rod do what it was designed to do, and employ its arc and power in both backward and forward cast motions. You can only do that if you're confident about your ability to control backlashes.

Wind is the bane of many bait casting tackle users, more so than spinning gear because of a heightened chance of backlash when casting into the wind. When casting with the wind everyone looks like a champ. When you have to cast into the wind with bait casting tackle you should try low trajectories (use a low sidearm cast, if possible, and/or release the lure a little later than you ordinarily do), increase magnetic spool control and/or thumb pressure, and use more aerodynamic lures. You will probably have to use more force to achieve normal distance in a strong wind, so greater thumb pressure, in addition to increased magnetic force, will likely be necessary.

RETRIEVING

When casting to any kind of fish, what you do after you get the lure in the water is critical. Proper retrieval and presentation often separates the casters from the catchers. The keys to successful retrieval of most lures are depth control, action, and speed, all of which vary in importance depending on the situation and the lure. Achieving the proper depth is perhaps the most important factor, since you can't hope to catch fish without getting your offering to the fish's level. In the case of many lures, the ability to achieve a certain depth is a function of the lure design and the way in which it is used.

Speed is often the most ignored factor in retrieval. In cold water it's best to fish slowly; speed up the retrieve in warmer water. Many species are less energetic in very cold water,

How a fisherman works the different types of lures that he uses will be a large factor in his ability to catch fish.

Some lures are primarily fished along a lake or river bottom, and do their best when worked over and around various objects.

especially those that relate to generally shallow environments. Fish bottom-crawling lures slowly at all times.

Retrieval speed is influenced by the diameter of line being used, type of lure, current, and retrieve ratio of your reel. To some extent, speed is a factor in the retrieval of all lures. A moderate speed for plugs generally catches the least fish, with more succumbing to high- or low-speed retrieves. Some lures can be retrieved too fast, at which point they lose their tight action and run off to the side. Achieving the proper action, of course, is a necessity in order for the lure to have its maximum attractiveness.

While every lure is designed to do a certain function, that function must be coordinated with the current fishing conditions, and

achieved through proper lure retrieval. Let's review retrieval techniques according to the major categories of lures.

SPINNERS. In moving water you generally don't fish a spinner downstream, but cast it upstream at a quartering angle (ten o'clock viewed from right, two o'clock viewed from left). The lure is tumbled by the swift water and also reeled forward at the same time. Fish spinners as slowly as you can under the circumstances; you should be able to feel the blade revolve with a sensitive rod. The depth of retrieve can be altered by raising or lowering the rod, or chan ging the speed of retrieval. Though spinners receive criticism for frequent hangups, this is often a matter of misuse. In shallow streams and when using heavy spinners it is important to get the lure working the moment it hits the water. Hesitation can mean hung spinners, particularly casting across-stream in a fast flow.

In lakes, spinners can be cast parallel to the bank and allowed to sink to the bottom, then retrieved just slowly enough to rotate the blade and keep the lure swimming over the bottom.

SPINNERBAITS. A spinnerbait is a good lure for fishing in and around cover, and its appearance evidently triggers a reflexive strike. Lily pads, grass, stumps, brush, treetops, boat docks, rock piles, logs, and similar fish-holding places can all be effectively worked with a spinnerbait, and shallow water is generally where they are most productive.

The most common technique of fishing a

Right: *Retrieval techniques vary with types of lures, some needing faster retrieve, some slower. Rod angle is varied, as well, with a high rod angle useful when using plastic worms, jigs, and some surface lures.*

spinnerbait is to retrieve it close enough to the surface so that you can see the lure through the water on the retrieve. The depth of water fished below the surface ranges from a few inches to several feet, depending on the clarity of the water and the structure present. When working the shallows, begin retrieving a spinnerbait the moment it hits the water for maximum effect.

Occasionally, spinnerbaits are retrieved out of sight along the bottom, or fished very deep by fluttering them down sharply sloping shorelines, dropoffs, rocky ledges, and the like, using a short-armed spinnerbait, and working it in a series of short hops or in a jigging-like motion.

For fishing weed beds and weedlines it is

The key to "walking the dog" is an adroit combination of rod tip twitching and reel handle turning that makes a stick bait turn repeatedly from one side to the other.

sometimes effective to crawl a spinnerbait slowly over the tops of the grass, when the grass is submerged a few feet. For grass beds with definable weedlines, however, cast parallel to the edge or bring the lure over the top and let it flutter down the edge. For lily pads it is best to work the channel-like openings, but don't be afraid to throw into thick clusters, work the bait in pockets, ease it over the pads, and drop it in another pocket.

SPOONS. Retrieving a casting spoon is a pretty straightforward endeavor since the action is derived from their size and contoured shape. Although spoons are primarily retrieved shallow, they can be fished at varied levels by letting them sink via the countdown method (count at a cadence of one second per foot) and then reeled steadily with an occasional twitch to alter the action momentarily. The heavier the spoon the deeper it sinks during retrieval. In

Fishing in weedy shallow water, these anglers have several lure choices available to them, and will likely retrieve their lures on or close to the surface.

retrieving spoons the most important factor is to establish the optimum swimming speed; in other words, reel the lure at the speed that produces the best wobbling action. The action of some spoons may be enhanced by adding a split ring to the line-tie hole. A weedless type of spoon is mainly fished in fairly heavy cover, like vegetation, and is retrieved slowly, with occasionally an added pumping or twitching motion.

DIVING PLUGS. You must know how deep any diving plug runs to be effective with it. Diving abilities depend on the lure, the diameter of line used with it, and the speed of retrieve. It is not necessary to crank the handles as fast as possible to achieve maximum depth with diving

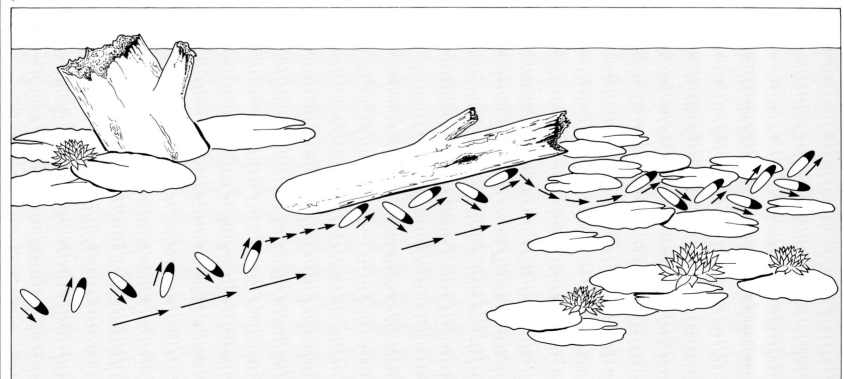

plugs. In fact, some lures lose depth when worked too fast. A moderate pace of retrieve will keep the lure as deep as it will go depending on your line. The heavier the line you use, the greater its diameter, which means it offers more resistance to the water and inhibits lure diving. The lighter your line, the deeper a diving plug will go. If you are flinging long casts, this will make a difference. Current, if it is present, will affect diving ability. Lures retrieved with the current or sideways to it don't run as deep as those worked into it.

Bottom scratching is usually critical in most fishing situations with diving plugs. Keep a plug rooting along the bottom, over objects, and along impediments. This is no problem with the right floating/diving crankbait. For the sinking version, let it settle to the bottom or count it down to a particular level and make your retrieve at a rate slow enough to keep the plug on or as close to the bottom as possible.

Floating/diving plugs are exceedingly buoyant, a feature that adds a different dimension to their fishability. If you stop your retrieve, these plugs will bob toward the surface like a cork. You can take advantage of this feature in your fishing techniques. A pull-pause action is easily accomplished by retrieving in the standard fashion and stopping momentarily, then repeating the procedure.

The twitch of a rod tip, stripping of line, or gathering of line in the non-casting hand are common retrieval actions for fly anglers.

There are many places that are well worked with diving plugs, including open-water locales and structural objects. With objects, fish to, from, over, and around them, and don't be concerned about bumping the lures against them.

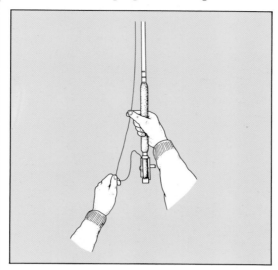

Fly fishermen sometimes use a stripping retrieve, especially when working streamers and poppers; to do this, wiggle the rod tip from side to side or up and down, and strip in short lengths of fly line.

Where possible, cast beyond targets so that when you retrieve, the lure will be able to get down to its running depth before it reaches the target. As with many lures, a key pointer for successful diving plug usage is proper positioning of the angler, especially when fishing from a boat.

SURFACE LURES. Fishing with surface lures is very exciting for many anglers because you

get to see the strike. You also get to see where your lure is and what it is doing at all times. There are many types of surface lures, and retrieval is quite different among the types.

Poppers generally are worked slowly. The actual popping or forward chugging motion is made by jerking your rod up, or back, not by reeling line in, to achieve the proper movement. Keep the rod low and pointed toward the lure; this helps reduce slack to work the lure well and puts one in the best possible position to react to a strike. When you pop this plug you can do so with varying degrees of emphasis. Seldom is it worthwhile to jerk the rod hard so as to create the loudest possible commotion. If it appears that bass are feeding fairly actively, you can shorten the time between pops, but generally it is best to maintain long pauses, of several seconds' duration, between them. Obviously, poppers are time-consuming lures to fish, and do not cover a lot of area very well.

Wobbling surface plugs are most commonly retrieved in a straight, continuous motion. It is a worthwhile technique, however, to make the lure stop and go at times, or to give it a pull-pause motion, particularly as it swims next to an object. Try to resist the urge to set the hook the instant a fish slashes at this lure and momentarily wait to feel the fish take your plug before setting the hook sharply. If the fish misses altogether, try stopping the lure in its tracks and twitching it a little, then moving the lure a bit and stopping it.

The basic technique for retrieving propellored

plugs is a jiggling, jerking, pausing motion that is erratic and representative of a struggling or crippled baitfish. Point the rod down, utilize the rod tip to effectively impart action, and make your wrists do the work. Retrieve either quickly or slowly, the latter perhaps when prospecting for unseen fish and the former when casting to a school of fish.

A buzz bait, which is also a propellered creation, is at its very best in areas with thick cover. Worked on a steady, moderate retrieve, it is employed primarily for largemouth bass in emergent vegetation that is not too thick to prevent free lure passage, submerged vegetation that comes fairly close to the surface, around brush, in timber, and around fallen wood. The closer you can work a buzz bait to such cover, the better.

A stick bait can't be tossed out with abandon and then cranked back in. The secret to its effectiveness lies in a masterful retrieval technique. All of the action must be supplied by the angler, making the stick bait foremost among lures for which retrieval skill is of ultimate importance.

The principal stick bait retrieve, called "walking the dog", causes the lure to step from side to side. To accomplish it, begin with the rod tip at a low angle, preferably pointing toward the water. This permits a desirable angle of pull and allows the head of the lure to lurch in and out of the water most effectively. The all-important lure action is achieved through an adroit combination of rod-tip twitching and reel-handle turning. Make a continuous series of short jerks while simultaneously advancing your reel handle perhaps half a turn with each rod-tip twitch to take up slack. By slowing the pace, you widen the lure's path of travel; by speeding it up you narrow it. A skilled stick bait angler can just about keep the lure in the same place, making it nod from side to side while barely moving forward.

An advanced technique of retrieving stick baits is one known as "half-stepping." This is the peak of stick bait retrieval skill and is a technique that can drive a fish wild. In the half-step, a stick bait moves repeatedly to one side instead of from side to side. To half-step a stick bait, first jerk the rod tip to bring the lure in the desired direction. Then barely nudge the rod tip, a maneuver that doesn't advance the bait, but causes it to turn its head just slightly outward. Now jerk the rod tip as before and the lure will dart back in the same direction it last headed. Nudge the rod once again, then jerk it. Again the plug will head inward.

Floating/diving lures are most effectively worked in a deliberately erratic fashion to imitate a crippled baitfish, but this is one particular type of lure where the action you put into fishing it is directly proportional to the results. The objective is to make a floater/diver gyrate as enticingly as possible in a stationary position.

Keep the rod tip pointed low toward the water and use your wrist to move the rod. Jiggle the rod tip in a controlled, not frantic, fashion. Then jerk the lure back toward you a few inches. Then gyrate it some more, all the time reeling in an appropriate amount of line to minimize slack. This is not very difficult to accomplish if you have a rod with a fairly soft tip.

Another way to use this lure type is on a straight retrieve, allowing it to run a foot or two beneath the surface. This is more like using it in the style of a diving plug. Still another retrieval method is making it run just below the surface in a series of short jerk-pause movements, running it forward half a foot with each motion. This retrieve is more in the style of darters, those plugs that float but have no significant surface action, and are used solely just below the surface.

FLIES. The art of retrieving flies is a fairly precise one in many circumstances but is nearly always dependent upon a proper cast and often

Flow

Nymph fishermen will flip their offering upstream then tight-line it downstream, systematically covering the breadth of water.

also upon a delicate presentation. The latter is especially important in small stream or river pool fishing for wary trout, when a dry fly must alight gently and the line or leader should not slap the water to alarm the fish. In flowing water especially, where the drift of the fly is a major component of the presentation, the fly often must be placed in a proper place upstream in order to drift into the right location. In order to effect a proper retrieve, the fly must be placed properly at the outset.

In a stillwater environment, a dry fly is usually cast to a rising fish or to a likely fish lair, where it may be allowed to rest momentarily or be slowly skimmed across the surface by stripping line in short segments. In moving water, a dry fly is cast directly upstream or up and across stream and allowed to float with the current while slack line is gradually picked up during the float. Occasionally extra line will be flipped

out to minimize drag (called mending). Drag occurs when the fly floats either faster or slower than the current; the ideal is to effect a drag-free float for the most natural-looking presentation.

Wet flies and nymphs, which are primarily used in current, are fished below the surface and often near or close to the bottom. They are primarily cast up and across current, sometimes more up than across in order to get the fly deep. Nymphs are fished on a tight line, often using a clearly visible strike indicator on the leader butt or end of fly line to detect strikes. They are usually fished on a free drift without drag but sometimes are jerked just a bit. Fish sometimes strike at the end of a drift as the fly line straightens and the angler is about to pull the fly out of the water to cast upstream again.

Streamer flies are meant to represent small fish, so they are retrieved in short darting or jerking movements, usually caused by stripping fly line in with your free hand. In current they are cast up and across stream, directly across stream, and downstream, and stripped while they drift. Elsewhere they are allowed to sink before the stripping retrieval begins, and this retrieval here may constitute foot-long strips, fine twitching movements, or short pulls.

Other so-called flies, fished on the surface, include an assortment of swimming or popping bugs. Poppers are fished with a pull-pause line-stripping motion or the twitch of a fly rod tip. More vigorous strips produce loud noises while slight twitches produce light popping sounds. Sometimes it is worthwhile to fish these flies in quick darting motions. The same is true of swimming bugs.

PLASTIC WORMS. Many people have trouble getting the retrieval down right when fishing plastic worms. To retrieve a plastic worm you should begin with your rod butt and arms close to your body, and with the rod held perpendicular to you and parallel to the water. Raise the rod from this position (we'll call it 9 o'clock) upward, extending it between a 45-degree and 60-degree angle, which would mean moving it from 9 o'clock to 10:30 or 11. As you raise the rod, the worm is lifted up off the bottom and swims forward, falling to a new position. Make this motion slowly, so the worm does not hop too far off the bottom and swims slowly. When your rod reaches that upward position, drop it back to its original position while at the same time retrieving slack line. Keep your motions slow. When you encounter some resistance, as would happen when crawling it over a log or through a bush, first gently try to work the worm along, and if this fails, try to hop the worm along with short flickers of the rod tip. The worm should usually be on the bottom, or right near it, although occasionally you may find it beneficial not to hug the bottom exactly, but to swim the worm slowly just off the bottom or above submerged cover.

JIGGING

A jig is one lure that many freshwater anglers have trouble getting acclimated to and therefore confident in using it. A jig requires patience to fish well, since it is often retrieved very slowly and methodically. It requires paying attention to technique and some finesse in use. One thing that a jig is not is a throw-it-out-and-reel-it-back-in kind of lure, one that can catch fish in spite of the abilities of the person using it. A fisherman has to put some work into making a jig catch fish, and into being able to detect strikes.

Jigs are primarily fished on or close to the bottom, as these anglers found when trying to catch this walleye; using the right weight jig for the conditions is important.

There is a bit of a knack to jigging, too. Good jig users have a certain feel for what is happening to their lure, and are razor sharp at detecting and responding to strikes. To the inexperienced, fishing with such an individual while attempting to duplicate his success can be exasperating.

The key to jigging success is establishing contact with your lure, getting and keeping it where the fish are, and using the right rod to feel a strike. The greatest concern is often how deep you need to fish a particular jig, and how effective you are at doing that. Jigs excel at being on or close to the bottom, which is where the majority of jig-caught freshwater fish are found. They also are productive for covering the area in between in vertical presentations.

It's usually important to maintain contact with the bottom, and to do so by fishing rela-tively slowly. Let the jig fall freely until the line goes slack. Reel up slack and lift the jig off the bottom. Once you are on the bottom, you need to maintain contact with it. Assuming that you have cast your jig out, let it settle to the bottom, and are now retrieving it toward you, you should keep it working in short hops along the bottom as long as the terrain and length of line out enable you to do so. If you are in a boat and drifting, the jig will eventually start sweeping upward and away from you and the bottom as you drift, unless it is very heavy, so you need to pay out more line occasionally until the angle of your line has changed significantly, then reel in and drop the jig back down again.

Choosing the right weight lure to use is critical to most types of jigging. The ideal is to have a lure that gets to the bottom and stays there under normal conditions, but which is not too large to be imposing to fish. Most anglers who fail to reach bottom not only don't use the right retrieval technique or compensate for wind or current, but also use too light a jig for getting down to the bottom under the conditions that they face.

Sometimes it is necessary to swim a jig by pumping it slowly and reeling, never actually letting it hop along the bottom. Other times it may be necessary to slowly drag it. When fishing a moderately sloping shoreline or point, for example, you should slowly pull the lure a little bit off the bottom, let it settle down while keeping in contact with it, take up the slack, and repeat this.

When working a ledge, or a sharply sloping shoreline, slowly pull the lure over the structure until it begins to fall, let it settle, and then repeat. Don't hop the jig up quickly here, as it will fall out and away from the bottom and likely miss a good deal of the important terrain. With some jigs, such as grubs, it is sometimes a good technique to make them jump quickly off the bottom rather than make short hops. You can also swim a jig on the edges of cover by reeling it slowly across the bottom and giving it occasional darting movements with manipulation of your rod tip. The majority of strikes while jigging come as the bait falls back down, so be alert for a strike then and keep both a good feel, and an eye, on your line to detect this.

Jigs also have a lot of value in rivers and where there is current. In a fair amount of current you should cast upstream or up-and-across-stream, engage the line-pickup system as soon as the lure splashes down, reel up slack and try to keep the line taut by letting the jig drift or by reeling in slack to achieve a natural drift. You virtually fish a jig in quick water the same way a fly angler works a nymph, keeping slack out and rod tip up, and feeling the lure as it bounces along. In deep, swift current, you actually need to swim the jig a bit by pumping the rod tip.

Jigging vertically, of course, is useful, especially when fishing through the ice or when angling for suspended fish in open water. Here, both leadhead jigs and metal or lead spoons are used and you needn't maintain bottom contact, though you might start at the bottom and jig your way up. Sometimes it's necessary to get to a particular depth and regularly jig at that spot.

If you know what depth to fish you can let the desired length of line out and commence jigging, never reeling in any line and only paying line out if you begin to drift. Here's one way to know how much line you're letting out: reel the jig up to the rod tip, stick the rod tip on the surface, let go of the jig, and raise your rod tip up to eye level, then stop the fall of the jig. If eye level is 6 feet above the surface, your jig will now be 6 feet deep. Lower rod tip to the surface and do this again. Now you've let out 12 feet of line. Continue until the desired length is out. With a level-wind reel with a freely revolving line guide you can measure the amount of line that is let out with each side-to-side movement of the line guide, then multiply this by the number of times the guide travels back and forth. If you use a reel that doesn't have such a guide, you can strip line off the spool in 1-foot (or 18-inch) increments until the desired length is out. Another method is to countdown the lure's descent. A falling rate of one foot per second is standard and may be accurate for medium-weight jigs, but you should check the lure's rate of fall in a controlled situation first to ensure accuracy.

For some vertical jigging you may need to let your lure fall to the bottom, then jig it up toward the surface a foot or two at a time. Bring the lure off the bottom and reel in the slack, then jig it there three or four times before retrieving another few feet of line and jigging the lure again. Repeat this until the lure is near the surface. The only problem here is that you don't know exactly how deep a fish is when you do catch one, and you can't just strip out the appro-

priate length of line and be at the proper level.

Discerning a strike when jigging can be difficult because so many fish don't slam a jig when they take it. Certainly some do, and there's no question then that a fish has struck, but in most light-jig usage where small fish are sought, something just a little "different" happens that signals a strike. That difference is often barely perceptible.

The job of detection is made even less obvious by the fact that most strikes come when a jig is falling, which is often when there is a slight amount of slack in the line. If you fail to detect the strike quickly enough the fish might reject the lure or you will be too late to set the hook properly.

In a sense, it's good to tight-line a jig backward as it falls, but not with so much tension

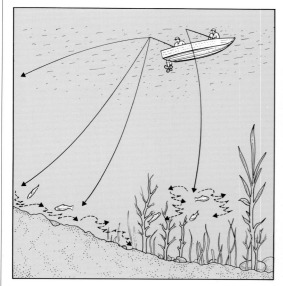

Casting toward shore and jigging a lure back along the bottom is a fairly standard jigging tactic; vertically fishing a jig on or just slightly above bottom or objects is another.

to make it fall unnaturally and stiffly. You need to slightly lower your rod tip as the jig falls, and when you feel something take the jig, set the hook quickly, keeping the rod tip high and reeling rapidly at the same time. A lot of jig-struck fish are lost because the angler, in reacting to a strike, raises his rod high but never gets the hook to penetrate the mouth of the fish. So the hook pulls out after a moment or the fish jumps and throws the hook easily. A forceful hookset that eliminates slack, coupled with constant pressure and rapid reeling, is the way to avoid losing fish on a jig.

Having the right rod is also a big factor, especially in freshwater where jigs are usually fairly light. Light jigs are rarely fished well on stiff, heavy rods, and vice versa; wimpy super-flexible rods don't make good jigging rods, nor do the pool-cue versions. This is where that elusive quality of sensitivity comes into play. A well-tapered rod with a fast tip is preferable, and

Left: An ice fisherman uses a jigging rod for vertical fishing.

Most strikes on a jig occur when the lure is falling; being able to detect a strike is often critical. These anglers are working light jigs along a rocky bank for smallmouth bass.

it's good to keep the tip angled upward.

Two conditions that make detecting strikes when jigging more difficult (as well as maintaining jig depth and control) are fishing jigs under windy conditions, and in and around weeds. Many fishermen tip their jig hooks with bait, and when fishing around vegetation, the best bait is a leech. The leeches work better for weed fishing than nightcrawlers because worms get torn up too easily through contact with weeds. That contact makes it hard to detect a strike, incidentally, especially if the wind is up.

Developing a keen feel, especially in weeds, takes patience and practice. Realizing that the 'tick' you feel is a fish (often a walleye or perch) sucking in your offering, takes some adjustment, although it is usually easier with larger fish, because they take in more water when they inhale a lure and thus there is a more pro-

nounced effect to feel. You will lose a number of fish, including a few good-sized ones, that you have on momentarily because you don't realize quickly enough that you have a strike instead of stroking a weed. Most of the time you feel it as you pull on the jig. Detecting that strike is made easier by using light jigs and light (6- or 8-pound) line on a spinning outfit.

If you must fish a jig in weeds, to counter detection problems when there is wind, try using a bobber with the jig in the weeds. An alternative is using a split shot and jig, which will keep the lure down but which is extremely hard to feel.

DRIFTING

It is a common image in television commercials to see a fisherman sitting in a boat with his feet propped up and a line dangling over the side waiting to get lucky. Although some anglers are like this, others who look pretty laid-back will fool you, and there are a lot of times when those who seem to be doing little, if nothing, have an uncanny knack for achieving success. Drift fishing from a boat, for instance, appears to be about as lazy a fishing method as you can find, but there is often more to it than meets the eye.

In fact, there are times when it is advantageous to drift with live bait or lures, rather than to be moving, such as when the fish appear to be spooked by engine noise. But the haphazard drifter, who pays little regard to how deep he is fishing, where he is headed, and what he is using, is not likely to do be as effective as the

Below: *Using the wind or current to drift quietly and cast, jig, or fish live bait is a common angling tactic.*

drifter using carefully selected tackle and making a calculated approach.

If you are drift fishing with live bait, for example, pay attention to the type of live bait rig that you use, and to the sinker. Bank, dipsey, pencil lead, and split shot sinkers are commonly used in live bait drifting. While split shot are often used for suspending bait at specific depths, the others are essentially used for keeping contact with the bottom, are good in deep water, and cast well. Split shot are preferred for light tackle. Dipsey sinkers are also used with light to medium tackle and where bait is suspended off the bottom above the sinker.

A very popular bait fishing rig, used for drifting as well as for trolling, and which is especially useful on perch, walleyes, and bass, is a spinner rig, which features a small spinner ahead of a worm, with a fixed sinker or sliding sinker above it. Another popular bottom-drifting bait rig features a three-way swivel attached to a bell sinker and a leadered hook.

Some fishermen who cast lures use a wind-aided drift to their advantage in combination with occasional electric motor use to help maintain a desired position. In plastic worm fishing for bass, for instance, one can successfully work an open weedy area this way with a variety of lures. Plastic worms, in fact, are especially good for some slow drifting work, and can be fished

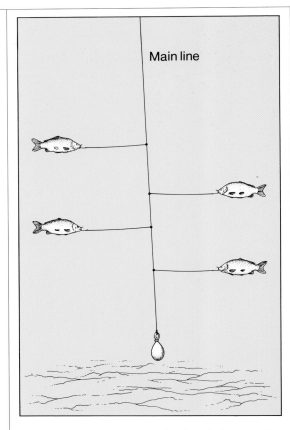

Live bait rigs are popular for drift fishing, using some type of sinker to get to the bottom, and often fishing with more than one bait at different levels.

on a slow retrieve that is combined with a drift. Generally, however, the best lure to use when

Above: *Anglers in a drift boat anchor and drift their offerings through a run while prospecting for salmon or steelhead.*

drifting is a jig, either with a soft-plastic attachment or strip of live or dead bait.

In order to properly drift over a particular stretch of water, you have to plan the approach properly, taking wind and current into consideration. Drift fishing is usually done on the windward side of the boat, particularly in deep water; it is preferable if the boat is in a position broadside to the wind, but this is not possible with some boats. Be sure to note where you start a drift and have success, as you should return and re-drift over productive stretches. The longer you drift, and the more the wind shifts, the harder it will be, especially in open water environs, to return to the proper place or to achieve the desirable drift.

River drifting is popular, too, and there is little haphazard about this. Using electric motors, outboard motors, or oars, boaters try to effect a downstream boat movement at a pace much slower than the speed of the current, allowing them to cast lures and baits and work them better or longer (or present them more often) in likely places. This is especially effective for salmon, steelhead, trout, bass, and walleyes.

The most critical aspect of river drift fishing

Right: *Maintaining boat position when drifting along a river breakline, as shown here, can be done with an occasional thrust of the electric motor, keeping along the proper contour.*

is proper bait or lure presentation through boat control. A premier method of doing such is called slipping, and it entails moving slowly backwards downstream while in complete control of your craft, in such a way as to allow passengers and boat operator to fish at ease. To do this, point the bow of your boat upstream and accelerate the outboard motor in forward gear. With the bow placed into the current, throttle the motor down to a point where your boat has begun to move backward downstream. The thrust of the motor is not enough to keep you going forward, and your boat slowly drifts backward, stern first. The boat moves very slowly, sometimes almost imperceptibly, and you have precise control over position and rate of descent.

With the motor at a steady forward thrust, the boat backs downstream with ease as you cast and retrieve. Cast upstream and retrieve slowly downstream. Upstream casting allows you to present lures in a manner similar to the movement of natural bait in current. The bow of the boat is always pointed into the current. It is a

position easily held, providing you don't allow eddies and backwaters to trap the boat, and you can readily move across current as necessary.

A similar thing can be done in moderate-to slow-flowing rivers by using an electric motor for positioning to face into the current and wind, and drifting with bait or jigs. Maintaining pace with the current allows for a vertical presentation that aids hook setting and gives the fish less of a chance to detet the offering. It also permits the use of lighter jigs, which many times are more likely to be taken than a heavier product.

Most river anglers who fish from shore, incidentally, are drift fishermen, though they don't think of it that way. The standard procedure for casting to nearly every river species, regardless of whether you are using lure, fly, or bait, is to cast across and upstream and then allow the offering to drift or swim naturally in the current. Proper presentation is one of the keys to success here, and it is effective presentation that makes drifting a worthwhile technique in various forms of fishing.

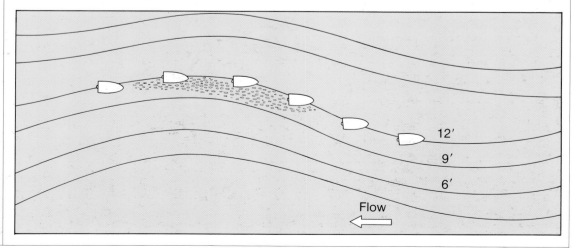

FLATLINE TROLLING

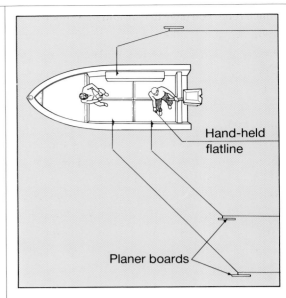

Hand-held flatline

Planer boards

An overhead view depicts the use of three in-line planer boards to separate trolling lures, while the boat operator fishes with a handheld flatline directly out the rear.

The simplest trolling of any kind is to run what is known as a "flatline". A flatline is simply one that is fished straight out behind the boat and for which there are no heavy ball sinkers, downrigger weights, diving planers, or other devices to influence the depth attainment of the lure. Anyone fishing out of a boat with a rod, reel, line, and a lure can run a flatline.

The key to flatline productivity is the length of line fished and how you manipulate your boat to position lures or bait. The clearer the water, the shallower the fish, the spookier the fish, and the more local boat activity there is, the longer the line you need. Lengths up to 200 feet may be used, but most trolling line lengths are under 100 feet, with 60 to 75 being standard.

The best success in flatlining usually results from altering the lure's path of travel by turning, steering in an S-shaped pattern, driving in other irregular ways, or by increasing or decreasing the speed of the boat. This enhances your presentation by altering the speed and action of the lure, and making it appear less mechanical and more susceptible to capture.

As you are making a flatline trolling presentation, you have to consider where the fish are and how to get your lures in close to them without alarming them. Many fish that are in shallow water near shore or that are close to the surface in open water characteristically move out of the boat's path of travel. That is one reason why you seldom see fish on sonar in less than 15 feet of water. These fish, particularly schools, swim off to one side of the boat as it approaches. They may continue swimming away, they may stay where they are once they have moved, or

Manipulating the boat, as in making S-curves, is a prime way to bring trolled lures into contact with fish, especially fish that are spooky and in shallow water.

they may return to their original location after the boat has passed.

If your lure is trailing directly behind a straight-moving boat, fish in the first two instances may never see your lure. If your line is too short, fish in the third instance may also not see it if they are slow to return to their position, or they may see it but associate it with the recently passed boat. This helps illustrate why a lure should be fished on a long line and how proper boat manipulation can bring lures into the range of fish that may not have been in the boat's path or that have moved out of it.

The true test of flatline trolling is to make such presentations in non open-water areas. Near shore, around reefs or shoals or islands, along grass lines and weed edges, and so forth are hard places to reach effectively due to limited maneuverability, yet you may not have success if you don't reach them. Consider, for example, a lakeshore that drops off fairly sharply and which may have boulders or stumps submerged just under the surface. If you bring your boat too close to shore your motor may hit these structures. The way to deal with this when flatline trolling is to sweep in and out from shore, and plan strategically advantageous approaches to such areas as points, sandbars, islands, shoals, channels, and the like. You may have to troll by many of these more than once, from different directions, to effectively cover the location.

There are devices that solve many of the difficulties of shallow trolling, and which make your presentations much more versatile than flatlining. These are sideplaner boards. They are plastic or wooden surface-running planers that evolved on the Great Lakes for trout and salmon trolling. Sideplaner boards work something like a downrigger on the surface. A non-fishing line or cable tethers the planer to the boat, and allows it to run at varied distances off to the side of

your boat. One or more fishing lines are attached to the planer or tow line via release clips; you are free to fight a fish unencumbered when it strikes your lure and releases the fishing line from the clip.

Another type of planer for flatlining is smaller and attaches directly to your fishing line. It can be set up to pop free when a fish strikes (which necessitates returning to retrieve the planer), or it can be set up so that the planer stays on the fishing line, being freed of it when a fish is played and the planer reaches the boat. Often referred to simply as a trolling board, this sideplaner has a calm water fishing advantage, but requires fairly stout tackle and moderately heavy line, and makes hooking fish a little more difficult.

Sideplaners can be used in trolling for all kinds of fish, but are mostly used for trout, salmon, and walleyes. They vastly increase presentation capabilities because they allow lures to pass near fish that may have been spooked by the passage of your boat (or would be spooked if you ran your boat near them) or are in areas where you can't or don't want to take your boat.

How far you set the sideplaners out depends on how close you want your boat to shore, how far apart you want to spread your lures, how

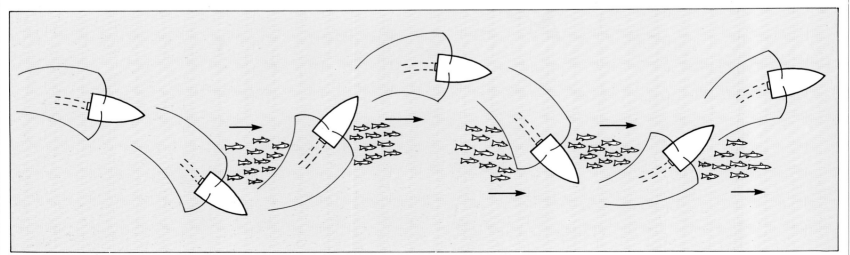

much room you have to fish, and how much boat traffic there is in the area, among other factors. Eighty to 100 feet out is a common distance. They can be run out as much as 200 hundred feet if you have a high anchor point in your boat for the planer line (some fishermen use a 6- to 8-foot pole).

To use sideplaners you must have a method of tethering them to your boat and retrieving them. You can use manual downriggers for that, though this limits your range. Sideplaner booms and reels are generally used. Double-runner planers are becoming more common than single runners because they track well and handle rough water better.

You can run lures any length behind a sideplaner that seems feasible. Because the lures are trolled well off to the side of the boat, and behind a relatively unobtrusive planer, they often don't have to be run as far back as when using a flat line. You still need a lot of line on your reel, however, since your fishing line extends first to the release clip and then back to the lure.

With sideplaners, a host of fishing combinations are possible. When fishing near-shore areas you can run two or three strategically spaced lines off the shore-sideplaner. On the open-water side of the boat you have the option of running a surface or diving lure on a long flat-line, running a lure deep via the downrigger, or

Flatline trolling is very common when seeking many species of freshwater fish, although some anglers do not maneuver their boats well enough when flatlining.

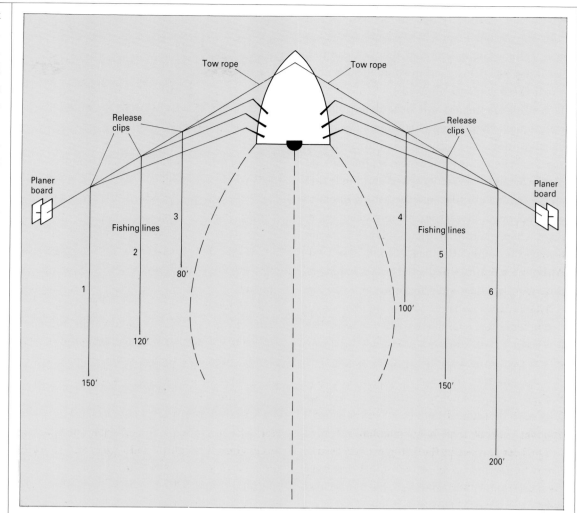

running one or more lures off the other sideplaner. Moreover, the amount of territory that can be covered is vastly increased. If you run two sideplaners, each 60 feet to either side of the boat, and have two fishermen in the boat, you might run four lines over a 40-yard span of water. If the bottom drops off sharply near shore, as it does in many trout lakes, you could be

A large boat could fish six flatlines using this system (seen from overhead) via sideplaners. Note the staggered line setbacks. Fish are played in the dotted area.

working over a few feet of water on the near-shore side of the boat, and over 40 feet on the opposite side, presenting your lures to fish that

would not ordinarily see them, and which would not be frightened by the passage of your boat. (This example assumes that you can fish two lines per fishermen; in some locales only one line per angler is allowed.)

Trolling strategies and boat manipulation techniques when using sideplaners are much like those described earlier for flatlining without boards. When you turn, however, the outside planer board increases its speed and the inside one slows or stalls. Because the fishing lines are well separated, there is less chance of entanglement when you turn, particularly if all lines are nearly the same distance behind the boat. Although a lot of sideplaner board fishing is done with shallow-running lures, you can use whatever lures are appropriate for the conditions; moreover, by adjusting the tension of the line release, you can troll a hard-pulling deep-diving plug or a line with weights on it.

Large boats accomplish similar things, incidentally, with the use of outriggers, which are long rods that are extended out to the side of the boat and sport a release clip that frees fishing line when a fish strikes the following bait or lure. These originated in big-game trolling, but have been used to troll small lures as well in the Great Lakes. Lines can't be spread or separated as far with this system, and the angle of line from release to water entry is much greater, affecting lure depth.

When you're fishing several lines, you can experiment with their distance from the boat and the distance the lures are set behind the tow line or outrigger. When running two or three lines off one sideplaner or outrigger, don't put short lines on the outside. If a fish were to strike a short outside line, there's a chance that he'd cross over one or more of the inside lines after the hookup. Take this into account when setting lines out and try to arrange them so that a fish caught on the outside line will drop back clear of the inside lines, and then be played up the unfished center alley. If you have three lines on one side, and the outermost one pops, you can slide the inner lines out, then put the released line back out as the inside line. This is all accomplished without having to pull fishing lines and the planer in.

To determine the length of line to set your lure out behind the boat, sideplaner, or outrigger (downrigger, too), you can use one of several systems. With levelwind reels you can count the number of "passes" that the levelwind guide makes across the top of the reel. Measure the amount of line that comes off the spool for one pass, then multiply that amount by the number of passes to arrive at a setback distance.

Another system, used with levelwind reels that possess a line guide that locks in an open position, and used with spinning and fly reels, is to count "pulls". Start with the lure or fly in the water, hold the rod in one hand and grab

the line just ahead of the reel with your other hand. Pull off line in set increments, either as far as your arm will reach, or in 1- or 2-foot strips. Count the distance let out as you pull to arrive at setback length.

A third method is to "sweep", by putting the lure in the water, pointing the rod tip back at the lure, and sweeping the rod toward the bow of the boat in a measured length. As the boat moves ahead, bring the rod tip back and then sweep forward again. If your sweep is 6 feet, multiply that by the number of sweeps you make

In-line planer boards such as those in use by the anglers in this scene above help spread lures away from the path of the boat to reach fish that are off to the side.

to approximate setback length. Sweeping is a bit less accurate than using pulls or passes, but quickly done. A final method is to use fishing line that is marked. At least one manufacturer supplies fishing line that is color-marked in 10-foot increments, and this can be counted to gauge distance.

DOWNRIGGER TROLLING

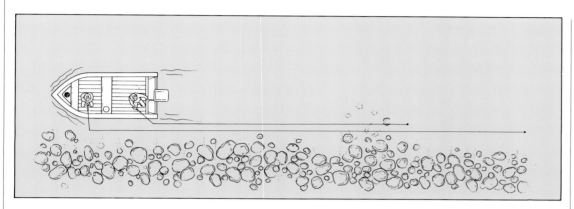

Controlled depth fishing is the hallmark of downrigger usage and something that should always be kept in mind when trolling with these devices. Using a downrigger is not difficult. Once you're on the water, you can be operating a downrigger and mastering angling depth in a

Downriggers are employed in conjunction with rod holders and sonar, with the objective being to control the depth placement of your lures.

When flatlining along a shore, one troller can run a shallow-running lure closest to shore on a long length of line, and another can fish a deeper outfit.

few minutes. To get started, open the bail or push the freespool button on your reel and let your lure out to whatever distance you think it should be swimming behind the downrigger weight. Keep the reel in freespool with the

clicker on if it's a levelwind reel; loosen the drag or keep the bail open with a spinning reel. Bring the downrigger weight and line release close to the boat where you can reach them without stretching far overboard. Grab the line at the top of the rod and place it in the release (the device used with a downrigger weight that holds your line till a fish strikes), twisting the line first several times and setting the loop that is then created into the release. Set the weight back overboard if you brought it onto the gunwale of the boat or swing the downrigger boom back to trolling position so the weight can be lowered. Take your rod in one hand and make sure that the line is not fouled at the tip and that line will freely depart the reel spool. Use your other hand to lower the weight, either by depressing the down switch on electric downriggers or lightly releasing clutch tension or back-reeling manual downriggers. Stop the weight at whatever depth you want, as indicated on the downrigger's line counter. Set the rod in a holder and reel up slack so that the tip is bowed over.

When you place the downrigger-set rod in a holder it's important to reel in slack line, then pull on the line near the first rod guide while you turn the reel handle, to bring the line from rod tip to release as tight as possible without pulling it out of the release. The rod should be well arched in an inverted J shape to increase hook-up efficiency as well as alert the angler to a strike (the tip momentarily springs upward as the line is pulled out of the release). Also, the reel drag should be checked for proper setting and the clicker on levelwind reels should be engaged. Long, limber rods are generally used in downrigger trolling in order to set them well into the holders and make them tight to the release, and also because they will absorb the punishment of bouncing in rough water better than a stiffer rod, which tends to snap the line our of the release in rough water.

That's all there is to the basic setup. The only thing you'll do differently each time you employ a downrigger is change the length of line between the downrigger weight or cable and the lure, and change the depth to which the weight is lowered. That depth can vary from just below the surface to as deep as the amount of line on your reel will allow. You determine desired

Following pages: Trollers run flatlines at all times of the day and during all seasons, although it is most effective when fish are relatively shallow.

When a strike is received on a downrigger, the rod tip pops up in the rod holder; the fisherman then pulls the rod out of the holder and is quickly fast to a fish.

to fish and the bottom depth of the water, and run the risk of snagging the weight.

How far back to fish your lures – called "setback" – varies greatly, depending on the depth being fished and the species being pursued. As a general rule, the deeper you fish the less line is needed between weight and lure, and the shallower you fish, the further you put the lure back. This is only a general guideline, as some fish can at times be caught shallow on short lines. Determining setback distance requires experimentation, as does the selection of lure type and color. Short setbacks, however, increase hooksetting efficiency, minimize possible conflicts with other boats in heavily trafficked areas, and make boat maneuvering easier.

The number of downriggers used and their location determines what horizontal spread can be achieved with lures presented on downriggers. If you troll with two downriggers, you needn't be too concerned with rigging systems, other than to realize that you may want to keep the weights at different levels, use stackers or sliders to maximize your opportunities per line or per downrigger, and vary dropback lengths. The more downriggers you employ, however, the more you should be concerned with systems or patterns of operation, not only to cover the water well horizontally and vertically, but also to facilitate fish landing, minimize line crossing and lure tangling, and better appeal to some species of fish.

Boaters with four to six downriggers who fish large open waters can employ some variation of V patterns in terms of weight depth and lure dropback length to avoid inconsistent, possibly confusing, and perhaps troublesome lure and line placement. Regarding depth, in a V-Down pattern the innermost weights are deepest, the weights to either side of them are shallower, and the outside weights are shallowest. A V-Up pattern is just the reverse. An Equal-Depth pattern would see the weights all set at the same level. As for line-to-lure setback from the weight, in a V-In pattern the innermost lures are closest to the weight, the lures to either side of them are further back, and the outside lures are furthest. A V-Out pattern is just the reverse. In an Equal-Length setback, all lures are set at the same distance behind the downrigger weight.

Why would you want to adopt a pattern? Because you'll always know where your weights and lures are. The more rigs you troll, the harder

Right: Large boats, such as those used in salmon fishing on the Great Lakes may use many downriggers and pattern their offerings to increase the chances of catching fish.

fishing depth by checking temperature levels to see at what depth the thermocline or preferred temperature of your quarry might be found, and by watching a sonar instrument to find fish and locate structure.

Sonar is to downrigger fishing what headlights are to driving at night. The purpose of

downrigger fishing is to control the depth of your lures and to place them in specific places and at specific levels. You use sonar equipment to find baitfish or gamefish and the levels at which they are located, as well as the depth of the bottom and other aspects of underwater terrain. Without sonar you have to guess the depth

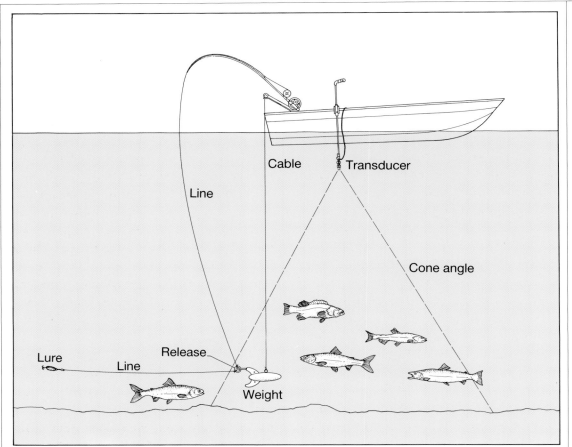

Depicted is a downrigger-set lure, and a hypothetical viewing area of a wide-angle sonar transducer. When a fish takes the lure, it will pop free of the weight and the angler will be able to play the fish unencumbered.

it is to keep track of things, and when a hard-fighting fish strikes, and lines are cleared, in the confusion it can be easy to lose sight of what weight the successful lure was on, how deep that weight was, and how far the lure was set behind the release. When you know these matters, you can rerig immediately in a similar fashion.

It is important to minimize the possibility of lines crossing over one another and tangling. Realize that outside lures speed up and inside lures slow down on a turn. Outside lures keep swimming high while inside lures rise or fall; this varies with the type of lure used (floating plugs rise while sinkers fall). Some fishermen troll for hours without checking their lures, only to find that they have been dragging a tangle. The problem was the way lines were set and how that affected their movement when turns were made.

A V-Down depth system is preferred by many fishermen. Deepest lines are directly below the boat. Shallower lines are more out of the boat's direct path of travel with this system, perhaps where fish that are spooked by boat passage or

A troller, whether using downriggers or flatlines, has to watch where he is headed, and be especially aware of changes in bottom terrain. Following this 20-foot contour means watching the sonar and maneuvering the boat in a way to keep the trailing lures along the edge as best as possible.

deeply set downriggers may have moved. The V-Up system might be the better approach when you are after fish that are not spooked by the boat and may be attracted to its noise or to the prop wash. Coho and Atlantic salmon are two such fish. An Equal-Depth presentation may be useful when fish are only being caught at a very specific level, such as when they occupy a narrow-band thermocline, and when you are not trying to locate fish by scouring all depth levels.

With setback lengths, there is seldom much reason to use a V-Out system, and the V-In pattern is favored. When fish are caught regularly on lures trolled at a fairly specific mid-range distance behind downrigger weights (especially when depths are nearly the same), there is little reason to stagger them much, so Equal-Length setbacks can be used. With the V-In system, the inner lures will run under the outer ones when turns are made and fish that are located on sonar directly below the boat may move up and out toward the lures set further back. When used in combination with either the V-Down or V-Up

depth settings, this setback system helps avoid line tangling when a fish strikes and releases deep lines from the release.

Naturally, you have to experiment with these patterns and see what's best for your type of fishing and boat. Where you only fish one or two downriggers, this is academic. Such patterns have their greatest use in mid- to large-sized boats, and the most common pattern is to use a V-Down/V-In combination. Keep in mind that depth and setback distances are relative. In a V-Down system the shallowest depth trolled might only be 12 feet, the intermediate depth 18, and the greatest depth 24, which is not really a significant variation, or it could see the same progression as 20, 40, and 60 feet. The same is true for setbacks. There are no limitations.

It is possible to fish two rods off one downrigger, and this is particularly important for the small boater or single downrigger owner. You can even stack three. To set up stacked lines, rig the first line as you would conventionally and as described earlier. Once the first line has been placed in the release by the weight, lower the weight down 10 feet and attach the stacker release to the cable. Put the second lure out the desired distance and set the line in the stacker release.

Place both reels in rod holders and leave the freespool clicker on, then place the boom in the proper position (if applicable) and lower the weight down to the desired depth. The two lines are now spaced 10 feet apart. Be sure to place rods in holders so that the lower line will not tangle with the upper line if a strike is received and the fish immediately comes toward the surface. The setback for the upper line should be shorter than for the lower line, again to minimize interference if a fish strikes the lower one. The vertical distance between the two lines is optional, although it probably shouldn't be less than 10 feet.

Where very deep water is fished, a difference of 30 to 50 feet may be useful. Another option for fishing more than one lure on one downrigger, although it does not involve using two rods is to use a slider. That is covered in detail elsewhere (see Special Factors).

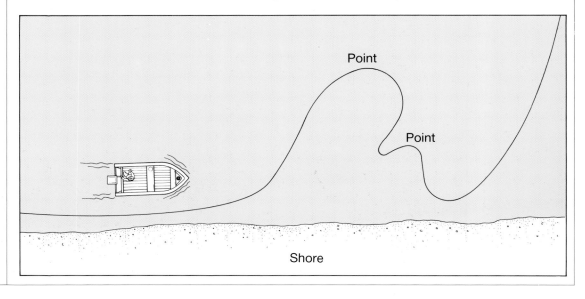

BACKTROLLING

"Backtrolling" is a fisherman's term used to refer to two vastly different fishing techniques, These are generally employed by small boats, and feature precise boat handling and boat manipulation as a means of presenting a lure or bait behind the boat in a precise way to make a thorough, slow, and careful presentation. It is used in both lakes and rivers, primarily by walleye, steelhead, and salmon fishermen. In lakes it is employed mostly by walleye anglers, who use a tiller-steered outboard motor in reverse or a transom-mounted electric motor (with lower unit turned so that the stern goes back when the motor is technically in a forward position), and move very slowly stern-first to maintain precise position around points, reefs, weed lines, sandbars, and along dropoffs.

By using sonar, a backtroller can maintain

Equipped with splash guards, and using a transom-mounted electric motor (hidden from view), two lake anglers backtroll slowly to put their offerings in a precise location.

position along specific depths, nearly hover over selected spots, and maneuver his boat to use whatever wind direction is present to position his boat in such a way as to keep his following bait in the proper place. This is very vital when a school of fish is packed into one small spot.

In many rivers, precise boat control and precise lure or bait placement is achieved by floating, drifting, or trolling slowly backward downcurrent. In some places this is called backtrolling, but in others it is called Hotshotting, which is a derivative of the West Coast technique of using a Hotshot brand of trolling plug for river steelhead and salmon, or "pulling plugs". And in still others it is called "slipping".

Whatever you call it the idea is to have the bow of your boat pointed upstream, using motor or oars to control the downstream progression of the boat. The boat moves very slowly—it actually drifts—downstream, and at times remains stationary in the current (some boaters anchor once they have caught fish in a spot), while lures are fished at varied distances (from a few feet

to 75) behind the boat. The lures dangle in front of fish that the boat has not yet passed over, and this is a big difference compared to upstream trolling, where the boat passes over fish and alerts them to your presence, probably spooking them. Additionally, lures that are backtrolled downstream ahead of the boat approach the head of fish, instead of coming from behind them and swimming past their head. Lures are usually fished in the channels and deep pools where bigger fish lie, and waver in front of fish for a much longer period than they would if cast and retrieved or if trolled upstream and away. The fact that fish have a better chance of being undisturbed and of seeing a more natural presentation (a small fish, for instance, struggling against the current and being slowly swept downward) makes this a highly effective river fishing technique.

Most of this downstream backtrolling is done with diving plugs for fish that take them. Some fish, such as shad, don't take plugs and you must use shad darts (a form of jig) or tiny spoons fished behind a torpedo-shaped bead chain sinker. Others respond well to bait; winter-run steelhead, for example, are caught with pencil lead-weighted spawn sacks, single-hook salmon eggs, or worms. Many different attractions, including plugs, spoons, spinners, flies, and bait, can be used, depending on the circumstances. Plugs may be flatlined or used with a

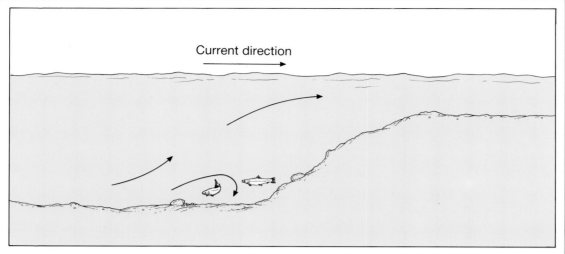

Current direction

In a river pool, backtrollers slowly work through the pool with plugs, and often catch their fish at the tail of the pool, either because the fish have been pushed there and do not want to go back downstream, or because they are resting there due to less current.

sinker, and bait is always used with some form of sinker.

When slipping, it's important to manipulate the boat properly in order to maintain precise lure position. The location and depth of your offering is critical to river fishing success. The lure must be on or close to the bottom, so you

Salmon fishermen (with a chinook on the floor) in a jet sled backtroll in a river to drift their plugs down in front of fish in a deep pool.

need to use the appropriate amount of weight or design of lure that will achieve this.

Pools and deep runs are the major locales that are fished with this technique, and often the boat needs to be positioned far enough upriver so the lure slowly works from the head of a pool or run down through the tail of it; it's not good enough to boat down to a spot and then hold position, as the fish you seek may have been located at the top of that locale. When working from side to side across the river, you should realize that it takes awhile for a trailing lure to catch up to the boat position; when you sweep close to a bank, for instance, hold that position because it takes time for the lure to get over to the bank. If you were to sweep in and out quickly the lure wouldn't get as far to the side as you might like.

Another point to remember is that you want

to troll backward in a slow, controlled fashion. When you stop rowing or throttle the motor back, a floating plug rises, a spinner doesn't spin, weights sink, etc. This is because there is now less pressure against those objects. Slow, controlled backward movement keeps lures working best and draws more strikes. Boat control is maintained with oars, especially in rafts, johnboats, and river drift boats (McKenzie River style dories), or with small tiller-steered outboard motors.

If necessary, in order to get lures into the right spots and to fish a hole without moving the boat over the whole run, the tactic of back bouncing is employed. To back bounce, a fisherman slowly lifts the rod tip upward and feels the lure working, then drops it down till it hits bottom and either reels up a bit or lifts and bounces the plug or bait with the current flow back as he drifts. Keep dropping it back to hit the bottom and then lift, always working the offering back.

It can be hard to get the hang of the backtrolling and back bouncing techniques, but anglers must remember to maintain contact with the bottom and constantly watch their rod tips for a strike and for the proper working action of a lure. In deeper holes, fish will not come up much for a lure and you must be down on or near the bottom. In shallower water, fish will come up a bit and get it. You will catch some fish almost under the boat, so they do not fear it, except when rivers are low and very clear.

OTHER TROLLING TECHNIQUES

MOOCHING

In the Pacific Northwest coastal waters, the most common technique for catching salmon is mooching. Mooching involves the use of bait, and is practiced in a way that includes a bit of drifting and some very subtle trolling.

There are a number of ways to mooch, with differences revolving around the size of bait used, the speed of boat movement, and the strength of tackle employed. A lot of mooching is done in areas where there is current, in rivers as well as in coastal areas where tides and eddies are prominent. Herring is the bait used for mooching, sometimes live, sometimes freshly killed and fished whole or cut, and sometimes fished as thawed/ treated/cut bait.

Cut bait is preferred in most areas, but the angle of cut is important and dictates the speed of the roll as the bait is drifted or trolled. An angled cut is made behind the gills by the pectoral fin and the innards are pulled or routed out of the cavity. Snelled salmon hooks in two- or three-hook rigs are used; the manner of placing them is important, but varies with number of hooks, size of bait, and speed of roll desired. The lead hook is impaled through the head, however, with point inserted inside the cavity behind several ribs and hooked out through the top of the bait.

Tackle consists of a long – generally 10 1/2-foot – rod and a reel capable of holding several hundred yards of line. In some locales, notably British Columbia, anglers are partial to so-called "mooching reels", which are direct-drive, 1 to 1 retrieve products akin to large fly reels. Levelwind reels and fly reels are also used, the latter with lighter line and shorter rods and smaller bait when smaller fish, especially coho salmon, are abundant.

Fairly heavy sinkers are used–from 2 to 6 ounces–being keel shaped and fished several feet above the bait. A barrel swivel is used a few feet ahead of the sinker and the length of the leader from swivel to bait is roughly equal to the length of the rod.

Boat control is very important in this fishing, whether drifting or trolling. Tides and wind and swells dictate positioning, etc., but you want to achieve a proper roll of the bait as well as keep it in the most advantageous locations. When trolling, or motor mooching, the boat operator frequently (in some cases constantly) puts the tiller-steered motor in and out of gear, sometimes going backward a short distance to maneuver.

Although some strikes are vicious and result in instant hookups, many are soft, in which fish bump the bait; one has to pay out line quickly to give the fish time to get the bait well into its mouth without feeling resistance. Most fish are hooked just inside the mouth to enable release without harm if that is desired.

DIVING PLANERS

Diving planers are objects that attach to fishing line a few feet ahead of a lure and dive deeply. There are no weights used to get the lure down; the resistance of the planer makes it dive. When a fish strikes, it trips a release mechanism that allows the diver to offer minimal water

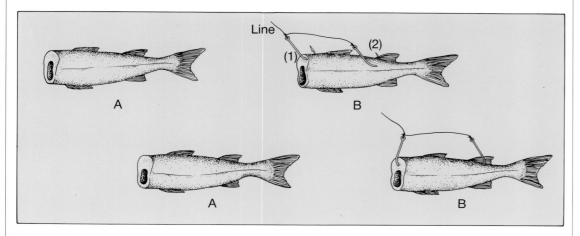

Above: *When mooching with cut herring, it is important to get the proper angle of cut when separating the head, as this governs the speed of the roll as the bait is drifted or trolled. Note the two different hooking methods, with snelled hooks being used.*

Below: *The type of planer shown can be adjusted to run straight or to either side.*

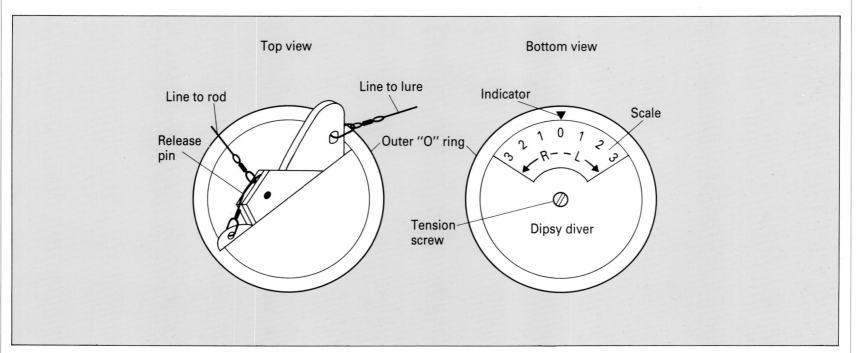

With mooching rods and reels in holders, two anglers slowly maneuver their baits.

resistance as the fish is played. For those without downriggers and for those who wished to avoid wire or lead core line or the use of heavy weights to get deep, these planers offer an alternative. The earliest diving planers, which predate the era of downriggers, were nondirectional and only dove straight down. The newest is a multi-directional product called a Dipsy Diver, which can be run not only straight down, but to the left or right of a straight path and still attain significant depth. Because these planers take lures out and away to the side of the boat, they are used by some trollers in conjunction with downrigger-set lines. Some fish that are in the path of the boat are spooked by downrigger weights and move down or out away from them. Directional diving planers bring lures off to the side of other presentations.

Diving planers offer several other benefits besides taking lures deep. They can serve as attractors to trout and salmon by their very size, color, and swimming motion. They offer an action that lures set behind downriggers usually don't get; the divers are more responsive to boat movements (turns and wave effects, for example). Because the lures are set a short distance behind them, they respond similarly.

To determine the depth that divers will run, consult the chart supplied with them by the manufacturer. Because divers run deep you cannot estimate the amount of line let out, but you must use the pull or pass system of line-length determination. It is important to accurately judge the how much line you have set out to know relative diving depth, especially for resetting after fish have been caught.

A diving planer is fished off of a very stout rod, because it pulls so hard when trolled, and is used with fairly heavy line. On big boats, beefy 9- and 10-foot rods are used, and 7 or 8-footers on smaller boats. The rods are placed in rod holders, which obviouslky must be able to withstand a lot of torque. These should be located on the boat's gunwale, several feet ahead of the transom, with the rods angled low and perpendicular to the water.

The lures to be fished behind a diving planer are quite broad. Spoons and cut plugs are especially favored because these products are similarly used for trout and salmon. Minnow-imitating plugs of various sizes also get the nod, as do dodger-and fly or squid combinations. Diving plugs are not usually worked unless they are very shallow runners and can withstand sometimes erratic planer action. Three to 5 feet is a common setback length. You need relatively short leaders because of the difficulty of netting a fish that is 5 or so feet behind a planer. Leader

An old-style method of trolling many lures on one weighted line is the Seth Green rig.

length should be as strong or stronger than the main line, preferably 17 or 20 pounds if big fish are likely to be encountered and perhaps 25 or 30 if a dodger is trolled. The main fishing line should be strong, at least 14 pounds; most people use 20.

OTHER TROLLING VENUES

While flatlining and downrigging are the most popular methods of trolling, there are alternatives to using a downrigger to get deep, or to simply using a lure or bait behind a nylon monofilament line or a fly line. These include:
WEIGHTS. This simply involves using some

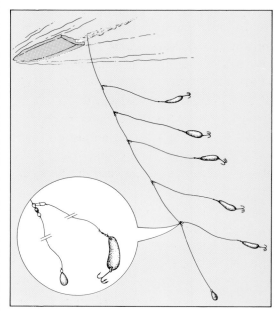

Using weights to get lures deep is a standard trolling tactic; this angler's weights are visible just above the barrel swivel on his line.

type of weight (drail, split shot, keel, bell, ball, or other type of sinker) to get a lure or bait deeper than it would achieve unaided or to control its use better. The latter is particularly true in current. Steelhead and salmon anglers especially use this to present both wobbling, diving plugs and bait in drift, backtrolling, and back bouncing techniques in current.

The rigs used with these often feature a three-way swivel, with a leader-to-lure or hook tied to one end and with a leader-to-snap/weight tied to another. Some are used in slow trolling, but most often they are used in current to back bounce and backtroll plugs (see previous section). The weights allow the plugs or bait to spend more time in the productive area and to be controlled better, especially when fished directly downstream with the boat up above.

The element of knowing actual depth fished is dependent on boat speed, line size, current, trolling line length, amount of weight, and so forth. In current, weights from 1 1/2 to 6 ounces may be used, obviously on stout tackle.

LEAD-CORE LINE. In this system, the weight of the line causes the object being trolled to sink. Depth achieved depends on how much lead-core line is let out. Some anglers use a long (50 feet or so) length of nylon monofilament line ahead of the lead core, or use the lead core mainly as backing for their other line.

Lead core is marked or color-coded at intervals; how much line you troll essentially determines how deep your lure will run, depending also on speed and lure type. While this can be a more precise method of fishing than using an unweighted flat line, it primarily puts the lure

or bait at a general trolling depth, and it is not as comfortable to use, since lead core line is strong and is bulkier than nylon or Dacron. Lead core isn't as supple as those products either, so it doesn't transmit the fight of a fish quite as well. Although there is relatively little use of lead core line nowadays, and this product only accounts for a small percentage of fishing line sales, it does have its devotees, including some modern walleye trollers who like to use this in open water trolling to augment their flat-line techniques. Also, some diehard New England landlocked salmon trollers will use this in the spring, as will some veteran lake trout trollers.

WIRE LINE. This is probably the least practiced and least popular trolling tactic, although still used in freshwater by some lake trout and musky trollers. As with lead core line usage, the weight of wire line causes the object being trolled to sink, and the amount let out determines the depth to be achieved. Wire can't be fished on just any rod or reel as it requires stout tackle; it is also subject to kinking, crimping, and spooling difficulties, and does nothing to enhance the sporting nature of fish being caught because the tackle blunts the fight of the fish, especially if it is small. It does, however, telegraph every movement of a fish quite well because of its high sensitivity.

RELEASEABLE CANNONBALL SINKER. This is a deep-trolling system where a large cannon-ball-shaped sinker is used to get down, with the sinker being released and dropping to the bottom when a fish strikes. You lose a lot of lead weight in this system, and need stout, heavy-line tackle. You also don't often know the depth

you're fishing when you're off the bottom.

SPOONPLUGGING. Spoon plugging is a flat-line trolling tactic that is specific to a certain type of lure used. You will be hard-pressed to find many practitioners outside of the upper Midwest, and would have to refer to a mail order tackle supplier to find Spoonplugs because very few stores carry them. These are sinking lures stamped from brass into a slightly arched position. They take a lot of abuse and can be trolled into all kinds of objects without changing their shape or needing adjustment. The size of lure and the amount of line employed determine diving depth. This technqiue employs high-speed boat work, and is geared toward people who are new to an area and scouting for fish while trying to learn bottom contours. Low-stretch line is employed as well.

SETH GREEN RIGGING. This is one of the oldest methoids of trolling and one developed over 100 years ago by New York fish culturist Seth Green. There are some deep-water trollers still using this technique, principally as an adjunct to other styles of deep trolling.

The Seth Green rig features five to eight lures, usually spoons or flies, on individual leaders that snap to the main fishing line and stay at a constant position in the main fishing line because they are attached to swivels. A heavy lead weight is used to get the rig down. Leaders are separated by a 10- to 20-foot distance. To fish it, you lower the weight and line into the water until the first barrel swivel is reached, then you take a leader and snap it to the barrel. Slowly lower it in the water until you reach the next swivel, and attach another leader. Continue in this fashion until all lures are out.

This requires a heavy rod and reel and some adroit manipulation to retrieve. When you reel in, you must stop to remove each of the snapped-on leaders. Leader length varies; old-timers used 15- to 30-foot leaders, but much shorter ones seem preferable. This setup has also been called a thermal rig and is primarily used in deep mid-summer trout and salmon fishing for covering a wide spectrum of water. It was adapted from commercial fishing applications. Sport fishermen should check state fishing regulations to be sure that they can use this many lures or hook points on a single fishing line.

Most of these systems can suffer from imprecise depth control; in other words, you often don't know exactly how deep you're fishing. Veteran trollers using these systems, however, have overcome that problem and have learned to have more mastery over their depth placement than inexperienced anglers. Getting a lure or bait down to a specific and proper level is the key aspect of any trolling system.

FISHING IN VEGETATION

Some species of freshwater fish are particularly attracted to vegetation because it offers them security, opportunities for food, and suitable water temperature, oxygen, and light conditions. Baitfish require food as well as protection from predators, and they, too, find this in the vegetation, so it is natural for gamefish to frequent such areas. Deep in the recesses of lily pads, hyacinths, and other masses of aquatic salad, the environs are protected and cooled to a tolerable level for such fish as largemouth bass, walleye, northern pike, muskellunge, and assorted panfish.

Below: *Weeds and flooded brush are some of the best places to fish for largemouth bass, especially if the water, as here, is murky.*

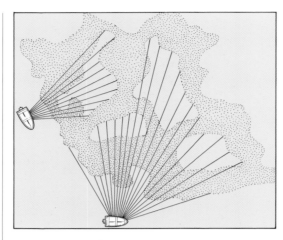

Above: *Work the edges of vegetation, as in the lily pads depicted here, and also all of the pockets and openings, positioning yourself in several locales to make appropriate casts.*

There are varying concentrations of weeds to contend with – thin, thick, thicker, and unbearable. All of this can be fished, though you can't get your boat through the worst of it except by poling. Some types of vegetation, such as grass, can be found extending through and covering the surface, as well as being submerged several feet, or it can be shallow or deep. You have to adjust to the peculiarities of each situation, but there are some patterns that hold true for all conditions, and some lure types that receive prominent usage. Pinpointing the location of weedlines is often a crucial element in determining boat position, lure presentation, and fishing technique. Sonar can be a big asset in this situation. The point is to be aware that there is both submerged and emergent vegetation.

When fishing in vegetation, it is good where possible to cast to the edges, irregular features and contours, openings, and the like.

Before fishing weeds it is a good idea to study things a bit to see where the water drops off and to find the weeds, weed edges, and perhaps bait, and other fish. When you are unfamiliar with a

A spinnerbait or surface plug can be worked on or near the surface over submerged vegetation, while a plastic worm or weedless jig can be fished deeper within.

particular lake, that is important to do. Even if you are familiar with a lake it isn't a bad idea.

Finding weeds, of course, is relatively simple, but studying them, looking over conformations and edges (the weedline) and depths is a little more involved. The objective is to find the better places to spend your fishing time, not just any stretch of weeds.

Weed density is one of the things to look for, seeking thick clumps as opposed to scattered weeds, because the former offer more cover. Clumped weeds is the easiest situation to fish. It may not be available, however, so scattered

weeds become the second choice. Look to see if weeds in a given locale grow in different stages or at different levels. Shorter weeds in moderately deep water, for example, are often preferred by such fish as walleyes than taller weeds in the same depth. Look for the weedline and its depth. An excellent situation to find, though not one as readily fished, is where the weeds are thick and the edge is close to a sharp bottom dropoff.

The most obvious, most often used, and most easily managed way to locate fish in vegetation is to work the edges. In large, fairly thick concentrations of grass, for example, many species of gamefish stick close to the outside line, most likely because they can see and ambush prey well there. This is especially true if the grass is so congested that you can't work any type of lure across the surface without it being fouled up. Milfoil beds are a prime example of this type of cover. Here, you may have to work the edges, with most strikes (from bass) occuring within a

Following pages: Some vegetation is submerged and hidden from sight, and must be found by scouting. This pike was caught from a submerged bed of cabbage weeds that was well away from shore.

foot or two of the edge. Any irregularity in the weedline, such as a protrusion, pocket, etc., may be an especially significant place to fish.

Frequently the key to unlocking the fish-catching secrets (especially with largemouth bass) in sparse grass is to fish isolated clumps, patches that are small but thick and that stand off from the main mass of vegetation (they may be within the main body as well as outside). If you find this to be the case, take care to identify and fish every likely looking isolated patch. Usually there is a lot of ground to cover in weed bed fishing, and if you find a spot that is more worthwhile than others, zero in on it and work it thoroughly.

When the vegetation is sparse and partly submerged, you won't be able to identify isolated patches such as these. However, if you are using sonar, you may be able to identify the thin and thick sections, as well as dropoffs or holes, by traveling across the area first. If the vegetation – either emergent or sumberged – is thick and has visible holes in it, start casting. Clearings in the grass are prime fishing locations, and they are easier to fish than the thick spots. Submerged grass that is at the see/no-see level is also a problem, particularly for the angler who's better off if he can watch what he's casting to. I've fished in areas where the only openings in submerged vegetation were afforded by large flat rocks, and you could only find these by hunting and pecking, watching the sonar, and dropping marker buoys, then fishing a lure (like a plastic worm or jig) on the edges of the openings.

The key to the success and enjoyment of vegetation fishing is a weed-free, or so-called weedless, presentation, and, naturally, your lure plays the lead role. There are relative degrees of weedlessness in lures, just as there are relative degrees of manipulative retrieving skills, but there is no out-of-the-box, guaranteed never-to-get-stuck fishing lure.

The plastic worm can be one of the most tangle-free lures, although it will hang up if the hook pulls through the plastic body or the sinker gets wedged. The key to using a slip sinker in vegetation is to fish the lightest one that you can toss and that will get the worm down adequately, and to also peg it with a toothpick. In grass or pad stems, or other types of vegetation, a free-sliding slip sinker pulls off the object, leaving the worm behind. You need to have the two working close together to effect a proper, natural presentation.

Worms are primarily used for bass. These fish and others may prefer something moving more

It is often very important to fish the edges of submerged grass, either by working a jig, plastic worm, or spinnerbait over the top and dropping it along the edge (presuming that you can see it), or casting to the edge and letting the lure fall straight down.

enticingly, with a flash of metal, to get a strike. The weedless spoon and pork rind trailer has justifiably been a long-time favorite of grass and pad fishermen. In moderately heavy cover it is fairly tangle-free, and its action is reasonably good when drawn into open pockets from the clustered vegetation. Another popular combination incorporates an in-line spinner, a spoon, and a skirt. There are also some good buzz baits on the market (these are fairly weed-free), some of which incorporate a buzzing blade and shaft with a spoon, or spoon-like, body. For good measure, you can also add a trailer hook to both of these arrangements. The trailer will mean more hooked fish per strike, though it also means more snagging on pad stems, grass clumps, and the like.

Spinnerbaits are a particularly effective lure when used near vegetation. When pads and grass are not too thick, as is usual in the spring or early summer, a spinnerbait is the best lure for bass and one of the best for northern pike and chain pickerel. For thicker grass and pads, a spinnerbait can be effective when worked on the edges, either fishing parallel along them or by fluttering it vertically along the breakline.

Some plugs have merit in and around vegetation, although they must be cast and retrieved judiciously. When fishing over the top of submerged grass, super-shallow-running floating/diving plugs, sonic vibrating plugs, and surface lures can be quite effective. Surface lures will also work in areas that feature openings or channels through which they can be retrieved. A crankbait might be worth using if the weeds are not thick; crankbaits are very popular in walleye fishing, for example, but in weedy environs are mostly reserved for earlier in the season. A fine time to catch these fish on plugs is when the first green weeds start to show. Jigs might also be worth a try, although they are not usually used in vegetation. A bobber-and jig combo works well on windy days in the weeds, and straight-lined jigs tipped with bait may also be

used, too, if you can keep a good feel with them.

Bait is fished in and near grass, too, of course. Shiners and worms are fished below bobbers in openings or just above submerged grass, as well as behind jigs and various bait rigs, with attention being paid to minimizing the fouling of these items in the vegetation that renders them ineffective. A bobber with a jig-leech/worm combo is a choice of walleye anglers. Fishing with large live shiners in vegetation is a specialty of many Florida guides, and they use these baits in heavily matted concentration of sawgrass, peppergrass, and hayfields, as well as fishing them around floating mats of hyacinths, where the bait can be freelined to swim well back and under this expansive cover.

When you are faced with the problem of fishing vegetation that is so thick that you could walk across it, and the edges don't produce (perhaps because they get a lot of fishing pressure), you have to deal with fishing deep within, which poses obvious boating dilemmas as well as presentation troubles, and is primarily a need of largemouth bass anglers. Sometimes there are small holes in the mass that can be readily fished, but more often than not, you wind up making your own hole and dunking your bait (worm or jig) in. There is no casting here, just reaching over a hole, dunking your bait up and down, and moving on. You may even use your rod or an oar to poke the hole. Flipping, yo-yoing, and doodlesocking are all terms used to describe the technique.

Vegetation fishing usually requires fairly stout tackle, incidentally. This is a place where you should leave the real light line and limber rod for other, more appropriate, situations, unless fishing for small species. Also, angling in vegetation often seems to be more productive in low-light situations than in bright daylight. Bright days tend to drive fish deeper and further into the vegetation, where they are harder to reach effectively. Dawn, dusk, overcast days and night offer the best fishing conditions.

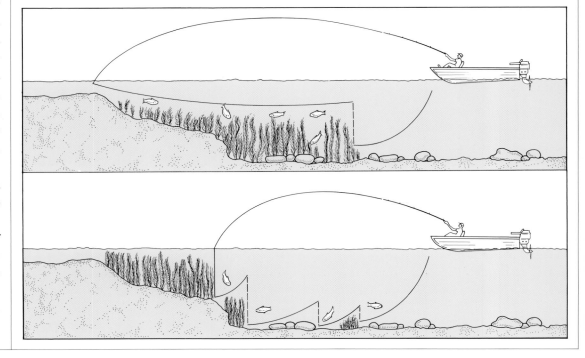

FISHING IN TIMBER

Standing timber, whether it is exposed to view and existing above the surface, or hidden from sight and at varied depths below the surface, is a prime place to catch certain warmwater species of fish. And yet, it is a bit intimidating, especially if you haven't encountered it before. Many anglers in northern environs, for example, have little or no experience with flooded timber because few large manmade impoundments exist there. They rarely encounter the flooded timber phenomenon until they venture to southern reservoirs. (Oddly enough, there are some big impoundments in Canada, especially northern Quebec, that have beaucoup flooded timber and harbor walleye and northern pike.)

The trouble with fishing in timber is that so much of it looks the same, yet there are certain locales that appeal to fish more so than others.

A lot of anglers take a pretty haphazard approach to timber, merely fishing various locales because they look good, because they've seen other people fish there, or because they have encountered some success in a particular place at a particular time, although they can't be sure why.

Fishing timber haphazardly is like mowing a lawn randomly. To assess timber fishing situations, look at the entire picture. When you do, you'll realize that not every tree is the same, that contours below visible timber vary greatly and may be a factor in fishing success, that timber follows certain conformations, and that there are a lot of subtleties to fishing timber.

Where timber sticks out of the water, there can be visible clues to good places to fish. The most conspicuous is the leading edge of the timber, which many anglers treat like a shoreline, keeping their boat out from it and casting lures to the edge or just beyond the edge and by it. In young reservoirs, where fish may be highly mobile and schools of wandering fish are likely to swim along this edge in search of bait, particularly shad, it may be good to spend a lot of time in such places, using relatively noisy, vibrating lures and covering a lot of territory. This is not as reliable in lakes where timber has stood for a long time and fish behavior is relatively stabilized, although it may be more likely for striped bass than for largemouth bass.

Almost as obvious, and for similar reasons, are timbered points. If a timbered point is being washed by wind, it could have a concentration of bait on it, so that would be a good spot to fish. Another prominent place in a stand of trees might be the edge of a clearing, which could be where an old pond existed. In many flooded timber environments, farmlands were inundated and old ponds or lakes with fish were important to early angling.

Where largemouths are the quarry, you frequently need to get into the trees and maneuver around, fishing deliberately in those areas that are just a little different. At first, of course, all flooded timber looks the same, but sit back a moment and observe and you'll see that certain things are really quite different. You should zero in on the differences.

This might be as simple a matter as finding leaning trees rather than perpendicular ones. Leaning trees offer more shade and are more conducive to hiding than straight ones.

It might mean looking for the largest, widest trees, again for shade, but also because of the underwater protection they might afford. Large multi-limbed trees eventually lose their limbs, which usually fall around the base of the tree. If enough fall and get stuck on lower below-water limbs, they form a canopy, which is a great hiding place.

Watch for different species of trees, too. Pines amongst hardwood usually signal a change in bottom depth. Pines usually grow on higher ground, such as a ridge; on the water this would be like a hump, and that might be the place to fish. Tight clumps of smaller trees can provide protection and may be the ticket as well. A clump of trees on the edge of a creek channel is a particularly good spot. Some channels through timber are fairly obvious, and can visually be followed through the trees, but in some flooded timber it is easy to lose the channel visually, in part because trees have fallen or are leaning or have disintegrated at the water line. That is

when sonar equipment becomes important.

Bottom contours and changes in underwater terrain may be more important than the trees themselves. Trees, after all, are just objects that provide some measure of cover. How they relate to the hydrography is another matter.

A channel is one of the most important terrain features to look for, with special emphasis on the outside bends, where it comes near a point or shore, and especially where two channels meet.

Even where you aren't searching for channels, an old roadbed, a dropoff, and other features are worth looking for, but in the simplest aspect, it can be beneficial just checking the depth. I've been in flooded timber where trees were 40 feet over my head and the water was 40 feet deep under the boat, and where you might not have realized this without sonar and would have wasted time or chosen the wrong type of lure.

Sonar is absolutely invaluable for fishing completely submerged timber, where you seldom have visual clues to depth or tree con-

The edges of timber, boat lanes, channels, and locales with sharp drops are places to focus fishing efforts.

formations. In deep, submerged timber, fish are usually suspended, sometimes at the treetops and sometimes among the branches. To prevent fishing haphazardly you have to know where you are and where your lure is.

Good sonar should be able to show you some fish in the trees, although such interpretation becomes tricky. A paper graph recorder does this better than any other sonar. Some liquid crystal recorders will show a fish in the trees, too, but most of the time you can hardly tell a fish from a limb unless it moves. The thicker the trees the more this is true. Some sonar won't read past the uppermost thick limb, so you can't see below it, but others will get past the upper signals and go to the depths.

If you can see fish suspended in the tree tops, you may want to troll a plug just over the tops (if they come close enough to the surface to allow this), or use a downrigger. Some folks will recoil at the suggestion of using a downrigger where trees exist, because of the obvious possibility (even likelihood) of getting the weight hung in the trees.

I've successfully used downriggers at submerged treetop level, but it is a two-man team operation. On Arkansas' Lake Ouachita, for example, friends and I have trolled jigs behind downrigger weights at submerged treetop level (20 to 40 feet). We watch the sonar constantly and raise or lower the downrigger weight quickly as needed. We don't try to run the weight or lure through the trees, although we have had skirmishes with them, but close enough to get the attention of some large stripers that lay in waiting.

You can vertically jig here, too, and where there are a number of fish in an area in the trees, or where you can't see fish on sonar but suspect they are present, this may be the best tactic. Some people recoil at this suggestion, too. Jigging in trees? You'll get hung up all the time and lose lots of lures. Well, you will get hung up some times and you will lose a few lures, but you will also catch fish you wouldn't get otherwise and it can be really exciting.

The way to do this is to use a fairly heavy lead jig or preferably a jigging spoon. Spoons have treble hooks whereas jigs have a single hook. Single hooks get hung up less so you might try replacing trebles with singles. Spoons have an O-ring between the body and the hook, and this allows for a bit of swiveling, which facilitates de-snagging. In any event, lower the lure through the limbs, retrieve by slowly jigging it; when it hits a limb, drop it down and then bring it back up over the limb. Keep jigging. As long as you haven't buried the hook it will usually come free when the weight of the lure falls back on it. When it gets wedged in a crotch, however, you may not get it free.

This tactic is most effective when you use an electric motor for positioning (or are tied to a tree), and where there is no breeze. You have to be able to jig vertically, and when you move off the vertical line, you greatly increase the chance of hanging the jig up. Doing this jigging gently, and using heavy line with a fairly stiff-tipped rod, can bring a lot of excitement in the tree tops with striped bass, hybrid stripers, or largemouths. Of course, you need to be able to muscle a fish out of the branches and limbs quickly.

Most of the angling done in trees is by casting, however, especially for largemouth bass and active schooling fish. Surface lures, when appro-

Flipping with jigs or plastic worms for largemouth bass is a prime tactic around standing timber or fallen trees.

priate, are especially productive. Because the water is usually stained or turbid in flooded timber, noise and action are important, so walking stick baits (like a Zara Spook), poppers, and buzz baits are good choices.

A rattling, vibrating crankbait is also a good lure choice, worked just below the surface. So is a spinnerbait. Floating-diving crankbaits have merit at times as well, although there's a knack to working these just right; don't set the hook when you tick a limb, and let the plug float up to get over obstructions.

For conventional casting as well as flipping, a plastic worm (use a pegged slip sinker) is a prime lure for largemouths in timber, as is a weedguard-protected jig with rubber tentacles and pork chunk. The latter is used for flipping in shallow to mid-depth water.

One thing about conventional casting in the trees is certain: you'll fine-tune your casting abilities. Spend enough time in the flooded timber and your accuracy will be sharp. On a parting, practical note, exercise some common-sense precaution while fishing in flooded trees. Watch where you put your hands, for example; ants, bees, snakes, tarantulas, and other critters may be about. Tilt your outboard up when in use and run only at low-throttle speed. When standing, be aware of bumping into trees and be careful not to fall out of your boat.

FISHING IN THE WIND

No matter what direction it comes from, wind is one of nature's phenomena that can be a blessing or a curse to anglers, although usually more of the latter. When there's no wind you usually wish for a light chop on the surface to make it easier to dupe fish. Yet when there's too much wind, boat handling and lure presentation can be so difficult that fishing may be impaired. Wind can direct a cast fly into your hat or your ear. It makes you throw more forcefully with a baitcasting reel, increasing the chance of backlash. It may cause you to troll too fast or too slow, depending on whether you're headed with it or against it. When the temperature is low, wind makes a fisherman cold and often uncomfortable, rendering him less able to fish properly.

Have you ever been anchored in a river, fishing downcurrent, when a south wind pushed your boat up above the anchor position? Have you ever been forced off the water because the wind blew so hard it was extremely uncom-

The wind-driven shoreline is often a good bet to angle, especially in large lakes, as baitfish get pinned against it, which attracts predators.

fortable, or worse, unsafe, to fish? Have you ever been angling a prime locale when the wind blew you by so fast you couldn't even properly fish out one cast? Those who have done a lot of fishing have been through all this, and more.

Should you get out of the wind or fight it? If the wind is a precursor to a front, changing several days worth of stable weather, it may signal the beginning of fish activity that you don't want to miss because that period before a new frontal system is often a good angling time.

In some places, you have no such choice. In winding or island-studded bodies of water, you often do. However, while getting in the lee may allow you to fish comfortably, you may not be very successful there or you may have to pursue a species of fish that you were not already after.

The wind-whipped shore may be, and often is, the place to be fishing. In large bodies of water, like the Great Lakes, several days worth of wind turns the temperature around, bringing cold water where there had been warm. This may bring trout and salmon in and you simply must fish the wave-beaten water.

Small fish and baitfish can be greatly disturbed by hard-driving winds, becoming

disoriented or finding it very difficult to move, sometimes even being pinned against wind-driven shores. Wind pushes minute organisms into the windward shore, which attracts small fish and in turn larger fish. Oxygen is enhanced on windward shores because of the continued wave-beating. Fish may be facing out toward deep water here and a controlled drift or troll is a good idea.

Fishing along those shores, or around the sides of wind-driven islands or shoals, may also be a good move. Baitfish may try to move out to deeper water to escape the turbulence, and predators sense this and move from deeper water to shallows to capture their prey. Casting crankbaits and jigs into the shallows and retrieving them outward may be the ticket, provided you can hold boat position. Keeping position is often hard, and sometimes impossible.

There will be times when you can't make any headway into the wind or are constantly being blown about, and fishing becomes a hardship. Recently while fishing for smallmouth bass, a cold front was followed by clear skies amd high winds, and the angling toughened. The wave-washed fish stopped hitting plugs and spinners and it seemed that a slowly worked jig was the answer, but that was frustrating to fish. You need to watch your line and be able to control a jig when you're trying to finesse it along bottom, and when the wind doesn't let you make as many casts as you'd like in a given spot, or doesn't let you fish a jig very far or hampers your ability to detect a strike, you can feel like your

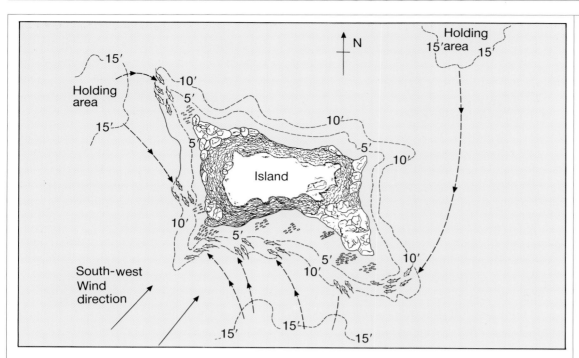

Gamefish will move into the windward side of a shore or island, as depicted here, because small baitfish are attracted to that spot or are pinned there.

efforts are wasted. Working into the wind, struggling to maintain boat position, using light line to sink a jig quickly, using a slightly heavier jig than I would have fished otherwise, and making shorter casts were some of the altered tactics I took that helped catch fish.

Fishing can be productive in the wind, although casting and retrieving are difficult and anglers find it hard to adjust.

There are a lot of anglers who are ready to give up fishing when they see that it's windy or when the wind picks up while they are out on the water. That's too bad. Perhaps they just don't like having to work a little harder for their catch. A lot of casting and trolling is done by people who want to, or must, fish, wind notwithstanding, and they learn to deal with the conditions as they exist, and as they change.

Trolling is one activity that can be done quite well in the wind if your boat is suitable, but you have to be mindful of several factors in order to make an effective trolling presentation. Probably the most important of these is the affect of the wind on speed.

A boat moving with a motor at a constant 500 engine rpms, for example, will go much faster with the wind than when headed into the wind. Many times fish are caught only when the boat is headed in one direction; this is because the lures being used aren't traveling at a suitable speed in the opposite direction (and don't have the proper action). You really have to pay attention to speed (using a trolling speed indicator rather than tachometer is probably the best way; checking lures beside the boat to see that they have the same action in both directions is another). Going into the wind at a moderate speed may bring lures deeper or shallower, depending on the lure, so depth attainment, rather than speed, can be the main factor.

The worst thing you can do is troll blindly in one direction, then turn around and head blindly in the other direction, not knowing much about either the real speed or the depth your lures are working at. Maintaining a course is another matter that trolling anglers don't anticipate a problem with, but which is affected by wind speed and direction. To counter the tendency of a quartering wind to push a boat forward and away, for example, you must get the boat slightly sideways to the wind. This can be a difficult position to steadily maintain.

This is why backtrolling is popular with walleye anglers. By using some type of sonar unit a backtroller can maintain position along specific depths, nearly hover over selected spots, and maneuver his boat to use whatever wind direction is present to position the boat

in such a way as to keep a following bait in the proper place, and worked very slowly.

Casting is an altogether different story than trolling. Depending on what you are tossing to the fish, the act of casting itself is difficult in a brisk wind and accuracy is often sacrificed. You may have to cast further upwind or cast low and sidearm to be more accurate, or use a heavier lure, or cast only with or quartering into the wind instead of directly into it.

High winds impact on just about every form of cast-and-retrieve angling, primarily because boat control and lure presentation are made much more difficult the greater the velocity of the wind. Wind particularly affects jig and plastic worm fishing, which are games of feel and depth attainment. With a bow in your line you don't have the sensitivity you need, and

often your lure spends far too little time in the places it should be.

Anchoring is one way to deal with the wind for casting, but few anglers who are accustomed to positioning with an electric motor and casting to cover a good deal of water are satisfied with repeated anchoring and re-anchoring. Electric motors are certainly very helpful for fishing in the wind and maintaining position, provided the motor is up to moving your particular boat (the more weight the harder) and the battery has enough juice. An electric motor's energy reserves are depleted more quickly in brisk wind – the motor is run more often and at higher speeds. With a bow-mounted motor it may be necessary to have a long shaft to keep the motor in the water as the bow lurches up and down.

A note on safety when dealing with wind is

in order here, as sometimes coping is not terribly prudent. For example, when there are whitecaps on the water, the wind is whistling, and the waves on a lake are moving with such swiftness that they look like river rapids, give the outing serious thought.

Your first concern when fishing in heavy wind – especially if the water is cold, the waves are high, your boat is small or tipsy or flat-hulled, or you have a far distance to go – should be safety. You're a fool if you don't put on and zip up a proper-fitting personal flotation device (PFD) that will keep your fully clothed body afloat and your head upright. Don't use a cushion or waist-worn foam skier's float. There is no alternative, and no excuse.

When the wind and weather is rough you have to consider whether you, and the boat you expect to use, are up to fishing. On the personal level, taking a pounding by running through heavy waves is hard on the back and neck, particularly for older anglers. And while the fish may be biting like crazy, that's of small comfort to someone who is vomiting because they've lost sight of shore, have sucked in engine fumes from a tailwind, or just have a sensitive inner ear.

But the boat's another story. You have to realistically assess what your boat can handle, going forth only if you're completely sure and prepared, or turning back when good sense demands. Of course, going out to fish under severe wind is much different than being on the water and angling when conditions change from calm to frothy. Too many anglers push their luck each year, not noticing shifts in wind speed or direction, or thinking they can run themselves out of trouble. Sometime they pay for it. Most of us, myself included, are guilty of not looking enough to the horizon for squalls and thunderstorms. That's one reason why on large lakes and rivers it's good to have a VHF radio or handheld weather radio to keep you informed of weather patterns, changes, and potential problems if you're in a locale where these devices function.

If the wind has picked up enough to put whitecaps on the water or, worse, a trail of foam, beware. It's already late, especially on large shallow lakes, which are among the most dangerous bodies of water because big waves build up quickly there. So are lakes with many reefs and shoals. Small boaters get caught in troughs, or get pushed up into shallows or shoals or boulders and bang up the outboard's lower unit or the boat hull, maybe even causing capsizing (especially watch out in a canoe). You have to recognize the dangers that lie ahead and be smart enough to avoid them.

A light wind, as seen here, is usually good for fishing, but when the wind picks up, anglers in boats should heed it, especially when fishing from small craft or on large bodies of water.

SPECIAL FACTORS

There are some elements of sportfishing that are intuitive by nature, things that many successful anglers do routinely, and which make them successful yet also separate them from those who are merely adept. Yet every angler can improve himself if he desires to do so. There are many factors that contribute to fishing success, some of which are totally unrelated to the equipment owned or used. Much of this is a bit intangible, having to do with the use of your brain in assessing situations or in accumulating some savvy as the result of considerable experience. These special factors are often not touched upon in angling literature, but they are worthy of attention.

OBSERVATION

A lot of anglers don't notice the little things that sometimes make a big difference in sportfishing. They don't see fish swirl after a lure. They don't see that quick moment when a fish spooks a bunch of bait and gives his presence away. They don't detect a strike until they feel the hard tug of a fish, and then it may be too late to properly set the hook. They don't notice things about the water that attract fish or stimulate activity.

Often this is a matter of not being observant or of not knowing what some signs may mean. Observation is an important factor in fishing success. But many people, especially those who do not have the opportunity to fish frequently, don't notice things that might make their fishing better. I don't mean noticing stream trout rising to the surface to take flies, or gamefish chasing schools of bait with birds working over them. Those are as obvious as rainfall and if you don't notice such matters you really have problems.

It is understandable, however, for many people to miss the subtle signs that would be helpful in catching fish. Working in an office environment or indoor job makes the average person less aware of natural phenomena, so when he goes fishing for the first time in a few weeks, or perhaps even longer, he has to get acclimatized to the outdoor world. It takes some folks longer than others to do this.

Many an angler, including this writer after a bit of a layoff, has gone fishing with a guide or astute nonprofessional angler and felt inadequate in certain aspects of the sport, especially failing to spot actual fish, or fish movements, and various activity as quickly as the other person or even after having it pointed out.

To some extent the power of on-the-water angling observation is a function of frequent fishing, but it is also a function of being in the right frame of mind and applying yourself to finding fish and thinking about what you are doing while you are fishing. This is especially so when the action is not fast and easy. For some anglers it also happens because they have various gadgets, such as sonar and temperature gauges, which they rely on a bit too heavily, forgetting that there are other aspects to fishing success besides what information is gleaned from instrumentation. Bass fishermen may be particularly vulnerable in this regard. I have seen more than one instance in which an angler with the latest in boating and fishing paraphernalia failed to take note of little signs that others (both with and without such equipment) spotted and used to help them catch fish.

Watching the water, for example, is very important in many ways and when pursuing many species of fish. This includes visibly watching for reefs, rips, near-surface vegetation,

---

Observation is one of the intangible factors in fishing that sometimes leads to productivity.

Fish feeding on a surface hatch are readily observed by stream anglers, although the type of fly they are taking may require a closer look.

current flows, shade, and water color.

Water color is an especially good example. The clarity of the water is sometimes very important to fish movement and/or location as well as to lure selection. If the water always looks the same to you in all places, you may not be looking closely enough at it.

Some species of fish are more likely to be in clear water (or the clearest possible) or are more prone to strike lures in clear water (because they can locate them better) and it would behoove a fisherman to look for such. The places where clear and turbid water mix—runoffs, creek mouths, tidal influxes, wind-affected edges, and so forth—and the immediate environs around them, are sometimes the best locales to fish.

In certain instances, where dirty water enters a clearer body of water, such as from a creek, the dirty water is carrying nutrients or small forage that attracts bait which in turn attracts predators. Another good place to put a lure is where there is a lot of baitfish (or perhaps to not put it if there is none). When fishing for some species of fish at certain times of the year, especially in waters that are unfamiliar to me, it is disconcerting if there is little or no sign of bait. That doesn't mean you won't catch fish, but if there is bait to be seen flitting on or near the surface or in the shallows, that will often direct you to the kinds of places to fish.

Weeds, for example, are a great place to find bait. Many species of fish orient toward weeds because they provide cover and protection for bait. If you are on an unfamiliar body of water

In clear shallow water, some fish are readily observed; these stream salmon can now be approached carefully and very deliberately.

and would be expecting to find certain fish (walleye and bass in particular) in or around vegetation, but you fail to notice any bait there, you should seriously consider looking in other types of habitat. The person who doesn't pick up on this little point might fish for too long in the weeds, thinking that perhaps the fish must be there or that they will "turn on" sooner or later.

When the water is calm, a fisherman can spot bait or baitfish movement without much trouble if he is being attentive. When the water is roiled by wind and waves, it is much more difficult to make visual observations. The presence of some species of birds, incidentally, such as a shorebird like heron, can indicate an abundance of bait or small fish in an area.

When bait are schooled and being pushed aggressively by predators it is quite easy to spot the action. Sometimes just one fish is pursuing a single prey or a few fish and the action is less obvious and perhaps more likely to be missed.

Probably every angler has noticed a fish swirl and create a commotion when it captured or chased some type of prey in either open water or the shallows. I wish I had a dollar for every time I had thrown a lure to a swirl, boil, splash, wake, or other type of water disturbance that indicated fish presence. It is the minority of times when that activity has resulted in a strike and hookup. In some cases, it wasn't even a game fish that caused the activity.

Nevertheless, fish that are stalking shallow water, that spook bait, that capture some prey item on or near the surface, usually give away their presence and often are aggressive fish which at that particular moment are highly susceptible to capture. If you look for the signs of the presence of such fish, you will probably be disappointed, but if you keep your eyes open and (just as importantly) listen while fishing, you will become aware of gamefish movement. This is especially true when casting and when fishing for most warmwater species of fish.

It is also true when fishing in coldwater streams. Both Atlantic and Pacific salmon, for example, will roll occasionally on or near the surface, sometimes very subtly, and if you are unfamiliar with the water that you are fishing, this movement, though unrelated to feeding activity, will give you an indication of a fish lie and point you toward an appropriate place to direct your efforts. Noticing a fish that jumps or rolls is obvious to many, but not to all, especially when there is merely a rise on the surface that can be confused with the swirl of current.

Noticing bait that is in an agitated state is really a subtlety that few master. A friend recently described such phenomena as being "nervous water", which is quite accurate although a tad hard to convey. Nervous water is a surface patch, usually just a few yards across, where there is some slight rippling on the surface, distinctly different from that caused

by current or light breezes. It happens when a pod of small baitfish is balled up and flitting about, neither feeding nor fleeing, but disturbed—usually because something is lurking nearby that means to maraud them shortly. If you see this, work the area hard, keeping a lure handy that might imitate a small fish that is injured or struggling.

On some occasions it happens that you are able to see certain fish in the water that are not actually in the process of chasing bait, but which may be foraging below the surface, or merely taking a feeding or resting position. Spotting such fish, which occurs in shallow water, is certainly helpful for making the best presentation in the proper locale.

When trying to spot shallow-water fish, look not at the surface but below the surface and at the bottom. Look for something that stands out as being different, and whose movement contrasts with some bottom locales enough for you to detect it. When you see the wake of a moving fish, note that the forward edge of the wake is behind the fish and take this into account when making a cast that is intended to intercept it.

Sometimes it's important to be able to see fish before you cast to them because you have to be able to approach them without alarming them. Other times it's important to see certain objects that might be harboring fish. Polarized sunglasses are a big help here; those with wraparound side-view protection are best. A cap with a wide bill and dark underside is also useful.

One of the easiest and best ways to have more success through being observant is to watch your lures when you retrieve them, especially as they near the boat. Some freshwater fish, notably bass, pike, pickerel, and muskellunge, are prone

Largemouth bass are one species that can often be caught with second efforts; a plastic worm, which took this fish, is an excellent lure for this.

to swirl after shallow-running or surface lures and create a sizable boil in the water after they miss the lure in an apparent attempt to stun it. Fishermen who aren't watching closely don't see the boil and cast elsewhere, though they might have been able to catch that particular fish or at least note its location for a later visit.

A lot of anglers just don't watch their lures all the way through a retrieve. I've seen fish strike and miss a companion's lure while he missed that behavior entirely. Some anglers become lackadaisical and inattentive, especially when the action isn't fast, and they often fail to notice something like this that might be instrumental in helping them be successful. However, it is precisely at the slower fishing times when taking note of things going on can make the day.

Another example of this would be noticing what your fishing companion is doing differently when he is catching fish and you aren't. Many times one fisherman in a boat has much better success than his companion although both are using the same lures and seem to be fishing in identical ways. But maybe the retrieve of one is a tad different (slower or faster), maybe he is letting his bait get deeper, maybe his line is a bit lighter and thus less alarming to fish, maybe he watches his line and rod tip more closely and can detect subtle pickups (worms and jigs especially) better. You should observe what differences exist in technique or tackle in order to emulate his success.

SECOND EFFORTS/CHANCES

Many anglers give up too easily on catching fish in difficult circumstances or where a little more effort or re-visits will pay off. Repeated and second attempts can catch fish, and the person who is prepared for such — whether he is the same angler or a companion — may just be able

Watching your line and lure during the retrieve may help you observe fish that strike but miss your offering, allowing you to try another lure or to re-visit that locale awhile later.

to catch fish he would not otherwise.

Most of the time, a second cast to a good spot, or to a fish that has struck and missed, or to a fish that has shown interest, isn't productive — with the same lure. That's the rub. Make another cast with a different lure, while the fish is still hot, and your odds are greatly improved.

Some of the best fish for second-chance opportunities are those that are primarily sought by casting and which are fairly aggressive. Bass and pike are premier examples. Largemouth bass often strike and miss a lure, especially when they come out of heavy cover, when they strike a noisy surface lure, or when the water is turbid. With bass that miss a lure, there is a difference between fish that have struck to kill, and those that are sending a warning or that make a half-hearted attempt simply because there is an opportunity. The latter especially happens in the spring when the water is cold and bass swipe at prey to stun it; you'll find many of these fish lightly impaled on one barb or a rear hook when multi-hooked lures are used. These fish are harder to coax into striking a second lure, and are more likely to need teasing. Largemouths in warmer water, however, are serious eaters and are often pugnacious enough to clobber a lure that is different than one they have just missed.

A plastic worm is the best second-chance lure for largemouth bass, perhaps because it is an unobtrusive, natural-moving type of bait. If a largemouth has just missed a lure that vibrates or makes some other commotion, it is likely still hungry enough to see the sudden appearance of a plastic worm as a bonafide meal. The best tactic is to go immediately to a plastic worm for a second-chance lure, if one is handy. If a bass misses a crankbait or spinnerbait in shallow water, or around cover, try throwing a surface lure out as a second-chance offering; a stick bait that can be walked slowly and tantalizingly is the best choice. When a largemouth bass misses a worm or jig, however, not much else is effective at second chances, although another color, size, or style of worm or jig is worth trying.

Much of the same is true with smallmouth bass as well. A jig, a spinner, or a spinnerbait is a good possibility after they miss a surface lure, with a jig best after a smallmouth misses other types of lures.

Northern pike perhaps offer more opportunity for second chances than any other freshwater fish. After having struck and missed a lure they will frequently follow or strike that same lure on a follow-up cast. This is especially true in lightly fished waters and in remote Canadian locales. Pickerel, which are a smaller cousin of pike, behave exactly the same way. This is partly

Moving to a new locale, or switching lures, or trying alternative tactics are all changes that should be made when fishing is slow or when standard tactics fail.

a matter of aggression, partly curiosity.

You are more likely to get pike to take a second offering than any other fish, and sometimes it doesn't matter what that second offering is. This is especially true with smaller fish. But with larger pike, especially trophy-sized individuals, it is best to go to an altogether different style of lure for a second attempt. Plugs, especially large minnow-styled versions, make great second-chance pike lures because of their realistic appearance and because they float and can be worked in a tantalizing manner, via stop-go or jiggle-jerk routines, acting much like a wounded or struggling fish. However, when a fish misses or follows a minnow plug, it may be best to toss something else back.

Another important element of making good on second chances is observation. The fisherman who watches the water where his lure is being retrieved will occasionally see a fish follow (pike, musky and pickerel); see a boil on the water's surface made by a fish that has swiped at a lure and missed it (stripers, largemouth and smallmouth bass, white bass, and sometimes trout); and see a fish make a pass at a lure (pike and largemouth bass). If you aren't

watching – looking on the horizon, watching something on shore, turning toward your fishing partner – you may miss an important clue. A lot of anglers do miss such clues; sometimes an observant companion takes note but usually neither of them notices and a potential opportunity is missed.

You have to meld attentiveness into your angling activities. Watch the fishing line where it enters the water; watch a lure during the full course of a retrieve; and be alert to feeling a sudden tick or bump that may signify a strike. The latter can be confused with the lure striking an object or behaving differently because it picked up a small piece of debris, but often it is because an unseen fish swiped at a lure.

Hooking a fish momentarily, incidentally, is not the same as having one strike and miss insofar as second chances are concerned. The percentage of fish that strike a lure, are momentarily hooked and then get off, and yet which come back to strike the same or a different lure, is very low. It may happen a little more frequently with pike or pickerel, in spawning situations, or with frenzied schooling fish, but creatures that feel the sting of a hook point, even

momentarily, are usually not as vulnerable to a second chance offering.

Certainly some fish can be teased or aggravated into striking, which enters the realm of chances-ad-infinitum, and situations exist where repeated attempts are legitimately part of the game. Sometimes it does take more than one repeat cast or a visit with a different lure to coax a fish into striking. The stream trout fisherman frequently experiences this when using flies or hardware, in part because it is necessary to make an exact presentation to bring an offering to the feeding lane of a fish, and in part because it is necessary to change lure or fly until finding what best represents the natural food that the fish are taking or looks and acts naturally under the conditions. When active stream fish are spooked and put down, they usually should be rested and re-visited at a later moment, with the same or similar offering.

But other circumstances exist in which there is a fine line between aggravating a fish and pursuing sporting-like second chances. Fish that are spawning and which can be spotted, such as bass on a nest or steelhead and salmon on a redd, may be caught by repeated efforts when an angler puts a lure or bait in front of them because the fish become irritated. Pursuing and catching fish in such a way may be effective and legal, but it can hardly be a prideful accomplishment. In such a circumstance, it seems reasonable to make a couple of presentations to see if a fish is interested, and then leave it alone. Where big fish are concerned, this is hard to do, of course.

In the majority of circumstances in freshwater fishing, you don't have an opportunity to sit on top of a fish and irritate it, so your encounters are brief. Making an attempt to get them to strike a second-chance offering is fair.

Keep in mind that not all second chances occur immediately after the initial encounter.

It may be most effective to return to places where you have previously had success, and/or where you have seen/moved/or had strikes from fish. This is a particularly worthwhile tidbit to remember when angling is tough, when fish are very scattered, and when large fish are located. Where big fish are concerned it is wise to note as precisely as possible where you saw the fish you didn't catch on either a first or second attempt. An hour later, or that afternoon, or the following day, you can return to that same spot, having the advantage of knowing how to best approach it.

CHANGES

Making a change – especially knowing when to make a change – is one of the real tricks to fishing success. This is true in fly fishing for stream trout, casting for bass in a lake, and in nearly all aspects of angling.

Some changes, like moving to a new place on a given body of water, seem obvious. Other changes, like lengthening a downrigger trolling line a few feet, are subtle. Changes involve places, techniques, and tackle, but they are often at the core of fishing success. The ability to make the right change to adapt to particular fishing circumstances is one that too-few anglers possess. It especially proves helpful when fishing is tough.

One of the reasons why people don't make changes is that they become complacent. They develop pet lures, favorite holes, or specialized techniques, and they either stay too long with those things when they aren't producing, or they are uncomfortable about breaking new ground and doing something that is out of their ordi-

Many anglers keep more than one rod, equipped with alternative lures, ready to be able to use different lures as situations dictate.

Catching two fish at a time as these anglers have done usually means the action is pretty good, but using systems to fish more than one lure at a time is what may turn the trick.

nary routine. Even when the fish don't respond, these anglers continue doing the same thing; they either hope that the fish will turn on and be receptive to the old tactic again, or they try to force-feed them. This stick-to-itness can be a self-perpetuating problem, and an angler who isn't well rounded will miss some very good fishing as a result.

Unfortunately, there are no commandments for when to change or what changes to make. Good anglers, regardless of the species they pursue, often do this intuitively. There is no substitute for experience in this regard, because the fisherman who has done a lot of varied angling under a wide set of circumstances can recognize conditions that he has successfully dealt

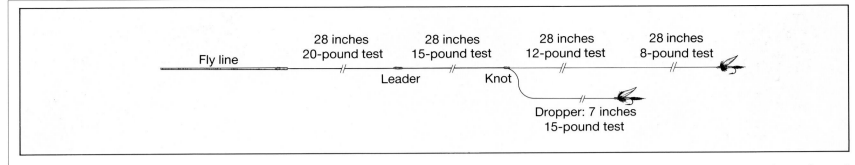

Although you can simply use a dropper loop knot to tie a second fly on one leader, some anglers prefer to leave a long length of line from a barrel knot on their leader, and attach the dropper fly to that.

with before, and be able to adjust better when faced with them anew.

Because there are so many variables that affect fishing success, it can be hard to develop confidence in different lures/techniques, etc., which is why it's a good idea to do some experimenting when the fishing is very good. That's how you can learn a lot. Sometimes when the catching is good in one locale, the fish suddenly shut down. Perhaps they get used to seeing a certain lure. Sometimes changing to a different color of the same lure, or simply to a different type of lure, will bring about action once again. But changing when the action is hot is one way to learn a little more about what to expect out of your lures and what to do under given circumstances, so that on another occasion, when you sense a need to change, you'll have some idea what to do.

The ability to make a change, of course, especially where lures are concerned, often makes change happen. Some casting anglers, for example, keep several rods ready so they can quickly pick up a different lure than they had been using and cast to a spot with something else or with a lure that may be more appropriate for that location. Different places call for different lures, and sometimes you go by a place while changing lures and don't get a chance to cast at it unless it's easy and you're ready.

You can facilitate some lure changing by employing a good quality snap. And you can avoid wasting time rummaging around in a tackle box looking for the right lure to try by having a few likely lures in holders or lying along the side of the boat (fly fishermen often keep favorite flies handy on their vest pocket.

Another reason to have alternate lures ready, and to use more than one lure in a given place, is obvious: the lure you are using at the time you go by a likely fish-holding locale may not be the one the fish want at that time. By making casts with several different lures, you are simply being a more thorough angler. That takes a little more time than using one lure and then leaving, so it means that you have to spend your fishing time wisely by concentrating on good locations.

Big-water trollers who fish out of large boats

and are able to run many lines simultaneously have a clear advantage over other anglers because when they are hunting for fish in open water they can try different lures, trolling line lengths, and colors all at once. This is like building a house yourself or building it with a crew of four; you can do it both ways but one gets the job done quicker. When such trollers have success they can fish more of the same type or color of lure and be still more effective. Thus, they are able to narrow the many angling variables down much more quickly than other small-boat anglers or casters.

And there are plenty of variables that affect angling: lake conditions, water temperature, water color, water level, type of habitat, disposition of fish, time of year, fishing pressure, current, tides, and so forth. That's why it's tough to say with absolute certainty that one thing alone contributes to fishing success on a given day. As a result, there can be a lot of changes to make in all kinds of fishing.

Maybe on a given day you don't need to change place or lure. Maybe you have the right lure but your line is too heavy and the lure isn't getting as deep as it needs to or doesn't have the best action or you can't cast it as far as necessary. You might need to change to a lighter strength line. Maybe while fishing you have several strikes, but don't hook the fish, or you see several fish that swirl after the lure but don't take it. That's an indication that the fish are not overly aggressive and you need to fish slower and use a trailer hook. Maybe you're trolling and you see fish on your sonar that come up as if they are looking at your lures but they don't strike. That's a good time to change boat speed, increasing or decreasing it to make the lures behave differently. This tactic often triggers a

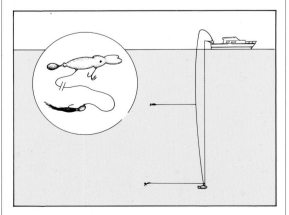

Trailing a jig off a diving plug is a popular two-lure rig; fishing a slider while downrigger trolling is another.

strike. Things that you do to alter the working of your lures, whether trolling or casting, are changes that may bring success.

DOUBLING UP

One of the best thrills in freshwater fishing occurs when you get a doubleheader; a doubleheader could be when two anglers in a boat both catch a fish at the same time, or when one angler catches two fish at the same time, either on one lure (fairly rare) or on two lures fished on one line. The purpose of fishing two lures on one line, however, is usually not to get two fish (although that happens often in striped bass and white bass fishing), but to double up on your chances of catching a single fish. Fishing an extra lure on a single line is sometimes a very good tactic. It's the "surf 'n' turf" combo of angling, and it has applications in many kinds of fishing. Multi-lure rigs are useful in trolling, jigging, fly fishing, still-fishing, or casting for everything from trout to crappies, white bass, stripers, landlocked salmon, and many others.

When trolling, it's possible to fish two rods (and lures) on one downrigger, in a process called stacking. But an alternative is to fish two lures on one line on a downrigger. The second lure is called a slider, or stinger. It lets you fish more than one lure on one downrigger without having to use two rods, which is especially useful if you are alone in the boat and/or are limited to the number of rods per fishermen that can be used (in most Canadian locales, you can only fish with one rod per angler; in most U. S. waters it is two rods per angler).

To rig a slider, tie a snap swivel to one end of a 3- to 5-foot length of line, then attach that to a fishing line already connected to a downrigger release below the boat. Carefully toss the lure into the water behind the main fishing line, and watch to see that it swims properly. The slider rig will drift out of sight, ultimately stopping well above the lower release, at a point where the main fishing line is bowed most sharply in the water. When a fish strikes the the slider, it pulls back on the main fishing line, popping the release and freeing the line from the downrigger weight. The slider then runs down the main fishing line and stops at the

Right: Using two lures via a three-way swivel, this angler has caught two striped bass while trolling.

Changing lure retrieval techniques, especially speeding up or slowing down a lure, may be the factor that triggers a strike.

lower snap swivel or lure. The precise running depth of the slider is unknown (a good guess is half the depth of the downrigger weight). The result is that you have a second lure being fished on one line and one downrigger.

Slider rigs probably are of little value when the lower lure is fished less than 20 feet down, since the slider may drop only 8 feet or less, and there may be little reason to expect to catch fish on such a short line so close to the boat. Therefore, the deeper the water, the more practical this tactic becomes.

When using a slider, you'll lose some of the fish that hit it because the hook doesn't.get very well set on the strike. On the other hand, this setup lets you put out a different type and color of lure in tandem with the one on the main line. If the slider lure draws a strike or catches a fish, it may point you toward changing the type or color of the other lure or lures being trolled, or to change the depth at which you are trolling.

Another way to accomplish the same thing is to use a device that connects the slider to your fishing line at a precise spot. There are only a couple of these being made, but they have the advantage of being set at whatever level you choose by locking onto the main fishing line but releasing and sliding to the end of the line when a fish strikes.

For fly fishermen, this mixed-doubles sort of tactic is an old trick, though it is not used that often these days. Dropper flies, tied to the main leader, are used in nymph, wet fly, and streamer fishing. A dropper can be affixed to the leader simply by leaving a few inches of overlap hanging down from the Blood or Uni knot used to connect different strengths of leader material. Tie a dropper fly to the protruding line and the main fly to the end of the leader.

Tying on two flies of the same type but in differing patterns is perhaps the best way to use the dropper technique. You can, however, mix fly types by using a streamer and a wet fly, or a nymph and a wet, or you can use a fly on a dropper head of a lure, particularly a small spinner.Instead of using the dropper technique, you can fish two flies, particularly streamers, on the same leader by tying a trailer fly directly to the bend in the hook of the main fly via a short leader. Many people prefer the dropper method to this, but it is possible that tandem-hooked streamer flies, which are a favorite of landlocked salmon fishermen in the Northeast, might have gotten their start as an offshoot of such rigging.

Incidentally, the use of a trailer, or stinger, hook by bass and pike anglers when fishing with spinnerbaits, buzz baits, in-line spinners, and weedless spoons is similar in principle, although the purpose of the extra hook is more to impale short-striking fish than to entice them to strike. Placing a stinger hook in such lure garnishes as soft plastic curl-tails or pork strips can

also be very worthwhile.

Some anglers use a castable multi-lure setup for the same reasons that fly fishermen use droppers or trollers use sliders: to double the attraction to fish. The prime way to set up such a double is with a three-way swivel. These swivels are primarily used for drift fishing with some type of bait, but they work well for putting out two lures at the same time. A diving plug on a relatively short leader is good for the lower line, while the other one (which rides higher) can sport a light spinner, spoon, or jig on a slightly longer leader.

This can be cast by careful anglers, although some tangling will occur, but it is probably more efficient as a trolling or drift-and-slow-retrieve technique. It can be dynamite for casting, however, when two jigs are employed. This is a popular method of fishing for white bass and is very effective at getting double, as well as single, hookups when those fish are concentrated. Here, 1/8- to 1/2-ounce hair jigs are used; one is tied to a 12- to 15-inch leader while the other is tied to a 24- to 30-inch leader, both fixed to a three-way swivel. A two-jig rig is also used in crappie and yellow perch fishing, and there are merits to similar combos (using jigs or jigging spoons) for fishing through the ice.

Besides using three-way swivels, spinning and baitcasting fishermen can run a floating/diving plug plus a small spoon or jig on one line by tying the latter onto the rear hook or the hook-screw connection of the former. This is an old

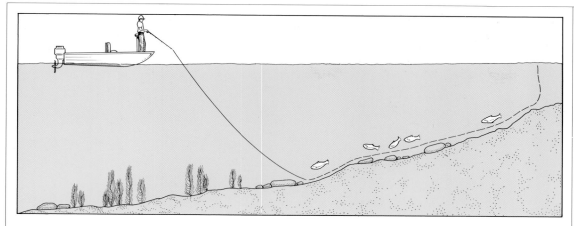

Utilizing a stop-and-go retrieve when fishing with deep-diving plugs is one way to trigger a strike.

inland striped bass trolling technique in which a heavy jig is trolled on an 18-to 24-inch leader behind a big-lipped deep-diving plug. The method is an effective one, although some anglers mistakenly believe that the the setup allows them to reach extraordinary depths on an unweighted line.

A tactic that seems to have potential for attracting fish which might not otherwise be interested – one that is overlooked by most fishermen – is the use of a small streamer or wet fly behind a crankbait. The fly is tied to a short leader that in turn is connected to the back of the plug, has no significant drag to affect either the depth or action of the main lure, and can be a way to entice such fish as crappies, perch, bluegills, or other panfish while casting for bigger quarry.

Some anglers who use popping plugs for schooling fish, such as small stripers or white bass, tie a light jig on a leader behind the popper; the trailing lure sometimes catches fish while the surface lure acts as an attractor. A jig trailing a wobbling surface lure may also have merit.

TRIGGERING A STRIKE

Is it actually possible to make fish strike? Sometimes. One of the most exasperating things that can happen to fishermen is to know that there are fish all around, yet not be able to catch even one of them. This is especially distressing when the sonar shows a host of large fish tantalizingly close to the boat, all of them ignoring the anglers' lure. At such times, frustrated fishermen frantically switch to different types or colors of lures, and sometimes this does the job. But often the only thing that will coax a strike from the indifferent fish is a totally different retrieve or presentation.

Often, this mean slowing down or speeding up a lure. Let's say, for instance, that you're fishing for largemouth bass, and the situation— warm, shallow water, weedy cover, overcast sky—seems to call for a buzz bait. You try it, but it doesn't produce or gets only an occasional boil. You can assume that if the bass were active,

they would pounce on the lure. For whatever reason, they don't. So it's up to you to make them strike. In this instance, you should try some type of stickbait (like one with a rear propeller) and fish it very slowly. The mild commotion and slow struggling movement of the lure can entice a fish when other techniques fail.

At other times, more speed may be required to trigger a strike, although creating erratic lure movement – strange or varied behavior – may be more important than merely changing the speed of your retrieve. When vertical jigging for stripers, for example, recalcitrant fish can be caught by speed jigging. To accomplish it, you cast your spoon out, let it settle to the bottom or a predetermined depth, then retrieve the spoon as fast as you can for five rotations of the reel handle. You then push the free-spool button and let the spoon go back to the bottom, with your thumb resting lightly on the spool (because the fish will almost always hit on the fall). When five cranks of the reel handle don't produce strikes, try seven, then ten, each time reeling as hard as you possibly can.

This is a tough technique to keep up for hours, but it's effective, probably because it imitates the struggles of dying baitfish. Whatever it imitates, it causes stripers to respond, even when they are showing little inclination to strike conventionally fished jigs, deep-diving plugs, or other lures that are dragged past them.

There are times when the only way to catch largemouth or smallmouth bass with plugs is to be very erratic. Most anglers tend to fish such lures as shallow-running minnow-imitation plugs and crankbaits in a less-than-frenzied manner, but when strikes are hard to come by, you may need to get a little wilder. Some anglers have specialized their plug fishing by effecting a ripping technique in which they violently jerk diving plugs in a pull-pause fashion. This violent jerking proves hard on the arms and shoulders after a few hours, but it does seem to produce larger-than-average fish.

In a less-wrenching manner, a simple stop-and-go technique for working deep-diving crankbaits can be the key to success. I've seen times when one angler would catch few, if any, fish, while a companion, using an identical lure, could catch a dozen or more simply because he was stopping his retrieve momentarily after

every three or four turns of the reel handle. This stop-and-go action is simple, and with a bait-casting reel with a slow retrieve ratio (meaning that you gain less line with each turn of the handle) it can be even more successful at catching fish that aren't very aggressive.

Erratic lure behavior can improve your chances while trolling as well as casting. Perhaps that is why the cut-plug-style of trolling lure has such appeal for salmon (especially in late summer and fall in the Great Lakes). These baits have a wide swing and can be worked at fairly fast speeds. Although they dip, dart, and veer, which would be abnormal and unproductive for most plugs, this designed behavior is what evidently appeals to chinook salmon, steelhead, and occasionally other salmonid species.

Because such plugs intentionally work erratically, the troller needn't do much to make them effective other than fish them at the right depth and speed. There are times, however, when trollers need to manipulate their lures to cause strikes, just as casting anglers do. This is more difficult when you're trolling, obviously, because you don't have direct contact with the lure while it is swimming down below. When using downriggers, this is especially so.

Increasing or decreasing boat speed (and thus lure speed) is one way to accomplish this, and you may have to put the engine in neutral or increase the throttle periodically in order to cause a strike. Fish often follow trolled lures, and while they may strike a lure that swims long distances in an uninterrupted pattern, they may be triggered into striking a lure only when it departs from that regular action. When you stop momentarily, for example, a spoon will flutter downward and a floating plug will rise upward. This change in behavior can prompt observing fish to strike.

There are times when you are trolling with downriggers and see fish on the sonar, that you can trigger a strike by changing the depth of the weight, popping the lure out of the downrigger release, or changing speed. Raising or lowering the weight is fairly easy with manual or electric downriggers, and with some can be done through a programmable oscillation mode that raises or lowers the weight specific heights at specific intervals.

Similarly, shallow-water trollers who fish for landlocked salmon and trout and hand-hold their rods should try jerking the rod periodically, especially if they are using streamer flies or spoons. Lake trout, which are notorious followers, respond especially well to this aberrant behavior. They may follow a lure for a long distance, even bumping or slapping it, but never

Following pages: *There are a lot of intangibles that go into fishing success, including having confidence in where, and how, to fish.*

really taking it unless the lure is twitched or jerked from time to time while being trolled; then they will pounce on it. Devices that electrically jig a trolled lure by sweeping the rod (placed in a holder) are available.

Popping a lure out of a release is less recognized, but also a very effective triggering trick. It is used primarily by downrigger fishermen, but also in sideplaner board trolling. It's a simple maneuver; all you do is pop the lure out of the release and leave it alone. With the boat moving forward, a spoon or plug will begin to move upward, perhaps even increasing in speed. The changes in lure behavior that result may prompt a strike from fish that are following. Obviously, if your lure is set well behind the downrigger weight, you don't know if a fish is present, and if you don't get a strike, you will have to bring the weight up to set the lure out again. But when you do see a fish at the level of your lure, deliberately popping it out of the release can be a very worthwhile tactic on days when you're not getting many strikes.

It is also good to use this tactic when you are about to change lures or even when you are going to quit fishing. Instead of reeling the lure immediately after popping it out of a release, put the rod in a holder and let the lure swim for a minute. You may catch fish this way that would not have otherwise struck.

CONFIDENCE

No matter what type of fishing you do, confidence is one of the most influential aspects of angling. It is an intangible quality that can't be bought, and which you can't dupe yourself into possessing. It is also an attitude or state of mind, since there are some anglers who have spent a lot of time on the water, yet still lack confidence.

Primarily you acquire confidence through learning and doing – by developing an understanding of the habits and habitat of your quarry, by mastering the intricacies of your tackle, and by slowly putting together the pieces of the fishing jigsaw puzzle. Hopefully, good advice and tutelage when you first start fishing will serve as a big help in upgrading your angling proficiency, and, if so, your confidence will soar. Just going out and catching a couple of fish (preferably the species that you are deliberately seeking) is a big boost to the neophyte's confidence. So is having, and knowing how to use, good equipment. Too many anglers, particularly novices, lose their concentration and conviction when the fishing is slow. They unreasonably expect to catch fish easily, and when they don't do so, or their favorite places or techniques don't produce, they lose interest, become sloppy or lackadaisical, or simply are flustered. Faith in your abilities, your equipment, and in your knowledge of where to seek various species of fish has to be acquired through experience, which is why so few beginning anglers can stand shoulder-to-shoulder with most veterans.

Ted Trueblood, the late and venerated writer for Field & Stream, thought that enthusiasm was one of the keys that separated consistently successful fishermen from unsuccessful or occasionally successful fishermen. In that magazine, he once commented that consistently successful anglers and hunters were enthusiasts. "Because such a man is enthusiastic," said Trueblood, "he does everything a little bit better than another who may be more or less indifferent or who doesn't honestly believe that he will kill any game or catch any fish....I think the difference stems primarily from the thought and effort each

Trollers should not just work in a straight line at the same speed constantly, but change speed, alter direction, and try other tricks to encourage a strike.

individual puts into his sport. And the enthusiast, the person who has faith and hope...does the best he can all the time. And it pays off."

Although Trueblood noted that success breeds confidence and more success, he also noted that there are ways to help your confidence along even when fishing is poor. Changing lures, for example, has an important psychological effect on the angler, giving him "new faith." Changing locations, and taking a rest to prevent fatigue and discouragement, were other suggestions.

Every move that a good fisherman makes is related to confidence – in the selection of which lure to use; in the selection of an area to fish; in the placement of his casts; in judging when to stay in, or leave, a particular spot; in determining what type of retrieve to employ; and so on. Because he is confident he concentrates harder on what he is doing, and is generally more attentive to the nuances of the fish's world.

At the same time he realizes that not every cast will produce a fish, nor will every day be a good one. He realizes that fish are unpredictable creatures and that he can't always figure them out, which is probably why he likes the sport in the first place. Yet, top-notch anglers are always convinced that there's a fish waiting to snare their very next cast, and that they're going to catch the fish. That's confidence.

Don't overlook the effects of feeling positive about your abilities and your understanding of the world of fishing. Perhaps your greatest tool is not in a tackle box, but in your head.

FINE POINTS

Angling is a sport with a lot of nuances to it, and while we have tried to be thorough, it is difficult to get every nugget of angling wisdom into this book. One thing that all anglers should have mastered is the fundamentals. Some fundamental items that we take for granted, and which many new or inexperienced anglers do not understand or appreciate, include how to set and use their reel drag, how to tie the proper kinds of knots, how to tune their lures to get the most out of them, and how to get out of snags. We'll cover those fine points here, plus give you some food for thought regarding the fine print on fishing regulations.

SETTING/USING DRAG

A lot of freshwater fishermen do not have much chance to use the drag mechanisms on their reels because they seldom encounter fish strong enough to pull line off the reel. Those who angle for big fish in rivers, and fish with light tackle, will have occasion to use their drag.

The purpose of the drag function is to let line slip from the reel at varying pressures when force is applied to the line. It serves as a shock absorber, or clutch. The looser it is set, the less force is required to strip line off. If the drag is set properly a strong-pulling fish may be able to take line from the spool by applying less pressure than would be required to break the line or knot. Thus, the drag acts as insurance, as a buffer between you and the fish. Properly set line drag is most useful when playing strong, hard-fighting fish; when using light line; and when reacting to sudden surges by fish. The latter is a very crucial time in playing a fish. Such surges may occur at the beginning of the fight, and especially as you bring a still-green fish alongside the boat.

Many large and strong fish are lost because of line breakage that occurs when a drag is set so tight (deliberately or through negligence) that there is no slippage. When the fish made a sudden surge, there was little shock absorbing effect. It would be like pulling at the end of a tightrope. The impact of this rush was more than the line could withstand, so it broke.

In partial defense of anglers who use very tight drags, there is sometimes a good reason to do so., usually because the habitat in which they are fishing (timber, thick grass, etc.) leaves little margin for error when a fish is caught in it or heads for it to break off and you must stop it before it gets into a tangle. This can't be accomplished easily with light line or if the drag is too loose, so you have to compromise in these situations.

The most accurate way to set the drag is to bring line off the spool through the rod guides and attach it to a reliable spring scale. Keep the rod up as if you were fighting a fish and have someone pull on the scale to watch the dial so you know at what amount of pressure the drag began to slip. Lighten or increase tension accordingly. Many anglers set the drag tension at between 30 and 50 percent of the breaking strength of the line for normal fishing conditions, raising it in heavy cover. If you think about

---

Large and strong fish will test a fisherman's tackle, and the drag on a reel has to be set according to the line strength to accommodate the action.

The star drag on a bait casting reel should be set before fishing; some anglers do so by feel, but there are more precise ways of setting it.

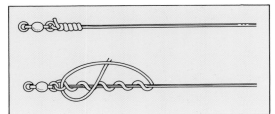

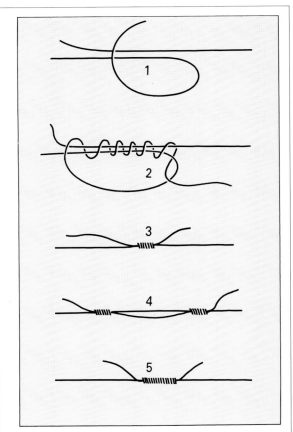

drag tension in terms of the breaking strength of your line, you'll realize that 50 percent of 12-pound line is still 6 pounds of pressure, and few fishermen exert 6 or more pounds of pressure even when setting the hook. Most anglers would be fooled if they were to pull line off their drag and guess the tension setting.

With a lot of experience you can set the drag by hand, adjusting the drag control and pulling line off by hand until you reach what "feels" like a good tension setting. Many people, including the author, do this all the time, but it is a bit imprecise. Another method is to catch your lure or hook on some solid object, like the underside of an oarlock or a handrail, and pull back on your rod to approximate the surge of a fish. Adjust the drag while doing this to achieve what feels like a suitable setting.

An important point to realize about reel drag tension is that the less line you have on the spool, the greater the amount of tension will be. As the diameter of the spool gets smaller, more force is required to pull line off it. This may not happen in most forms of freshwater fishing, where line capacity is not much of a factor in playing fish, but in some cases you will need to be aware of this and to compensate accordingly by not having too tight a drag at the outset.

Some anglers like to set their drag on the loose side, although not so loose as to impede hook setting, especially when using light and ultra-light tackle and when fishing in open-water areas. You can always apply more drag if need be, although it is imprecise to do so by quickly changing the drag setting to increase pressure because on some reels you can easily increase the tension too much too quick. By cupping the palm of your hand over a spinning reel spool or

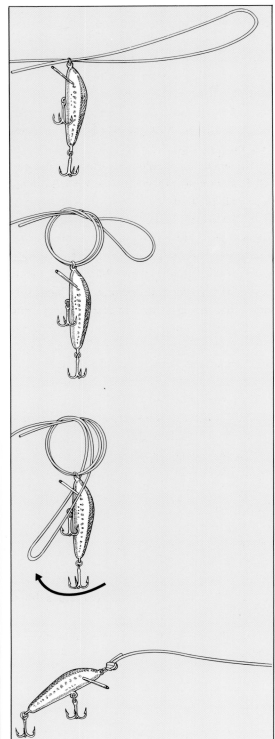

Top left: *The Improved Clinch Knot.*

Top right: *To form a Uni Knot to join two lines, (1) overlap both lines about 6 inches. Hold these in the middle of the overlap with your left hand while making a circle with the line to the right. (2) Bring the tag end around the double length six times. (3) Pull snugly. (4) Repeat in reverse on the other side. (5) Pull the two sections away from each other to draw the knot tight.*

by putting your thumb on a bait casting reel spool or by placing your fingers on the inside rim of a fly reel spool, you can apply some

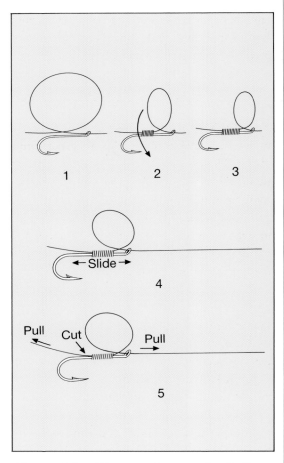

Above right: How *to form a Snell Knot: (1) First bring line through hook eye, lay along shank, and form a loop. (2) After that pinch both sections to the hook with one hand, and with the other hand wrap the looped line tightly and closely without overlays toward the eye. (3) After making ten wraps, snug down the knot. (4) Slide the knot to the eye if it is not being used to hold bait and to the mid-shank if it is to be looped to hold bait. (5) Lastly, pull the line in opposite directions and trim tag end.*

Above left: *The Palomar Knot.*

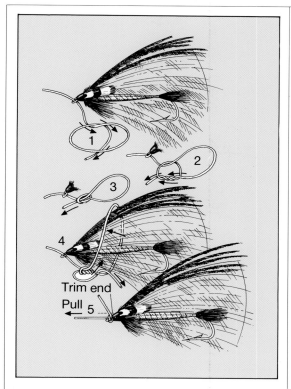

The Turle Knot, which produces a straight pull on a fly with a turned-down eye.

amount of tension in addition to that which your drag is applying. Do this judiciously, however, and backoff quickly as necessary.

KNOT TYING

As with drag, many freshwater fishermen are under the mistaken impression that their knots are good because those knots have never failed them. They don't realize, however, that they rarely test their tackle to its fullest or make the greatest demands on a knot. It's when you get to light tackle use, angling for very large and hard-fighting fish, and fishing under shock-loading circumstances, that you prove a knot, and these times are precisely when less-than-perfect knots fail. Furthermore, even the best knots don't perform adequately unless they are tied properly and uniformly time after time. Fastidious attention to detail is rewarded with superior knot performance.

Please follow these pointers to ensure good knot tying:

* Keep twists, spirals, and all tying steps uniform so that when you draw a knot closed, it is neat and precise.

* Snug knots up tightly with even, steady pressure. Watch for evidence of slippage and re-tie the knot if necessary. Don't pop the knot to tighten it.

* Wet the line as an aid to help draw it up smoothly.

* Don't nick a knot with clippers or knife when you cut off the protruding tag end.

* If your knot breaks repeatedly when you tighten it, check your hook eye or lure connection for rough spots that are cutting the line.

* Check the end of the line and clip off a damaged section.

The steps in forming an Improved Clinch Knot; good knots must be tied uniformly and properly every time.

* Use plenty of line to complete tying steps without difficulty.

* When using double lines keep them as parallel as possible and avoid twisting them as the knot is being tied.

* Test your knots occasionally with a scale to see if you are getting the performance you need. You can do this by tying wet line to the hook of a reliable spring scale. Have someone wrap the unknotted line around his hand several times, using a towel or cloth to keep from getting cut. While your accomplice pulls on the line, you hold and watch the scale, noting at what amount of pressure the line or knot breaks. If the line broke, your knot held; if the knot broke, check your tying.

There are many knots that anglers use, some of which accomplish the same thing, some of which have specific applications. There are terminal knots, for tying line to lure or hook eye; line-to-line knots; knots to create double line leaders; and loop knots.

The Improved Clinch is perhaps the most popular of all fishing knots, and is an excellent knot. Other highly rated knots include the Palomar, Uni, Albright Special, and Bimini Twist, although the latter two are seldom employed in freshwater.

The Improved Clinch Knot can give 100 percent strength if tied properly, and is perhaps the most popular terminal tackle knot in use. The

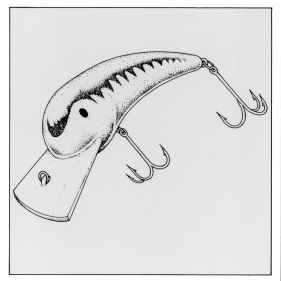

Using pliers, bend the line tie screw of a crankbait to the left or right to correct the action.

Palomar is a runner-up in popularity and is extremely reliable, though a little tough to carry out where large lures are used. The basic Uni Knot has many uses, but is especially valuable for tying two lines of similar diameter together. The Albright Special is a superior knot for joining light and heavy line. The Bimini Twist creates a double length of line that is especially valuable as a leader and with ultralight lines. There are many other knots that exist, and you might want to look into these by checking the literature of line manufacturers.

LURE TUNING

With few exceptions, lures must run true to be effective, or at least to be as effective as they are capable of being. This is true for all lures. Some, such as spinners and spoons, need little tuning and are easily corrected. Plugs pose a problem for many anglers, some of whom do not realize that their lure is not running right when they are using it. Plugs must run straight on the retrieve, not lie on their side or run off at an angle; spoons must have the right wobble, not lay flat and skip. But lures don't always work right, even when brand new from the factory. Some that have been working properly may run awry after you catch a fish on them, or someone steps on them, ot they get bashed against a hard object. Some lures work perfectly out of the box and some, especially plugs, do not. Moreover, you can buy a dozen identical plugs and find that several need alteration to work just right.

There are ways to accomplish this alteration, or "tuning", of lures to make them run true. It's not difficult, but it does take a few moments to accomplish, and it takes some observation to know when to make alterations on a lure to make it fish better.

The majority of plugs have clear plastic bills of various lengths and shapes for diving/swimming. Into these bills are attached line-tie screws, and virtually all running problems center on these little screws. That screw must be placed vertical to the mean horizontal plane of the bill of the lure. Because this screweye is positioned partially by hand at the manufacturing plant, the element of human error can be introduced. If the screw is placed a fraction of an inch out of position, the lure will not run perfectly true.

A well-designed plug that sports a lip should have a good wiggling action. Some lures have a tight action and some more of a wide wobble. Whichever action it possesses, the plug should come back in a straight line to you on the retrieve. The body of the plug should be vertical, not canted off to either side. It is a good idea to check each plug before you fish it. Tie it on your line, drop a few feet of line from the tip of the rod to the lure, then run the lure through the water next to your boat. If it does not run properly, adjust it immediately.

To adjust a plug you need only a pair of pliers, preferably needle-nose, to bend the line-tie screw. If, as you watch the path of retrieve head-on, the lure is running to your right, you must bend the line-tie screw to the left (again looking head on) and vice versa. Adjust the screw in stages, bending it slightly and then casting and retrieving once to see the change. Keep adjusting and changing until the lure runs true. Be careful not to loosen the screw.

Incidentally, a split ring, a rounded snap, or a loop knot will improve the action of some lures, in addition to proper tuning.

HOOK SHARPENING

If you look at a standard fish hook under a powerful microscope you'll see that it has many rough spots. This is especially true of hooks that have been used and which have been in a tackle box for a while. Sharpening new and previously used hooks smoothes out the rough spots and makes it easier to get the point and barb deep enough in the fish when it strikes to keep it on your line.

You can improve the sharpness of a hook by grinding the point over a sharpening stone or file. Be careful not to prick or hook yourself with the point by holding the stone and hook firmly and making smooth, deliberate motions.

Tackle stores carry several different types of hook sharpeners, most of which are inexpensive. Some stones have a groove through which the hook point is repeatedly ground, which will make the point sharper. It is best, however, to hold a hook firmly in one hand and run the edge of a sharpening stone or file over the hook point with the other hand in a back and forth motion.

If a snagged lure doesn't come free, try pulling the line taut, and then snapping it free.

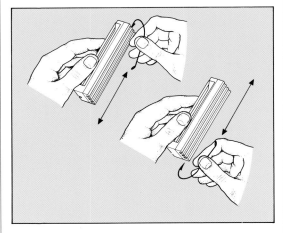

Hand-held hook sharpening stones are commonly used to touch up the point of a hook.

Do this in three positions, first grinding on the inside of the point, then on the left and right sides. This triangulates the point and sharpens the cutting area to improve penetration.

Test for sharpness by carefully — very carefully — running the hook point lightly over your thumbnail. If the point glides over the nail, it needs more sharpening. If it hangs up and digs in, it's ready to use.

Large, thick bodied hooks, including cadmium and stainless steel, and hooks that are forged (flattened around the bend on both sides), require more effort to sharpen. Different tools, like a diamond stone or file, may be necessary.

GETTING UNSNAGGED

Getting snagged is part of the fishing game. Many species of fish orient to bottom and different types of structural cover and, as the saying goes, if you aren't getting snagged ocasionally you're probably not angling where the fish are. Therefore, getting unsnagged is a practice you'll have to master unless you don't mind losing lures and breaking your line a lot.

An important point to realize about unsnag-

ging your lure is that it doesn't pay to use brute strength and just yank on a stuck plug unless you have very heavy line (and then you may straighten the hook) and/or are just stuck on something flimsy. You usually can't muscle that lure free. Moreover, in so doing you probably will sink the hook deeper into the snagged object; may break your line, meaning that you've probably lost the plug; or may free the bait but send it speeding perilously back to you.

A lot of lures will come free if you simply jiggle your rod a bit. Another tactic is to take line from the rod between the reel and first guide, pull back on the rod to get the line very taut, and then snap the line in the other hand free, which may jolt the lure free, especially if it is a jig or single-hooked spoon or spinnerbait.

Sometimes it pays to give the stuck lure slack line. A floating plug may float free, or another bait might fall back from the object it was hung on. If your lure is stuck in water that is no deeper than the length of your rod, and will not come free by any other means, stick your rod tip in the water and reel the slack line up till the tip of the rod hits the lure, then gently push or wiggle it free. You might try using a long pole to poke a stuck lure free, or one of several weighted objects that slide down the fishing line and tangle around the hooks, and which are pulled up with a heavy line or rope. In deeper water get yourself into a position 180 degrees from where you were when you got stuck and simply pull.

When you can't get free you have to try pulling up on the lure as a last resort. Because of the distance of water between you and the lure, you don't have to worry about it rocketing back at you if you are successful in freeing it. For last-chance unsnagging, try tightening the drag, pointing the rod directly at the lure, and pulling back. When you have been stuck on an object, check the first few feet of line to make sure it isn't abraded.

ABOUT THOSE REGULATIONS

Have you read the regulations brochure/booklet/guide that pertains to the places you fish? It is your obligation to know and to abide by the regulations that are detailed in that literature. Yet, many people are not aware of many of the regulations particulars or take things for granted from one season to the next. Size and creel limits, seasons, and other matters sometimes change, and are not the same from state to state or necessarily from one body of water to the next.

Right: *Fishermen need to be aware of angling regulations no matter where they fish; this New York angler is required to have his name on the tip-up that he is using.*

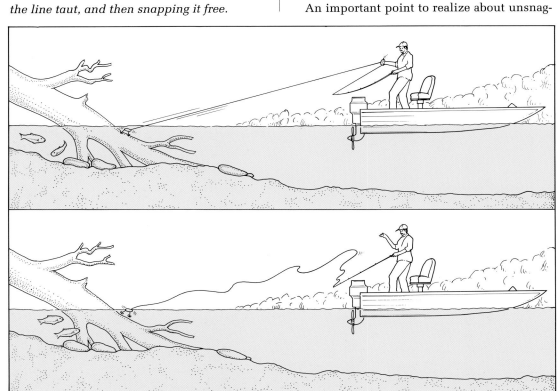

Fishing without a license is the No. 1 violation in virtually all places, but using illegal methods, possessing more fish than the law allows, and possessing undersized fish are also frequently experienced problems. Fishing on private waters is a common problem. In most states you need a license to fish on privately-owned waters. In many states you can fish on private waters without a license if you are the owner, a direct relative of the owner, or a tenant. In a lot of cases it depends on whether the private water has been stocked with public fish; has public water flowing in or out of it; is navigable; is an agricultural pond; or possesses fish purchased from commercial sources. It may also be legal for residents but not for nonresidents.

Regarding licenses, it is known that children under a certain age (14, 15, or 16 usually) don't need a fishing license, but does an adult need a license to take children fishing? The general answer is: no, if he is just supervising; yes, if he assists or fishes himself. There are limits to how much supervising one can do, of course, but this varies widely.

The number of fishing lines that an angler can use is an often overlooked subject, and one that varies widely. Don't assume that what applies in your state also applies in a neighboring state, or in a place where you vacation and fish as a nonresident. Some states have no restrictions on this matter; most allow two, some only one.

Most states have restrictions on the number of hooks that can be used on fishing lines. In some places you may be required to personally attend fishing lines (especially important for ice fishing). As for measuring fish, measurement is generally from the snout to the tip of the tail, but in a few places (New Mexico and Florida), it is from the snout to the fork in the tail.

Regulations vary widely as to whether gamefish may be used as bait. Buying or selling gamefish is prohibited in all states, although some species are not classified as "gamefish" even though they are popular with sportfishermen. Anglers may catch their own bait in all states provided they conform to accepted methods, but there are some exceptions. The deliberate snagging of fish is prohibited in all states, except in some states for certain non-game species or for Great Lakes salmon in specified areas and seasons. However, fish are sometimes unintentionally foul-hooked; in most states you cannot keep fish that were so captured, even if they conform to other existing regulations, such as size.

And, of course, there are exceptions to all regulations. It can seem like a confusing mess at times, though it usually is not that bad. However, it is the responsibility of the angler to know what is allowed and what is not, and to abide by the regulations.

Check line and knots before fishing; sharpen hooks when new lures or flies are tied on.

HOOK SETTING

Although some angling situations and techniques cause a fish to hook itself when it strikes bait or lure, most of the time, and always when casting and retrieving, an angler must react to a strike by setting the hook. This seems rather obvious and easy to accomplish; you just jerk back. Not quite.

It is harder to set the hook on some fish than on others, and there are enough variables — whether the fish is swimming away from or toward you, whether you are sitting or standing, whether you are using a stiff or limber rod, etc. — to make a non-studious appraisal very risky. Indeed, few anglers have an accurate notion of how much force they generate when they set the hook to the best of their ability. Actually, the average fisherman is quite inefficient when he punches the hook home, as tests using instruments that gauge the amount of force applied have demonstrated.

Consider that you may not set the hook as effi-ciently as desired each and every time, especially when caught unawares by a strike or hampered by a bony-mouthed or strong-jawed fish, or that some other factors (such as a bow in the line while river fishing or having a striking fish run toward you) will impede your effort, you see that it is imperative to do all that you can to execute the best hook-set possible.

This starts with proper technique. Hook-setting effectiveness has little to do with physical stature or with brute strength. If you doubt this, tie a barrel swivel to the line on any fishing rod, and have a friend stand 40 feet away from you holding the swivel clenched between his thumb and forefinger. Raise the rod slowly and apply all the pressure you can to try to pull that swivel out of his hand. If you don't jerk back violently, you can't pull it out.

Effective hook setting has to do with timing and hook point penetration. Pulling back on the rod with steady pressure after you detect a strike is not how you should set the hook, although this is how many anglers react to a strike even though they think they have done something more definitive.

There are two recognized and effective techniques in hook setting, one with a no-slack approach and the other with a slight, controlled amount of slack.

With a no-slack hook-set, you lean toward the fish, reel up slack till the line is taut, and then punch the hook home. This is accomplished in the blink of an eye, and it is crucial that you only reel slack up till the line is taut but not pulling on the fish; if you tighten up the connection to the fish so far that it feels tension, it may quickly expel your offering. This takes timing, which is acquired through experience.

With a controlled slack-line set, the line is not reeled taut to the fish, but nearly so, and the hook is punched home quickly to provide shock penetration. The theory here is that you get better hook-point penetration from a snappy shock force than from a tight-line pull. Try pushing a nail into the wall with the head of a hammer rather than by striking it sharply with

Set the hook by bringing the rod tip up sharply, keeping the butt in your midsection and not lowering the rod to produce any slack line.

Reel, strike, keep the rod-tip up, and, if neces-sary, keep reeling as the hook is being set.

the hammer, and you'll see the significance.

In either method there is a common denomi-nator of speed, particularly rod-tip speed. But that alone isn't the key. A principal reason why many people are ineffective at hook setting is not their inability to respond quickly, but the way they use their body and contort themselves while doing so. Hook setting is not a whole-body maneuver, but an exercise of wrists and arms. Back and legs have little to do with this. Someone thin and short might deliver more hook-setting force and better penetration than a much larger and more powerful individual.

It also helps a great deal if you are prepared for what is about to happen before it happens. Start by keeping your rod tip down during the retrieve (in some instances, such as when working a jig or plastic worm, this is not always best for accomplishing a proper retrieve or for detecting a strike). With the tip down, you're in the best position to respond quickly to a strike, even, as often happens, if you are distracted from what you're doing when the strike occurs. If there is little or no slack in the line you can make a forceful sweep up or back when you set the hook, and then be in immediate control of a fish to begin playing it.

When working some lures, however, it is usually necessary to keep the rod tip up to work the lure properly and readily detect a strike. When setting the hook you can compensate for a high rod position by bowing the rod slightly toward the fish while reeling up slack; this enables you to get a full backward sweep and be in the proper position for the beginning of the fight.

Where possible, you should be reeling and

striking all in one motion, keeping the pressure on constantly and not yielding unless the fish is strong enough to pull line off the drag. Good hook-setting technique is never more important than when long distances are involved, and the same is true for fish-playing tactics. Fish that are a long distance off are harder to control than those up close. It is more difficult to keep a strong fish away from an obstruction when it is 125 feet from you than when it is 40. When fishing from a boat it may be necessary to maneuver the boat to change the angle of pull on a large fish in order to help steer it away from obstructions. You have to anticipate and react

In most freshwater situations, a fly fisherman simply holds the line tight to the handle and raises the rod tip sharply to set the hook, although with large flies and big fish, it may be necessary to strip line with the free hand and also strike forcefully with the rod hand simultaneously.

quickly, however, to do this.

Hook setting should be a quickly accom-plished maneuver. When a fish strikes, the angler reacts reflexively, bringing his rod back and up sharply while holding the reel handle and reeling the instant he feels the fish. The position of the rod is important. The butt is jammed into the stomach or mid-chest area and the full arc and power of the rod is brought into play, without having hands or arms jerk wildly over your head. In order to countermand line-stretch it is important to be reeling hard and fast the moment you set the hook.

Nylon monofilament lines have about a 30 percent stretch factor when wet, which in part explains why you can deliver more force when a short nylon monofilament line is used rather than a long one (also with a dry line versus a wet one). By comparison, a low-stretch braided Dacron or cofilament line, if it had other desir-able fish line qualities, would be better for hook setting over all distances, though you would still generate more force on short lengths. Fishermen are more effective at setting the hook at short and mid-range distances than they are at long distances due to line-stretch. It is harder to counter the effect of stretch when setting the hook if you have a long length of line out. So you can generate more force and be more effi-cient at setting the hook at short distances, and are less efficient at long distances.

Good hook-setting procedure, however, doesn't end once you have reacted and feel the fish. Like a golf swing, the follow-through is usually important and sometimes critical. The line must remain tight; people who bring their rod tip back behind their head or raise their arms up high often put some slack momentarily into the line when they bring the rod back down in front of them. Not having to do this is the advan-

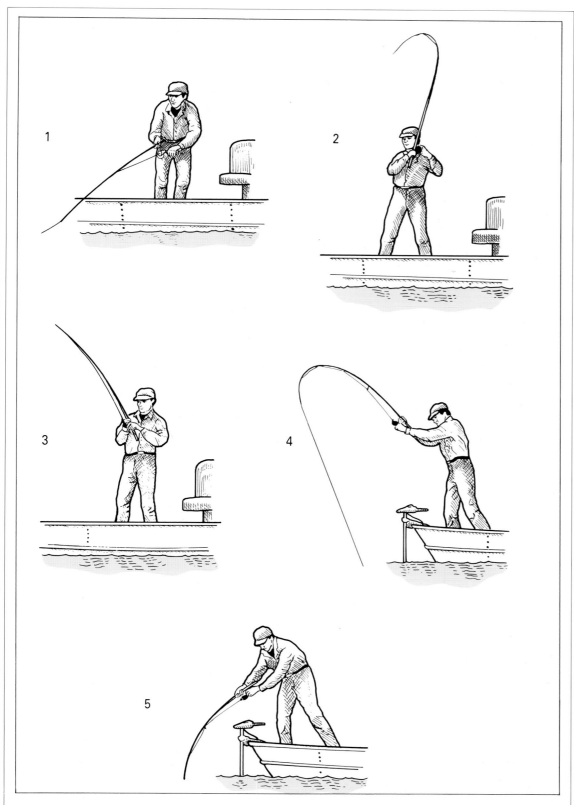

Good hook setting and fish playing begins with the rod tip angled down on the retrieve when possible (1), then reacting swiftly (2) to the strike and keeping the rod butt in the chest area. Keep the line tight and the rod tip up (3) throughout the fight. Keep slack out of the line (4) and guide the fish away from the boat or other objects (5).

tage of keeping the rod in front of you, and also of reeling continuously until the fish is firmly hooked and offering some resistance.

The type of rod that is used can aid or impede hook setting efforts. Generally speaking, limber rods decrease your ability to generate hook-setting force while stiff rods increase it. The soft and somewhat spongey response of a limber rod does, however, make it harder to break the line and to cast light lures, so there are functional tradeoffs in tackle used. A stiff rod can aid strike

detection, but it could lead to breaking light lines if the hook is set particularly hard. Is there a difference in hook-setting effectiveness between types of rods? Less so than we like to think. The difference is really one of rod action.

Light lines can pose hook-setting problems, incidentally, especially for those who are accustomed to heavier tackle and jaw-breaking hook sets. Again, that's usually a problem of using a rod that is too stiff for the line. Where light line is used, you need a rod with some cushioning effect. With a medium or light action rod that is used with light line, and the appropriate drag setting that must necessarily be employed, it's almost impossible to break the line when setting the hook.

You can prove this to yourself when you're hung up on some obstruction while using such tackle; try setting the hook to break the line and

you'll find that it is extremely difficult to do so.

If your line has a belly or bow in it, as it might when river fishing or when a fish takes your offering and runs laterally with it, you may not have time to take out all or most of the slack when you set the hook and still not alert the fish, so this is where you might execute a slack line snap, being sure to keep the line tight after the hook-up. Fly fishermen using light tippets and fishing in current don't want to muster much force anyway, so they'll use this method. A line that is impeded by some obstruction, is also hard to deal with, since your hook setting force is directed more at that impediment than at the fish beyond. There isn't much you can do about this situation except realize the problem, fish with heavy line in thick cover, and regularly check your line for damaged spots that might be a problem later.

Drag slippage can also be an impedance to hook setting. Some anglers who use bait casting tackle put their thumb on the reel spool when setting the hook so they can prevent slippage, but it is best to have the drag set precisely for the line strength so you don't have to do this.

One way to deliver better-than-average hook-setting force is to set the hook with both hands on the rod, one on the handle around the reel and one on the foregrip. Most anglers set the hook with one hand on the rod handle, and the other on the reel handle. Usually this is adequate. There are special circumstances, however, that necessitate using two hands to reef the hooks home. There are also a few occasions when it is desirable to set the hook two or three times in rapid succession.

What about when trolling? The fish already has the lure when you pull the rod out of its holder; should you set the hook then? It depends on the situation and fish. Where the quarry are large and hard-mouthed, yes. When using very light line or angling for soft-mouthed fish, no, because you run the risk of pulling the lure out. In either case you will still have to concentrate on keeping pressure on the fish and not making a mistake when playing it.

Paying attention to these matters will help you be more efficient at setting the hook. It you want to put this information to work for you in the best way possible, however, be sure to sharpen new and used hooks. A super sharp hook can make all the difference in landing or losing a fish. Most fish are lost because the hook slipped out or was thrown when the fish jumped. A super sharp hook penetrates easier and increases your chances of landing a fish. The primary benefit of having a sharp hook is to gain penetrating effectiveness.

Maximum penetration. translates into optimum hook-setting efficiency and better hook retention, which ultimately means more fish hooked and landed and not lost when you are in the process of playing them

LANDING FISH

.Many of the fish that are caught in freshwater are fairly small, being a pound or two at most in size. Few people have much trouble landing such fish on any type of equipment. Since the great majority of all fish caught are small, most freshwater anglers do not often get to experience difficult fish-playing situations, and unfortunately are ill-prepared to handle them when they do occur. That partially explains why many large fish are lost after being hooked. Salmon, large trout, steelhead, and large striped bass will test a freshwater fisherman's playing skills fully and anglers who frequently fish for these crea-

Left: The better the condition of your equipment, including line and reel drag, the better able you will be to land fish, especially large fish in strong current.

When an energetic fish is close, the angler has to be prepared to direct it away from the motor or steer it out from under the boat.

tures learn to handle their tackle and use the proper fish-playing skills.

Generally, fish-playing activities take place in a short period of time and the action is often fast. Your reactions must be swift and instinctive, and your tackle, particularly line and reel drag, must be capable and of good quality. Many fish are lost as a result of the way in which the angler plays the fish. A big fish, for example, will often run for cover or some obstruction and an angler must do his best to prevent the fish from getting to those places. Within the capabilities of your tackle, take the fight to the fish; don't sit back and be casual.

Line breakage is often the reason for losing large fish. Certainly it is possible to have purchased an inferior quality line, but more often breakage is due to line that is old and poorly conditioned, or line that is worn and weakened, or the use of poor knots or badly tied knots. Fishing line isn't good for angling indefinitely. Old line, especially if it has been left in the sunlight for a long time or it has been severely stressed in the past, needs to be replaced. Line that is frayed or sports little nicks or burrs has lost a good deal of its strength; check it occasionally and cut off affected sections.

When you have a line problem, did the main stem of the line actually break or did the knot slip or break? Poorly tied knots weaken fishing line, causing you to fish with line that is not as strong as you expect and that is unable to take the strain of playing a big or hard-pulling fish. Many anglers don't tie fishing knots as well as they should, and some don't realize that there are knots and then there are fishing knots (see knot tying in this section).

Another reason for losing fish is an improper reel drag setting. When the drag is set too tight, line won't freely come off the spool under the surges of a strong fish. This feature, which is akin to shock-absorption, helps prevent overloading the line, causing shock breakage. When the drag is set too loose, however, there is not enough tension on the fish, so a middle ground, based on the strength of line and fishing conditions, is best (see drag setting in this section).

Playing, or fighting, a fish starts with hooking them well, of course. From the moment that you set the hook, the position of the rod is important. The butt should be jammed into the stomach or mid-chest area and the full arc and power of the rod should be brought into play. You cannot play and land a fish well if your rod is held up over your head. You do have to keep the tip up, however, throughout the fight and constantly maintain pressure on the fish.

A technique that is used for playing all but the smallest fish is called "pumping", and is critical when fighting a large or strong fish and/or when using light line. To do this, keep the rod butt in the stomach, lower the rod tip and reel in line simultaneously, then pressure the fish as you bring the rod back up. Once the rod is up, lower and reel. Continue doing this.

Often when a fish is fairly close to you it is still energetic. Continue to keep the rod high. This is a time to be directing the fish. If you're in a boat and the fish streaks toward it (perhaps to swim under it) you could be put at a disadvantage, particularly when using light tackle. You must reel as fast as possible to keep slack out. If the fish gets under the boat, stick the rod tip well into the water to keep the line away from objects and possibly being cut.

You should anticipate that a fish will rush the boat and should be prepared to head it

When steady overhead rod pressure doesn't budge a large fish, you may need to lower the rod to the side and change the angle of pull.

around the stern or bow. In some cases a companion can manipulate the boat (especially with an electric motor) to help swing the stern or bow away from a fish, which is a smart maneuver that can aid the playing of a large fish. If possible, go toward the bow or stern to better follow or control the fish. Don't hang back in a tug-of-war with a large, strong fish; use finesse rather than muscle.

When a fish swims around your boat, keep the rod up (sometimes out, too) and apply pressure to force its head up and to steer it clear of the outboard or electric motor and their propellers. (Sometimes it's best to tilt motors out of the water.)

At times it may be necessary to change the angle of pull on a strong and stubborn fish, perhaps to help steer it in a particular direction, or to make it fight a little differently. Apply side pressure then, bringing the rod down and holding it parallel to the water, and turning your body partially sideways to the fish. Fight it as you would if the rod was perpendicular to the water. With very large fish that get near the boat but are still energetic, or with big fish that stay very deep below the boat and can't be budged by the fisherman, it may be necessary to move the boat a fair distance away and rather quickly, letting line peel off the drag. This changes the angle of pull on the fish and usually helps bring it up from the depths. This does not happen very much in freshwater.

In current, a big fish that gets downriver and through rapids where an angler is unable to follow, may return upriver if he releases line from his reel and allows slack line to drift below

the fish. The line below the fish acts as a pulling force from downstream (instead of ahead), and may cause the fish to head upstream again.

With some species of jumping fish (Atlantic salmon, for example), and when using fly tackle, it is necessary to slacken the tension when the fish jumps by bowing the rod toward it so the jumper cannot use taut line as leverage for pulling free of the hook. Sometimes you can stop a fish from jumping by putting your rod tip in the water and keeping a tight line, which changes the angle of pull and may stop a fish from clearing the surface.

Eventually the fish is next to you and may be ready for landing. If it still has a last burst of energy, however, this will be a crucial moment. Because of the short distance between you and the fish, there will be a lot of stress on your tackle. You must act swiftly when the fish makes its last bolt for freedom.

As it surges away don't pressure it. Let it go. Point the rod at the fish at the critical moment so there is no rod pressure. A large fish will peel line off the drag, which, if set properly (and does not stick), will keep tension on the fish within the tolerance of the line's strength, and provide the least amount of pressure possible. As the surge tapers, lift the rod up and work the fish.

If you are alone and without a net, you must be careful when landing the fish. Keep a taut line, extend the rod well back behind and over your head, and reach for the fish with your other hand (landing it by hand with some species, or gaffing or netting others). In this position you are able to maintain some control over the fish, even if it is still active, and avoid creating a momentary slack line situation that may give the fish its freedom.

When landing a fish, perhaps the greatest mistake of new anglers is reeling their catch right up

to the tip of their rod when the catch is at boatside, as if they are going to spear it; better to leave a few feet of line between the rod tip and fish to direct it to a net or swing it onboard. Applying too much pressure on an active fish near the boat is another mistake. Finesse, not muscle, is the secret. The key to properly landing fish is to employ common sense, anticipation, and finesse.

An easy way to boat small fish that are well hooked is by simply lifting them aboard with the rod. This is only practical for small- to medium-size fish caught on tackle that is sturdy enough to permit it. Landing fish by hand is a tricky maneuver for some species, but a practical and desirable method for those that have no teeth. Fish that are small, and that are to be released immediately, are best handled at a minimum, leaving them in the water while unhooking them.

Toothless species, like bass, crappie, and stripers, can be landed by grasping the lower lip, provided the fish is well tired before the attempt is made. Simply insert your thumb over the lower lip, with remaining fingers outside and underneath. This immobilizes the fish and is good for unhooking as well as landing. Be sure not to plant your thumb on the hooks of the lure.

For other species, particularly large ones, netting or gaffing is required. Most small fish don't need to be netted but some, such as scrappy stream trout, are often netted because they are difficult to land by hand. Proper netting technique is as much a matter of knowing what not to do as it is knowing what to do. Under most circumstances you shouldn't put the net in the

Landing a fish by yourself requires reeling up just the right amount of line and holding the rod behind you as this angler is doing.

water and wait for the fish to come close. Nor should you wave the net overhead where a fish might see it. A net in the water or moving above it is foreign and alarming to fish. It's best to keep the net solidly in hand at the ready, either motionless or out of sight, until a fish is almost within reach.

Don't attempt to net a fish unless it is within reach, and not if it is going away from you or appears to be able to go away from you. The fish should ideally be headed for you so that it must continue forward, or that if it turns you may still be able to move the net in front of it. As a general rule, don't try to net a fish unless its head is on the surface or just breaking to the surface. A fish that is up on the surface has little mobility, and cannot do as much as one with its entire body in the water, particularly if the fish isn't played out.

Don't try to net a fish from behind. If a fish is completely exhausted you may be able to net it from the side, but the most desirable position is from the front. And don't touch the fish with the rim of the net until it is well into the net. Touching fish, particularly if they are still lively, often initiates wild behavior.

If the fish acts wild, it could roll on your line

This fish was not netted head-first, as most should be; however, the large, multi-hooked lure might have fouled on its way into the net, and the big fish could have twisted free.

and break it, or simply snap it from the force of its getaway rush. Therefore, resist taking a fish that may be technically within reach of your net, but not in the best position for capture.

A major problem that occurs when anglers try to net a fish that is in a poor position to be netted, or when they don't get a fish coming squarely into the net, is snagging a multihooked lure on the mesh or webbing of the net bag. This is one of the surest ways to lose fish, particularly those that are heavy and cannot be readily hoisted into the boat or scooped up in the now-tangled net.

The angler can help the netter by making an effort to get the fish's head up so that it is near or on the surface and not deep in the water. When the fish comes up and is being worked toward the net, the fisherman should back up in the boat, put more pressure on the fish to gain line, raise the rod high to keep the fish's head up, and tell the netter that the time is right, attempting to lead the fish closer as the netter goes into action. The angler should be prepared for miscues, too, when his fish is to be netted. It is a good idea to back off a bit on the reel drag, or perhaps open the bail of the reel, when a fish is brought into the net. If it flops out, runs through it, or charges away, there may be a lot of pressure on your tackle, so anticipate this possibility and don't count the fish as caught until it is solidly in hand.

Netting a fish by yourself is often a tricky chore, made more difficult by the influence of

current, wind, and tide. Bringing a fish to net or boat as quickly as possible may not be feasible when you are alone and have a large fish, and it is often necessary to play the fish out thoroughly before you can slip the net under it. Try to get the fish to within several feet of the tip of the rod, then raise the rod high over and behind your head while you reach for the fish with net extended in your other hand.

Netting efforts are sometimes more arduous in fast-moving waters because fish are usually below you and it is hard to get big fish back upcurrent and positioned for proper netting. Another problem is that when you don't gain on fish in current, they rest momentarily and recoup enough strength to prolong the battle or give that last extra kick just when you think you have them. For this reason, those who net a fish for someone else in swift water usually get a reasonable distance downriver, in a position to land a tired fish as it wallows near the bank, still resisting but unable to swim off with vigor.

If it isn't feasible to try to land a fish because the net is too small or because you are without a net, you always have the option of landing it by hand or beaching it. In either case the fish must be thoroughly whipped and under your control before you can do so.

Fish that are netted usually can be released alive if desired. Gaffing is another option for landing fish, however, although one that is seldom used in freshwater.

HOW TO RELEASE FISH

As the result of diminishing resources, increased fishing pressure, and more sophisticated and experienced anglers, there is, within reason, a greater need for releasing fish unharmed.

The concept of catch-and-release has become one that is very widely embraced and supported in the past few decades, in part out of necessity because of depletions in some fish in some waters, and in part because the general angling public has come to realize that while the fisheries resources are renewable, they can be destroyed by overfishing and overharvest just as they can through habitat degradation.

Anglers as a group release more fish voluntarily today, meaning that they release fish that they could keep but choose not to. They also release more fish out of necessity. There are many more situations in which freshwater anglers must release fish: slot limits, minimum size limits, fish caught during closed seasons, catch-and-release waters, fish that may not be kept in any size, fish that should not be consumed, etc. Thus, there are many more fish being released because they have to be released.

Whether fish are released voluntarily or mandatorily, it is essential that they be treated as well as possible to ensure their survival after release. Proper care of the fish you want to, or must, release goes a long way toward helping perpetuate quality angling, as well as marking you as a sportsman, in the real sense of the word.

The suitability of a fish for release is sometimes affected before it is landed. When very light tackle is used, or when exceptionally large or strong fish put up a lasting and determined fight, fish will be exhausted upon landing and harder to rejuvenate. Such a fish experiences shock, probably from the buildup of lactic acid, which increases the fish's need for oxygen; if placed back in the water immediately, it may turn belly-up and sink out of sight. It may not right itself, and then will not recover. This is as true for small fish as for large ones, though the latter may take much longer to revive.

Whether fish are tired or not, the best thing for their survival is that they never leave the water, a feat that few fishermen do often enough. In some instances, fish can be shaken off at boatside by leaving some slack in the line and jiggling the rod tip. This is especially true if single-hooked and barbless lures are used. Wading fishermen can accomplish this easier than boat or bank anglers, but it is possible to unhook some fish in the water by grasping the hook with needle-nosed pliers and pulling the barb out.

A minimum amount of handling is desirable in all cases, particularly in warm water or warm weather. If fish must be taken out of the water, be conscious of their inability to breathe and of the length of time that they are forced to forego oxygen while being unhooked. Many of the fish that are held by anglers shown in this book were released, even though they were held briefly out of water to take the photograph. You simply have to be quick and careful, and it helps if the fish are caught quickly and the water is cool.

Don't let fish flop onshore or in a boat if you intend to release them; their protective mucuous coating can be removed, increasing the possibility of an infection that will be grotesque and life threatening. Don't grasp fish tightly around their midsections to prevent movement during the unhooking process, as this can cause internal damage. Don't put your fingers in their eye sockets or grab them by the gills, although you can carefully slip a finger between gills and gill plate to hold a fish (this is advisable for toothy species), as well as hold some fish by the lip. Don't keep fish that are to be released on a stringer or cooped up in a warm, poorly oxygenated container or well; you're cutting down their survival chances significantly by doing this. In a well or container, cool water and abundant oxygen are vital. And don't cull — replacing a fish on a stringer or in a well with another —

Some fish may need more help at recuperating for release than others; shown is an angler about to release a musky after it was revived for a while in the water.

unless you are keeping an injured fish and releasing a healthy one. Generally a fish that has been detained is not as suitable for release as one that has been freshly caught.

While it is seldom beneficial to keep fish in so-called livewells for later release (as opposed to instant, on-the-spot release), there are many people who do this in freshwater. In this case, it is good to use Catch and Release, a granular chemical that stabilizes fish, causing them to require less oxygen, and which fights fungus infection and mucous loss. Using ice, non-iodized salt, and some drugs (available from aquarium supply stores) are other measures that can be taken to aid fish that are detained for a long period prior to release, though this is something that relatively few anglers need to be concerned with other than tournament fishermen.

When releasing some fish and keeping others, keep the ones that are caught in deep water rather than those caught in shallow water. Fish caught in deep water are usually harder to revive than those caught in shallow water, so be thoughtfully selective. Keep a fish that is bleeding rather than one that is not; bleeders, particularly those hooked in the gills, are less likely to survive than unharmed fish.

By not using bait you can significantly reduce the chances of killing fish that you must, or want to, release. However, when it is not prudent to remove a bait hook from a deeply caught fish (because you may damage internal organs and/or cause bleeding), cut the line or leader and leave the hook inside. The hook will eventually corrode (bronze, blue, and gold hooks corrode much faster than cadmium or stainless). This may not guarantee the fish's survival, but the odds will be increased significantly.

Be particularly careful with netting. A net can remove some of a fish's mucous coating and scales. Also, a plug-caught fish often gets

The quicker that fish get back into the water, and the less time they spend flopping onshore or in a boat, the better for their survival when released.

enmeshed in a net because some of the loose hooks catch in the webbing during the netting process. As the fish thrashes around he pulls against the stuck plug, which can bend the hooks and/or tear the mouth of the fish where it is caught, prolonging release efforts. Fish caught on single-hooked lures are much easier to release, whether landed by hand or net. Hooking-mortality studies have shown that single- and treble-hooked lures are about equal in terms of causing fish mortality, but it can take longer to remove treble-hooked lures from a fish, and in the case of fish that are netted, this may really cause problems. Barbless hooks, therefore, if fish are to be netted, make sense, especially when using multi-hooked plugs for fish that are likely to writhe and struggle a great deal after capture. (Incidentally, there is a very good way to determine the weight of a fish without having

to keep and kill it: multiply the length by the girth squared, then divide by 800.)

While it may not be harmful to toss some fish back in the water, it cannot be helpful either. A gentle release, head-first, and after having certified that the fish has pizzazz and will scoot away, is desirable. It may be necessary to take the fish by lip or tail and lead it around head-first so that water flows thrrough the gills. Keep the fish upright, minimize vertical holding, and don't let it go until the fish tries to pull away from you. With fish that are exhausted, this can take awhile, up to 30 minutes for large fish.

Seeing a fish swim off is no guarantee of its survival. That's merely short-term survival. What the long-term survival, or delayed mortality, may be is open to speculation, but it certainly depends on the treatment of the fish prior to and during the release.

TAKING CARE OF THE CATCH

The key to enjoying fish isn't necessarily having a particularly good recipe or using a certain method of cooking. Once the fish is in the kitchen, you can increase or decrease its palatability, but if you harbor any hope of enjoying its fullest taste and nutrition, you must give it proper attention from the moment you catch it. The advantage that anglers have over people who buy fish is that they get this food as fresh as it can possibly be found, and they control its preparations and treatment. The end results will only be as good as you want them to be, and make them.

This starts with proper care from the moment that you decide to keep the fish. Once you've caught a fish that you're going to keep, you have to decide what to do with it. Where are you going to put it? On the floor of the boat? On the pier? In a tub or bag? That's okay—if it's cold out, if the sun isn't shining on it, if it will only be there for a few minutes, or if you don't particularly care what it will taste like.

The worst you can do is pay no attention to fish you've just caught. Leaving fish exposed to air and sun for a long time is undesirable, as is leaving fish ungutted overnight. Unaerated livewells, livewells filled with warm water, and stringers that are overcrowded or trolled or hung in warm surface water do not aid the edibility of fish they contain.

Ideally you should clean fish immediately after they've been caught, then put them on ice. But that isn't always practical. Maybe you can't clean fish at the place where you catch them. Or you simply don't want to stop fishing to do so. Or you don't have ice, or a fillet knife, with you. Do so, however, as soon as possible.

Air and water temperatures are keys to good fish care. The warmer both are the harder it is to keep fish alive and/or fresh till you stop fishing or reach the place where you will be cleaning and storing them, and the sooner you need to begin preparations. Do whatever you can to keep fish protected from heat and warmth. At the very least that may mean putting them in the shade, stopping fishing after a reasonable length of time to clean them, covering them with a wet cloth, or taking care to keep them alive in a protected, cool environment.   A stringer or rope is the most common way to contain whole fish until you bring them home or to the landing site. If you string fish, make sure they are allowed to breathe so they stay alive. Don't run the stringer through the gill. Put it through the lower jaw (and in the case of big fish or weak stringers, put it through both jaws). Try to keep the stringer away from gasoline in the water or any other substance that might affect the flavor of the fish. Take the stringer out of the water when the boat is underway at full speed, and try not to leave it out of the water for a long time. If you're going a long distance, stop for a minute and put the stringer back in the water. Whether in the water or boat, keep stringered fish in a shaded locale.

There is merit to killing some fish immediately, even if you have the option of keeping them alive, and also to keeping some fish alive rather than killing them. Some fish that die slowly, and struggle and bruise themselves in the process, won't taste as good as they might if they were simply dispatched with a couple

These char have been dressed and will be placed in a pool of cold water. The sooner you care for fish after keeping or killing them, the better for edibility.

of quick blows to the top of the head with a billy and stored temporarily in an appropriate environment. Still other fish are pretty hardy, and if you have the option, for example, of keeping them alive in cool water rather than dead under a cloth on the floor of the boat, opt for alive. You have to make this decision based on the circumstances.

Once fish are dead, the inevitable natural process of spoilage through bacteria growth begins. Fish are among the most perishable of foods. With this in mind, it sometimes pays to use a livewell to contain the fish, especially if the water is cool and if there is a fairly constant water circulation.

If you're not keeping fish alive, and you have an ice-packed food or beverage cooler, you should place freshly caught fish in the cooler for later cleaning. You can leave ungutted fish on ice all day and clean them at the end of the day without sacrificing freshness or taste. Plan for this eventuality at the beginning of the day by obtaining ice before going fishing. For short-term storage, cube ice is best, because you can cover fish fully with it.

You can tell when fish have lost their freshness if they are dried and shriveled, if they smell, if their eyes are glossy, if the skin is bleached, and so on. Fish that exhibit these conditions may be edible, but the manner of handling has contributed to some loss of freshness and therefore tastiness.

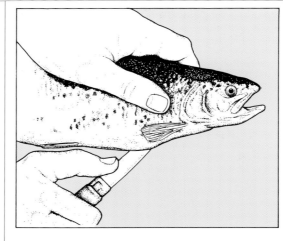

To clean small fish quickly by streamside, slit the belly open and remove entrails, then keep fish cool.

How you clean fish depends to some extent on the species, its size, and how you expect to cook it. Some fish, especially small, pan-sized species, need only to be gutted and scaled for frying. Larger fish that will be baked require the same treatment. Fish to be pan-fried or sauteed should be filleted.

If you'll be baking the fish or if you want the skin, you'll need to remove the scales. (A few fish, such as small trout and salmon, don't need scaling.) Scaling is best accomplished when the fish is whole, and by working from tail to head. You can use a fillet knife blade to scale fish, though a spoon, a tooth-edged scaler, or some equivalent implement will suffice. If you're at an outdoor cleaning station, which can be found at some piers, landings, marinas, and fish camps, you might be able to run water on the fish to facilitate scale removal and keep them from flying all over. In any event it's best to scale fish outdoors.

If you aren't going to fillet a fish, you need to gut it by removing the entrails from its body cavity after it has been scaled. Insert the point of a sharp knife blade in the anal area and move it forward until it is near the base of the pelvic fin. Clean out the contents of the body cavity, being especially careful to completely remove the bloodline (kidney) recessed in the cavity.

Cut the head and tail off if they aren't needed. For small fish that will be pan-fried, you should remove the dorsal and anal fins; slice along each side of the base of these fins, then pull free. Flush the cavity with clean cool water. At this point, a fish that has been gutted and scaled is ready for eating or freezing.

Generally the quickest method of cleaning fish is to fillet them, which removes the rib cage bones that anguish many reluctant fish-eaters. When properly done filleting causes little loss of meat, and is accomplished easily. One of the keys to good filleting is having the proper instrument. A sharp, moderately flexible blade with

This lake trout, pike, and landlocked salmon (from the bottom) appear freshly caught; the fins are not discolored and the eyes are clear.

an upwardly turned point is best. A 7- to 8-inch blade is standard for most freshwater fish. A smaller blade would do if you filleted nothing but pan-sized fish, while a longer blade is helpful for big-bodied fish.

The first filleting step is to make an angled cut behind the pectoral fin down to the backbone. Reverse the direction of the blade so that it is facing the tail and lying flat on the backbone, and slice back toward the tail along the backbone. A smooth cut, rather than a stop-and-go sawing motion, is best. If the fish has been scaled, cut through the skin at the tail.

If the skin is to be removed in the filleting process, do not cut through the tail, but slice to the end without severing and flop the meat backward. Angle your knife through the meat to the skin, then slice along the skin, separating the meat while exerting pressure on the skin with your free hand. If you accidentally cut through the tail, freeing the fillet from the carcass, you will find it a little more difficult to remove the skin. In this case, press the thumbnail of your free hand on the tail of the fillet (or use a fork), and skin it with your knife hand.

Now, with either scaled or skinned fillet, cut behind the rib cage, slicing the whole section away. Use the same procedure for the other side of the fish. Rinse fillets and prepare for the freezer or for eating. This filleting technique can be used on nearly all fish, except those with additional Y-shaped bones.

There are some other fish that require special dressing treatment. Catfish, for example, pose problems to many people, yet can be simply dressed. To skin and gut small catfish for pan frying, make a thin slice on the top of the fish, from behind the adipose fin up to the dorsal fin, and continue with a vertical cut from the dorsal fin down to the backbone. Put the knife aside, grab the head with one hand and body with the other and bend the head down to break the backbone. Hold the body portion firmly, with finger over the broken backbone, and pull the head away from the fish toward the tail, removing skin and entrails in the process. Cut the tail off and rinse the fish.

With larger catfish it's best to slice the perimeters of the skin. Hold the head firmly. Slice completely around the fish behind the pectoral fin. Slice along the top of the fish and around both sides of the adipose fin, then slice along the belly and around both sides of the pectoral fin. Use a pair of snub-nose pliers to grasp the skin near the pectoral fin, and pull back firmly toward the tail to remove it. Repeat on the other side. Sever the head and tail and remove entrails. You can now fillet the fish, keep as is, or steak it.

Steaking fish for frying or broiling is a good way to deal with large specimens. To steak a fish, scale and gut it first, then make a slice on both sides of the fins and pull them free. Cut the head and tail off and make the steaks about

1-inch thick. A fillet knife won't do an adequate job of steaking fish. Steaks should be neatly cut, not ragged and hacked. Use a butcher's knife, or cleaver, for steaking.

A final suggestion about cleaning fish: some fish contain a dark lateral line that has a different flavor than the rest of the meat. If you fillet these fish and remove the skin, you can also

Some beautiful fillets are coming off these chinook salmon, which are being cleaned not long after capture and prepared for storage.

slice away this dark flesh. For some fish that have a fairly high fat or oil content (such as lake trout) it's a good idea to trim the belly section. With Great Lakes salmonids, and occasionally

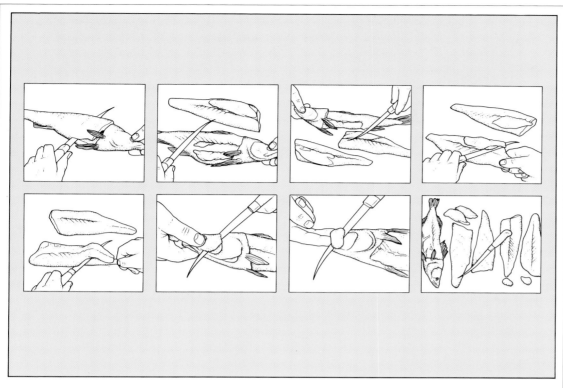

Here is a simple and quick method of filleting fish while removing the skin, and also cutting the meat from the cheekbones. Rinse and store fillets when finished.

other fish, slice off a little of the back tissue and as much fatty belly tissue as is evident. These portions are known to harbor the principal concentration of pollutants such as PCBs. By trimming this flesh you can minimize the amount of potentially harmful chemical (not detectable by taste, incidentally) that you consume. This procedure is recommended by many state health and fisheries agencies for a wide range of fish in many different waters.

If you bring home fresh fish that will be eaten in a day or two, you can wrap them tightly in freezer paper and foil, or in a sealable plastic bag, and place them in the refrigerator. Let them stay like this no more than two days, and then only if they were refrigerated the same day they were caught.

For longer storage, fish must be frozen. Remember that fish are very perishable, so they must be wrapped properly, and won't stay fresh when frozen for extremely long periods of time. Fatty or oily fish should be eaten within a few months of freezing. Other fish should be eaten within six to eight months for best taste, and frozen smoked fish can last up to a year. Generally, however, it's wise to eat fish as soon as possible. By labeling and dating packages you can consume stored fish on a rotational calendar basis, using the oldest fish first.

You can store fish simply in one tight wrapping of aluminum foil for a short period. But if they're in the freezer like this for very long, they'll develop the white-tipped symptoms of freezer burn, plus it's easy to puncture or scrape corners of foil packages and expose the contents. Better to double- or even triple-wrap fish using wrapping paper, foil, and/or freezer paper. The

delicatessen wrap, in which the ends of the paper are brought over the fish to meet one another and then are folded together several times, ensures a good seal.

Be sure to pack fish so there is enough for yourself or your family for a single meal, and, if possible, put wrapping paper in between fish or fillets to make them easier to separate and thaw. Also, label each package by writing on the outside with an indelible marker (or put a piece of masking tape on the package and label that).

Another method of storing fish is freezing in blocks of water in plastic containers, empty milk cartons, etc. If you don't have much food in your freezer, or only put a few fish in it occasionally, you might try this.

MINIMIZING HEALTH RISKS

It is a sad commentary when a book such as this must address the issue of edibility of fish to be consumed from freshwater environs, but there has been a great deal of concern about the wisdom and safety of eating fish in the past few years. Headlines in the media about contaminants in the waters, attention to oil spills and the like have raised the consciousness of people toward eating fish that they catch from any body of water, but especially those in major rivers and the Great Lakes. The health advisories and warnings issued by certain groups and governmental agencies regarding fish consumption have ranged between extremes; some of this, in my opinion, has been warranted and some not.

Unfortunately, no scientist has explained what the consumption of fish once a week, once a month, or at whatever frequency, is equivalent to in terms of inducing health problems, especially cancer. For example, is eating fish from Lake Michigan once a month equal to smoking a pack of cigarettes a month, a day, an hour, what? People are confused and concerned

about these scares because everything they hear is technical and too abstract.

Nonetheless, it is certainly known that some fish in some waters contain an element of so-called organochlorine contaminants. It is also known that you can greatly minimize the possibility of consuming what environmental contaminants may exist in the fish during the cleaning process by properly trimming them before cooking. It is wise, therefore, as a health precaution, to do so.

State fisheries agencies advocate trimming away the fatty parts and skin from fish fillets, which is very effective in reducing the intake of certain environmental contaminants.

We are not talking about the taste or the flavor of fish flesh here. This is about the hidden and tasteless elements with such foreboding names as mirex, PCBs, dioxin, and chlordane, contaminants that have a long residual life in the aquatic environment and which work their way through the food chain into the flesh of food and sport fish.

A high percentage of contaminants is found in the fatty portion of fish, so the best policy is to trim the fatty area of the back, belly, and lateral line away. A recent study evaluated before-versus-after fat and contaminant levels. In evaluating untrimmed brown trout fillets versus trimmed fillets it was found that trimming resulted in an average 62 percent reduction in fat content and 45 percent reduction in contaminants.

Filleting is a very popular method of cleaning fish, and one in which the flesh is separated from the carcass and from the rib cage to result in a boneless piece of fish. The skin may or may not be removed, but it is better to do so, as fat concentrations are high in the area between flesh and skin and along the lateral line, which in some species is composed of visually darker flesh. The fact that with a few extra slices of a sharp knife during the filleting process, an angler can remove the areas with the highest concentration of fat and possibly contaminants is good news.

Researchers note that cooking trimmed fillets in a way that allows some of the remaining fat to drain out and away from the flesh will further reduce levels of contaminants. Some studies suggest that baking or broiling on a rack will result in further reductions in fats and the contaminants stored in them, although the exact percentage varies.

Depending on where you fish and what you keep for consumption, you can take some steps to lessen potential health risks.

You can't ask for anything fresher or better tasting than fish that almost literally go from the water to the flames. Many freshwater fishermen experience this on northern expeditions each season.

INDEX